VOYAGEUR CLASSICS

BOOKS THAT EXPLORE CANADA

THE LETTERS AND JOURNALS OF
SIMON FRASER
1806–1808

EDITED AND INTRODUCED BY W. KAYE LAMB
FOREWORD BY MICHAEL GNAROWSKI

DUNDURN PRESS
TORONTO

Copyright © Dundurn Press, 2007
Originally published in 1960 by Macmillan of Canada as one of a series called Pioneer Books

All rights reserved. No part of this publication may be reproduced, stored in a retrieval system, or transmitted in any form or by any means, electronic, mechanical, photocopying, recording, or otherwise (except for brief passages for purposes of review) without the prior permission of Dundurn Press. Permission to photocopy should be requested from Access Copyright.

Editor: Michael Carrroll
Proofreaders: Marja Appleford and Allison Hirst
Design: Jennifer Scott
Printer: Webcom

Library and Archives Canada Cataloguing in Publication

Fraser, Simon, 1776-1862.
   The letters and journals of Simon Fraser, 1806-1808 / edited and introduced by W. Kaye Lamb.

(Voyageur classics)
Includes bibliographical references and index.
ISBN 978-1-55002-713-6

1. Fraser, Simon, 1776-1862—Travel—British Columbia—Fraser River. 2. Fraser River (B.C.)— Description and travel. 3. British Columbia— Discovery and exploration. I. Lamb, W. Kaye (William Kaye), 1904- II. Title. III. Series.

FC3212.1.F73A3 2007   971.1'302   C2007-902100-X

1   2   3   4   5   11   10   09   08   07

  Conseil des Arts   Canada Council
         du Canada   for the Arts

We acknowledge the support of the Canada Council for the Arts and the Ontario Arts Council for our publishing program. We also acknowledge the financial support of the Government of Canada through the Book Publishing Industry Development Program and The Association for the Export of Canadian Books, and the Government of Ontario through the Ontario Book Publishers Tax Credit program, and the Ontario Media Development Corporation.

The Dundurn Group and Michael Gnarowski wish to express their thanks to Mrs. Elizabeth Hawkins, executor of the estate of Dr. W. Kaye Lamb, for permission to reissue Dr. Lamb's edition of Simon Fraser's letters and journals.

Care has been taken to trace the ownership of copyright material used in this book. The author and the publisher welcome any information enabling them to rectify any references or credits in subsequent editions.

J. Kirk Howard, President

Printed and bound in Canada.
Printed on recycled paper.
www.dundurn.com

Dundurn Press	Gazelle Book Services Limited	Dundurn Press
3 Church Street, Suite 500	White Cross Mills	2250 Military Road
Toronto, Ontario, Canada	High Town, Lancaster, England	Tonawanda, NY
M5E 1M2	LA1 4XS	U.S.A. 14150

VOYAGEUR CLASSICS

BOOKS THAT EXPLORE CANADA

Michael Gnarowski — Series Editor

The Dundurn Group presents the Voyageur Classics series, building on the tradition of exploration and rediscovery and bringing forward time-tested writing about the Canadian experience in all its varieties.

This series of original or translated works in the fields of literature, history, politics, and biography has been gathered to enrich and illuminate our understanding of a multi-faceted Canada. Through straightforward, knowledgeable, and reader-friendly introductions the Voyageur Classics series provides context and accessibility while breathing new life into these timeless Canadian masterpieces.

The Voyageur Classics series was designed with the widest possible readership in mind and sees a place for itself with the interested reader as well as in the classroom. Physically attractive and reset in a contemporary format, these books aim at an enlivened and updated sense of Canada's written heritage.

CONTENTS

FOREWORD by Michael Gnarowski	11
ACKNOWLEDGEMENTS	19
INTRODUCTION	21
Ancestry and Early Life	22
The North West Company	29
Three Years of Exploration	35
The Fraser Manuscripts	52
Later Years	58
Family and Fame	72
THE GREAT JOURNEY: EXPLORING THE FRASER RIVER	81
Journal of a Voyage from the Rocky Mountains to the Pacific Ocean Performed in the Year 1808	83
From the original manuscript in the Toronto Public Library	
Fort George to the Thompson River	83
Thompson River to the Strait of Georgia	109
Return Journey to the Thompson River	127
Thompson River to Fort George	139
Second Journal of Simon Fraser from May 30th to June 10th 1808	151
From the transcript in the Bancroft Library, University of California	

BACKGROUND OF THE GREAT JOURNEY 181

First Journal of Simon Fraser from 183
April 12th to July 18th 1806
From the transcript in the Bancroft Library, University of California

At Rocky Mountain Portage	183
Rocky Mountain Portage to McLeod Lake	204
At Fort McLeod	218
Fort McLeod to the Nechako River	223

Letters from New Caledonia August 1806 to February 1807 247
From transcripts in the Bancroft Library, University of California, and from manuscripts in the Archives of British Columbia

MISCELLANEOUS PAPERS 275

1. Fraser's Notes on His Family 275
2. Isabella Fraser's Claim for Compensation, 1787 278
3. Jules Quesnel's Description of New Caledonia and of the Journey Down the Fraser River in 1808: Letter to J.M. Lamothe, May 1, 1809 280
4. Fraser's Declaration to the Earl of Selkirk, August 16, 1816 282
5. Petitions for Land Submitted by Fraser in 1818 283
6. Letter from Fraser to Donald Æ. MacDonell, 1840 285
7. Fraser's Application for a Military Pension, 1841 287
8. Memorandum by Simon Fraser and John McDonald of Garth, 1859 290
9. Letter of John A. Fraser, son of Simon Fraser, to the editor of the "Hastings Chronicle", 1862 290
10. Memorial of Fraser's Last Will and Testament, 1862 294

11. Petition Submitted by Harriet Fraser, Daughter of Simon Fraser, in 1887 and again in 1890	298

PORTRAITS OF FRASER   301

SELECT BIBLIOGRAPHY   303

NOTES   305

INDEX   323

MAPS

Fraser River, Fort George to the Sea	82
Part of Fraser's Course	150
New Caledonia	182

THE LETTERS AND JOURNALS OF
SIMON FRASER
1806–1808

FOREWORD

Tucked away in southeastern Ontario, in a Scottish corner of the province now known only to its inhabitants and to those "Macs" who with kilts and pipes gather every year for the Highland Games in Maxville, lie the small towns and villages from which went forth and to which returned Duncan Cameron, John McGillivray, Hugh McGillis, and David Thompson — men whose intrepid exploring and canny factoring in the great west and northwest of this country stitched Canada together. They came to Glengarry County and left their imprint on villages and hamlets with names like Dalkeith, Dunvegan, Apple Hill, Williamstown,

St. Andrews Roman Catholic Church, built in 1861, where Simon Fraser is believed to have been buried.

and St. Andrews. The stone fences laboriously piled by generations tell today's traveller that it is not the best of land, but the Scots endured; some farmed, and some went into the fur trade, seemingly thinking little of the back-breaking voyages between Montreal and points west — Athabasca, the North Saskatchewan River, Michilimackinac, and the Columbia. All but forgotten now, these men's bones lie in small village graveyards, the headstones leaning this way and that, their legends barely decipherable, blackened and time-worn.

Simon Fraser (1776–1862) lies in a tiny triangle of tended land between the highway and the Raisin River, across the road from the rounded walls of the oldest field stone structure in Ontario, which was built around 1801 to serve the Roman

Front and rear views of the oldest surviving stone structure, originally a Roman Catholic church, circa 1801, across the road from Simon Fraser's burial place.

FOREWORD

Catholic Highlanders. Raised under the leadership of "Spanish" John Macdonnell and the Reverend Roderick Macdonnell, with contributions from the local citizenry as well as members of the Montreal-based fur trading North West Company, it had its un-ecclesiastical moment as a field hospital during the War of 1812. Fraser shares the small country cemetery with some thirty or forty settlers of his time, among whom is Sandfield Macdonald. There is a log replica of the first Catholic church built by the earliest settlers, many of whom were Loyalists who had crossed into Canada after the American Revolution to take up land in the region in the late years of the eighteenth century. The original headstone that marked the resting place of Fraser and his wife has been replaced by a more modern monument, which looks, perhaps, slightly out of place beside its modest neighbours.

Corner of the graveyard in which Simon Fraser is buried, with log replica of the very first Catholic church erected by Scottish settlers, circa 1784, St. Andrews West, Ontario.

Simon Fraser's tombstone in St. Andrews West, Ontario. It replaced the original stone, which had fallen into disrepair.

FOREWORD

For a long time in the study of Canada, the written record of the fur traders remained the almost exclusive preserve of historians and geographers. Their journals, diaries, and reports of "this adventurous Traffick" (John Inglis, May 31, 1790), which they filed to their business partners and sundry commercial masters, were seen as the fundamental substance of the story of the opening up of the northern half of the North American continent. Nothing acknowledges the importance of this record more resolutely than the defining study *The Fur Trade in Canada* (1930) by the undeniably great economist historian Harold Innis. This study was preceded by the pioneer work of Louis F.R. Masson (1833–1903), sometime member of the government of Sir John A. Macdonald, senator of Canada, and lieutenant-governor of Quebec, whose collection of journals, letters, and documents relating to the western fur trade was published as *Les bourgeois de la Companie du Nord-ouest* in two volumes (1889–1890). This area of study was popularized engagingly by Lawrence J. Burpee (1873–1946) in his *The Search for the Western Sea* (1980).

Important as these works may have been to our understanding of a critically significant activity in the founding of Canada, the fur trade was also well served in the apparent interest in, and the popularity of, the published record when it became available. From the apocryphal insistence of the French admiral La Pérouse that Samuel Hearne publish his notes on his arctic travels in *Journey from Prince of Wales's Fort in Hudson's Bay to the Northern Ocean* (1795), to Alexander Mackenzie's *Voyages from Montreal ... to the Frozen and Pacific Oceans...* (1801), to Alexander Henry's *Travels and Adventures in Canada and the Indian Territories [Countries]...* (1809), to Daniel Williams Harmon's *Journal of Voyages and Travels in the Interior of North America* (1820), to name a few of the more engaging accounts, we note the unpretentious unfolding of a tradition of narrative that would lay claim to the critical and literary imagination. Recognition of the value and significance of this writing had become well established among historians and geographers in the late nineteenth century and, especially, the early decades of the twentieth century. Besides the occasional and random publication of some material by local historical societies and interested individuals, the most impressive and generous treatment of these records has been accorded to them by the Champlain Society, the Radisson Society, and the Hudson's Bay Record Society. Distinguished by a certain exclusivity and by high production and editorial values, the publications of these societies became repositories of much explorer writing of early Canada.

Transition from what was purely history and geography into the domain of literature began in the first decades of the twentieth century. In *A History of English-Canadian Literature to the Confederation...* (1920), Ralph Palmer Baker devotes a chapter of modest length to "Travels and Exploration," in which he fixes on the work of the major explorer writers, such as Hearne, Mackenzie, Henry, and Harmon, noting that they had "no pretensions to literary skill" but recognizing, nevertheless, their energy and vitality, their occasional stylistic excellencies, and their charm and naturalness, all of which invited comparison with the material of Daniel Defoe. Stephen Leacock had also dipped his literary toe into these waters with his *Adventurers of the Far North* (1914), which was part of a three-volume contribution to the Chronicles of Canada series. In spite of the fact that literary historians seemed to be teetering on the verge of appropriating explorer writing for Canada's literary heritage, one is hard-pressed to find it reprinted in whole or in part in key anthologies, or as the subject of extended critical appraisal. It was not until Victor Hopwood engaged this material in a key chapter, "Explorers by Land to 1867," of Volume One of *Literary History of Canada...* (1965), that criticism and scholarship received the prompting that saw, from the 1970s onward, a grad-

FOREWORD

ually widening set of critical perspectives and the coining of terminology that expresses itself in articles in literary journals such as *Canadian Literature* and *Ariel*, and in university courses labelled "Canadian Exploration Literature."

The present volume of the journals and letters of Simon Fraser belongs, in spirit, to the same family of works that gave us the voyages of Alexander Mackenzie, although at the same time it has to be said that it lacks the deliberate literary architecture with which, we surmise, Mackenzie's collaborating editor(s) endowed his work. Fraser's account, nevertheless, is not devoid of dramatic flourish or of an author's artifice. In that sense it is not only an account of exploration, with all that such geography implies, but is also very much interested in letting the reader in on the sheer adventure of an unknown country, strange people, and the incredible physical courage and challenges in navigating a wild and seemingly un-navigable river.

This edition of *The Letters and Journals of Simon Fraser, 1806–1808*, was prepared, edited, and introduced by W. Kaye Lamb (1904–1999), for many years the Dominion Archivist, whose talent as an archivist-historian resulted in much valuable scholarship, especially, in the context of this foreword, his superb work editing *The Journals and Letters of Sir Alexander Mackenzie* (1970) and the materials of Simon Fraser that we have here. The latter, first published in 1960 and now being reissued, was part of a short-lived series called Pioneer Books, which included Harmon's account of his sixteen years spent in Indian country, also edited by Lamb, and Hearne's search for the Northern Ocean. The problem with almost all explorer writing is that it rarely makes its way into readily available editions. A glance at the two key paperback series of Canadian writing, the Laurentian Library and the New Canadian Library, fails to strike gold as far as explorer writers are concerned, a fact that has undoubtedly contributed to the difficulty of structuring university or college courses featuring this material. It is only lately, with Germaine Warkentin's groundbreaking anthology *Exploration Literature*, first published by Oxford University Press in 1993 and now available in the Voyageur Classics Series, that there has been an improvement in the situation.

Michael Gnarowski
Voyageur Classics Series Editor

ACKNOWLEDGEMENTS

I am much indebted to the following persons and institutions, all of whom allowed me to secure copies of documents in their possession, and to print them in this volume: Mr. H.C. Campbell, Chief Librarian, and the Board of Trustees of the Toronto Public Library; Dr. G.P. Hammond, Director of the Bancroft Library, at the University of California, Berkeley; the Provincial Archives of British Columbia, Victoria; Mrs. I.M.B. Dobell and the McCord Museum, Montreal; Mr. Donald C. Fraser, of Fargo, North Dakota; and the Public Archives of Canada, Ottawa.

Mr. Willard E. Ireland, Provincial Archivist of British Columbia, who originally undertook the preparation of this book, very kindly allowed me to use his corrected copy of Fraser's narrative of the 1808 expedition. This was of great assistance in establishing an accurate text.

Mr. A.C. Tuttle, Chief Topographical Engineer of the Topographical Survey, Ottawa, was good enough to plot Fraser's route from the courses and distances given in his second journal (1808).

I am much indebted for help and advice received from Mr. Donald C. Anthony, Librarian of the Fargo Public Library; Mrs. Mabel Tinkiss Good, of Montreal; Mr. T.R. McCloy, of Calgary; and Mrs. J.H. Hamilton and Dr. Dorothy Blakey Smith, of Victoria. The staff of the Manuscript Division of the Public Archives of Canada searched many files at my request, and a special word of thanks is due to my Secretary, Miss Doris Martin, who made a first draft of many of the documents.

W. Kaye Lamb

INTRODUCTION

Simon Fraser is the most neglected of the major explorers of Canada. No biography of him has been written, and the versions of his writings that have been printed hitherto are without exception inaccurate. Although his major journey of exploration took place a century and a half ago, the present volume is the first attempt to present his letters and journals in a complete, annotated edition.

Of the interest and importance of his explorations there can be no question. His was the third expedition to span the continent of North America. The first, led by Alexander Mackenzie in 1793, was essentially a reconnaissance trip, to spy out the land in the interests of the fur trade. The second, the famous Lewis and Clark expedition of 1805–6, was sent out by President Jefferson soon after the United States acquired the vast and somewhat indeterminate Louisiana territory from France; it, too, was a reconnaissance trip, although Lewis and Clark had the political future of the Pacific region in mind as well as its trading possibilities. Fraser, on the other hand, was not merely a bird of passage; he crossed the Rocky Mountains in 1805 and again in 1806 to take possession and to build trading posts. His great journey down the Fraser River in 1808, though the first exploration of one of the world's most difficult and dangerous rivers, was undertaken primarily to find supply routes for those posts. He was the pioneer of permanent settlement in what is now the mainland of British Columbia.

Ancestry and Early Life

The Clan Fraser is one of the oldest and best known in Scotland. Simon, the explorer, was a kinsmen of Simon Fraser, fourteenth Lord Lovat, who was beheaded on Tower Hill in 1747 for his share in the Jacobite rising of 1745. He came of a cadet branch of the family, the Frasers of Culbokie and Guisachan.[1] William Fraser, Simon's grandfather, kept out of the rising, but in spite of this Guisachan House, his mansion in Strathglass, Inverness-shire, was burned by the Duke of Cumberland's troops.

William Fraser married Margaret Macdonell, of Glengarry, a woman noted for her beauty, her poetical talents and her interest in Gaelic language and literature. She had in her possession a collection of manuscripts of Ossianic poetry that figured in the famous controversies over the authenticity of *The Works of Ossian*, published by James Macpherson in 1765. Sometimes she read bits of the poems to a young son of a cousin, who passed her door on his way to and from school. Years later this small boy, Alexander Macdonell by name, was to become the first Roman Catholic bishop of Upper Canada.[2]

The Frasers were destined to have other and more direct relationships with Canada, some of which were to be of importance to their grandson, Simon. William and Margaret Fraser had nine sons. Most of them were in the army at one time or another, and served in far corners of the world. One of them was a victim of the famous Black Hole of Calcutta, in 1756. Two other sons — John and Archibald — joined the celebrated 78th Regiment (Fraser's Highlanders), and fought with Wolfe at Quebec in 1759. Archibald soon left Canada, but Captain John Fraser was one of the three hundred officers and men of the unit who settled permanently in this country. He became paymaster of the British forces in Montreal, and in 1764 was appointed

INTRODUCTION

judge of the Montreal court of common pleas. In 1775 he became a member of the Legislative Council of Quebec, and in 1792 a Councillor of Lower Canada.

Simon, the explorer's father, was the second son of William and Margaret Fraser. In 1752 or 1753 he married Isabella Grant, daughter of the laird of Daldregan. In his *History of the Frasers of Lovat*, Alexander Mackenzie states that Simon had "received a classical Education, and cultivated the taste which he inherited from his mother for Gaelic poetry and music." When he decided to emigrate with his wife and children to the American colonies, he seems to have taken with him most of the old Gaelic manuscripts collected and prized by his mother.

The Frasers joined a celebrated migration of Highlanders, almost all Roman Catholics, who in 1773 crossed the Atlantic in the ship *Pearl* to seek their fortunes in the New World. Both Simon and his wife had relatives there; in addition to Judge Fraser, in Montreal, there were Fraser cousins in the American colonies, and Isabella Fraser had two brothers and an uncle in America. They went first to Albany, New York, and then moved on another thirty miles to the vicinity of Bennington, in what is now Vermont, where Hugh Fraser, a kinsman of Simon's father, had settled some years before. In 1774, in the little community of Mapletown, Simon took a perpetual lease on 160 acres of land, at an annual rental of a shilling an acre. Here he settled, and on this property was born in 1776 his eighth and youngest child, Simon Fraser, the future fur trader and explorer.

The Loyalist claim submitted on behalf of young Simon's mother in 1787 gives some details of the Fraser farm. When they leased the property, 112 of the 160 acres were cleared; by their own exertion the Frasers increased this to 124 acres. They had paid £240 for the improvements on the place. Their livestock consisted of about 20 head of cattle, including three yoke of oxen, a horse, mare and colt, and 24 sheep. The picture conjured up is that of a modest, comfortable farm, where life would be free of privations, but where there would be little in the way of luxuries.

Unfortunately life at Mapletown was soon beset with many anxieties. For one thing, the lease of their property involved the Frasers in a bitter dispute over land titles. For some years before the American Revolution, and before the creation of the State of Vermont, New Hampshire and New York both claimed the Bennington area. In 1749, New Hampshire had chartered Bennington township; in 1764, an Imperial order in council had rejected the claims of New Hampshire and placed the township and its settlers under the jurisdiction of New York. The transfer itself need not have caused much difficulty; but the New York authorities took the view that the order in council had wiped out all the land titles that had been issued by New Hampshire, and they proceeded to issue new ones to many of the same properties. The Frasers took up their lands under New York titles, and as local sentiment favoured New Hampshire, they were highly unpopular in the neighbourhood. In 1775, within a year or so of their arrival, a local tribunal was able to reassert some of New Hampshire's lost authority; a boundary was fixed, beyond which New York titles were no longer valid. As luck would have it, the line passed through Simon Fraser's farm, and sliced off sixty of his best acres.

The loyalty of the Frasers to the British Crown soon added to their unpopularity in a community that was strongly in sympathy with the rebel cause in America. The first action of the Revolution was fought at Lexington in April of 1775; thereafter the Frasers found themselves increasingly subject to suspicion, abuse and persecution. Hugh Fraser fled to New York towards the end of 1776. Simon stayed behind, and became more and more active in the Loyalist interest. A summary of evidence given by his eldest son in 1787 states that he "Collected many persons who came to an agreement to join the British forces as soon as they could". The opportunity came when General Burgoyne led

INTRODUCTION

his ill-fated expedition into the region in 1777. Simon Fraser actually joined the colours of Skenesboro in July, and he quickly received a commission, first as a lieutenant and then as a captain.³ Only a month later a British detachment attempted to seize supplies and a magazine in Bennington. This precipitated a battle on August 17, in which the British were decisively beaten. There is a tradition that Fraser was wounded in the action, but no definite evidence seems to exist. Both his brother, Judge Fraser, and William, his eldest son, state that Captain Fraser was taken prisoner at the time of the battle, but John Spargo, Director of the Bennington Historical Museum, insists that this is not so. He believes that Fraser "escaped by way of the mill bridge at Cambridge" and that he remained at liberty until December 1777, when he was arrested in Bennington by order of the Albany Council of Safety.⁴ Certain it is that his case was considered by the Albany Committee of Correspondence on December 24. The official record reads as follows:

> Simon Fraser an Inhabitant of this State, and who has taken a Commission under the King of Great Brittain, and joined his Forces, having been apprehended, and sent to this Board to be dealt with as they shall Conceive proper, by the Council of Safety.
>
> Thereupon Resolved, That the said Simon Fraser be put in Close Confinement there to remain till farther information is received concerning him from the Committee of the District where he last resided.⁵

Fraser was imprisoned at Albany, and the conditions of his confinement were so rigorous that his health was soon undermined. His plight evidently aroused some sympathy, for a petition asking for his release was circulated in July of 1778. But nothing came of this, and he died after an imprisonment of 13 months and 10 days. If he were arrested in December 1777, as Spargo contends, his death must have occurred in January 1779.

His widow, who was in poor health, was left in desperate straits. She could expect no help from her relatives, for her uncle and brothers had all joined the rebel forces.[6] The fact that William, the eldest of her eight children, had joined the British Army in August 1777, must have added to her difficulties. According to Judge Fraser, repeated efforts were made to persuade Angus, her second son, to join the American Army, and the family was heavily fined each time that he refused.[7] Several of the children were too young to be of any assistance to their mother; little Simon was not yet three when his father died. Many of the Frasers' possessions were evidently confiscated or stolen. The list of furniture, utensils and livestock given in Mrs. Fraser's claim for compensation is followed by the note: "All taken from the Premises after the Battle of Bennington." Mackenzie's *History of the Frasers of Lovat* states that Captain Simon Fraser's house was "broken into and wrecked, and the family manuscripts which he had taken along with him from his home in Strathglass were destroyed".[8]

Even when the war ended in 1783 persecution continued, and the Frasers prepared to leave the United States and join the Loyalist trek to Canada. In the spring of 1784, Angus travelled to Montreal, and there enlisted the help of his uncle, Judge Fraser. The judge advanced him 50 louis, to assist the family to move to the wilds ("se rendre dans les bois") of what was soon to be Upper Canada, and got in touch with William Fraser, who was then at Kingston, and who had served throughout the war as a lieutenant in the King's Royal Regiment of New York. Judge Fraser also wrote to Governor Haldimand, in the hope that he might grant Mrs. Fraser a modest pension, but nothing of the sort was forthcoming.[9]

INTRODUCTION

Mrs. Fraser was able to sell the farm at Mapletown, and the whole family moved to Canada before the end of 1784. William, the eldest son, settled at Coteau du Lac, west of Montreal, and the other children seem all to have been with him there as late as 1787. Meanwhile, however, both William and Angus had acquired land grants in the Township of Cornwall. Patrick McNiff's famous map dated November 1, 1786, which shows all grants made up to that date, indicates that the brothers had taken up lots 20 and 21 of the 7th concession, each consisting of 200 acres. These lands run down to the Rivière aux Raisins, and they are of special interest because it was upon part of this property that Simon Fraser, the explorer, came home to settle over thirty years later, after his long years of service in the fur trade.

It has been said that Mrs. Fraser spent her later years in Edwardsbourgh, in Grenville County, but this seems unlikely. The family's closest associations were with Cornwall and Cornwall Township, and in 1796 she is referred to in an official document as "Mrs. Isabella Fraser of Cornwall". That same year she applied, as a United Empire Loyalist, for land grants for herself and her six younger children — "Peggy, Bell [Isabella], Nancy, Jenny, Peter and Simon" — none of whom had as yet drawn any land "except one Hundred Acres located to the said Peter". Grants of 200 acres to her and each of the children were recommended, and these were approved and authorized by order in council in March of 1797.[10]

When this order was passed, young Simon was far from Cornwall, carving out a career for himself in the West. Only the barest details are known about his life at this time. It is believed that his uncle, Judge Fraser, took charge of him, and that he attended school in Montreal. Masson states, on the authority of the Hon. R.W. (later Sir Richard) Scott, that he went to Montreal at the age of fourteen. As we shall see, this would limit his schooling to a little more than two years at the most. Two of his mother's brothers, Peter and Donald Grant, were engaged in the fur trade, and this may have turned his thoughts in the direction of the North West Company. This growing concern was headed by that commanding personality, Simon McTavish; he and his associates in McTavish, Frobisher & Company were its chief agents; they purchased its supplies, marketed its furs and engaged many of its staff. They must have been well known to Judge Fraser,[10a] who perhaps wondered if they did not offer a solution to the problem of what to do with young Simon. The Judge had a nephew in need of an occupation; the North West Company was in need of sturdy young clerks who seemed to have talents that would enable them to serve the Company well, and who perhaps might ultimately aspire to a partnership in the concern. In 1792, at the age of sixteen, Simon was apprenticed as a clerk to the North West Company.

Having taken this step, he virtually disappears from view for a decade. True, the name Simon Fraser is found now and then in the scanty surviving records of the North West Company. But virtually every family of Frasers included a Simon: at least four men of that name are known to have been connected with the Company in one capacity or another in the 1790s. Only two entries refer with certainty to our Simon. One states that in 1799 he was serving as a clerk in the Athabaska Department. The other — vastly more important — is the entry in the minutes of the meeting of the partners of the North West Company held at Grand Portage on June 20, 1801, which records that "It was unanimously Resolved" that Fraser and five others "should be admitted Partners of the North West Company for one Forty sixth share each, their Interest in the same to Commence with the Outfit of the Year 1802 ..."[11] Even though we have no details, this tells us a great deal. It is obvious that Simon had served the concern faithfully and well, for to gain a partnership at the early age of twenty-five was no small accomplishment.

INTRODUCTION

The North West Company

Fraser became prominent in the North West Company at an important period in its history, and a word should be said about its origin and character.

Following the Treaty of Paris, in 1763, British merchants and would-be merchants began to appear in numbers in Montreal. Many of the newcomers were Scottish, and for them the fur trade, which the French had carried on over a vast area to the West, soon proved to have a strong and peculiar attraction. Within a few years the so-called "pedlars" from Montreal had not only taken the place of the French in the West, but were steadily expanding the territory over which the fur trade was carried on.

Inevitably this expansion brought the Montreal traders into contact and competition with the Hudson's Bay Company, which for a century had been established in trading posts on Hudson Bay and James Bay. The Hudson's Bay Company claimed that its famous charter of 1670 gave it exclusive trading rights over the whole of the vast Hudson Bay watershed. The Montreal merchants, on the other hand, adopted the old French contention that the Company's rights were confined to a narrow strip of land around the rim of its two bays: the great expanses of territory in the western interior were to them a projection of Canada, Neither side ever retreated from its point of view, and as trade expanded, both in volume and in territorial extent, it was inevitable that competition between the two should become increasingly sharp. For many years the Hudson's Bay Company had contented itself with expeditions into the interior from trading posts on the Bay, but it came to realize that something more was required. In 1774 it built Cumberland House, on the Saskatchewan River, its first inland trading post; and thereafter other posts were established in the interior in rapid succession, to compete with the posts of the Montreal traders.

Meanwhile the latter had been struggling with competition of another sort — that which had developed amongst themselves. This had proven to be both dangerous and costly: dangerous, because the more unscrupulous traders were not above encouraging the Indians to attack their rivals, a policy which would soon create a state of affairs in which the life of no white man could be safe; costly, because it demoralized the trade, raised prices and increased transportation costs. Before long traders began to enter into agreements with one another, their two motives being to lessen dangers and to increase profits. The first agreements were no more than short-term arrangements between a few traders in a limited area; but the wisdom of larger and more enduring combines quickly became apparent. The first large-scale partnership came into being in 1779, and this continued in effect for several years. The original North West Company, a still larger partnership, was formed in 1784. The agreement upon which it was based was intended to run for a period of five years; but in 1787, after only three years, the advantages of the arrangement had become so obvious that the partnership was reconstituted and still further expanded, and this happened again in 1790. By the time Simon Fraser joined its ranks in 1792, the North West Company dominated and virtually controlled the western fur trade as conducted from Montreal.

Its success was due to the ingenuity and efficiency with which it adapted its organization to meet trading conditions. Most of the furs secured by the Nor'Westers came from west of the Great Lakes. Distances were so great that it was impossible for individual traders both to barter furs in the Indian country and to dispose of them and secure supplies in Montreal. Experience had shown that the traders should remain in the West, and that business details should be entrusted to others in the East. The partners of the North West Company, consequently, fell into two distinct groups: the "wintering partners", or *bourgeois*, who were responsible for the

INTRODUCTION

Company's posts and the practical details of securing furs from the Indians, and a group of agents in Montreal, who purchased supplies and marketed furs. By degrees Simon McTavish and his associates gained a dominating position amongst these agents, and this control became absolute in 1790, when the new partnership agreement provided that they were to do "all the business of this concern at Montreal".

Once a year, representatives of the agents, and as many of the wintering partners as could leave their districts, met to discuss their problems, to determine policy, and to exchange the latest harvest of furs for the supplies that had been carried inland from Montreal. For years the scene of this great annual rendezvous was Grand Portage, on the northwest shore of Lake Superior. When the fixing of the international boundary placed Grand Portage in the United States, the rendezvous moved to the "New Fort", which in 1807 was named Fort William.

Transportation costs were a constant worry to the Nor'Westers, and many of their journeys of exploration, including those of Alexander Mackenzie and Simon Fraser, were undertaken in the hope of finding better supply routes. In this respect the Hudson's Bay Company enjoyed a great advantage over its Canadian competitors; it could use cheap sea transport, and deliver supplies by ship to its posts on Hudson and James bays, in the very heart of the continent. The North West Company, by contrast, was compelled to use long and expensive overland canoe routes. Costs naturally became higher as the Nor'Westers extended their operations farther and farther to the west and north. In Athabaska, in spite of the richness of its fur resources, costs of transport finally threatened to swallow up profits entirely.

Anyone who reads the *Voyages* of Alexander Mackenzie will feel that his two great journeys were due in part to a simple desire to explore and to see new country. But he was also deeply concerned about the future of Athabaska, and the chief purpose of his journeys was to find a shorter and cheaper supply route for that department. He hoped that supplies could be brought to the Pacific coast by ship, and he was looking for a practicable route by which they could be taken from the coast to Athabaska.

From Mackenzie's point of view his first voyage in 1789 was thus a complete failure. He had found a great river, soon to be named in his honour, and he had reached the Arctic; but for his immediate purpose the Mackenzie River was useless. Determined to try again, he spent the winter of 1792–3 at a fort on the Peace River, near the mouth of the Smoky River, and in May 1793, set out upon the amazing journey that brought him to Bella Coola, on an inlet of the Pacific Ocean. But here again he had met failure. The very difficulties and dangers that make his account of the journey so interesting, and which revealed the immense courage and physical stamina of the man, made the route he followed impracticable for supply purposes. Mackenzie's expedition was the first to complete the crossing of North America north of Mexico, and as such it was an historical event of major importance; but it was nevertheless disappointing and a failure from his own immediate point of view.

Still convinced that cheaper transportation was essential to the prosperity of the western fur trade, Mackenzie next turned his attention to the sea route controlled by the Hudson's Bay Company. In the last pages of his *Voyages*, published late in 1801, he proposed that the Company and the Montreal traders should unite and form a great new concern that should seek from the Crown a charter covering the whole of what is now the Canadian West. Failing this, he hoped that it might be possible to persuade the Hudson's Bay Company to grant the North West Company transit rights through Hudson Bay. The coalition plan came to nothing, probably because Simon McTavish and his associates saw in it a serious threat to Montreal and their interests there. The second proposal met with greater favour and

INTRODUCTION

was under active consideration for several years. The Hudson's Bay Company naturally took the view that it could not grant so important a concession "without sufficient indemnity & security"; and in 1805, at the annual rendezvous, the Nor'Westers agreed to offer what they thought were generous terms. But in the end no agreement was reached, and it would seem very doubtful if the Hudson's Bay Company ever thought seriously of sharing its commanding advantage with its rival.

Meanwhile the end in view had almost been gained in another and somewhat roundabout way. After his two voyages of discovery, Mackenzie gradually became unhappy in the service of the North West Company. He retained his partnership, but joined McTavish, Frobisher & Company, and for a number of seasons represented the agents at the annual rendezvous. In 1799, when the current partnership agreement expired, Mackenzie withdrew and spent several years in Great Britain, where he published his *Voyages* and received the honour of knighthood. Returning to Montreal in 1802, he joined the New North West Company, better known as X Y Company, which for the past four years had been competing with the old concern. Mackenzie's influence and ideas showed up clearly in 1804, when the X Y Company's London agents failed by a narrow margin to gain financial control of the Hudson's Bay Company. This proved to be the swan song of the New North West Company. History had repeated itself; competition with the old company was proving costly and dangerous to both, and in November 1804, the two agreed to join forces.

In spite of Mackenzie's discouraging reports about a travel route overland to the Pacific, it is clear that the North West Company never abandoned its ambition to extend its activities to the country beyond the Rocky Mountains. The cost of supplying posts there from Montreal could, it was true, be extremely high; but one senses that hope sprang eternal that some navigable river would be discovered that would provide a supply route from the coast. The Columbia River was much in men's minds at this time. Mackenzie thought he had been upon its upper waters when he followed the Fraser River as far south as Alexandria, in 1793. Even thought he felt that the part of it that he had seen was useless as a trading-route, he insisted in his *Voyages* that it was "the line of communication from the Pacific Ocean, pointed out by nature, as it is the only navigable river in the whole extent of Vancouver's minute survey" of the Pacific Coast.

Even before these words appeared in print, the Nor'Westers were probing the approaches to the Rocky Mountains. In 1797, James Finlay had followed Mackenzie's footsteps up the Peace River to Finlay Forks, and had explored long stretches of both the Finlay and Parsnip rivers. David Thompson, in a letter written long after the event, stated that "In 1801 the northwest company determined to extend their Fur Trade to the west side of the Rocky Mountains, and if possible to the Pacific Ocean; ..."[12] It may be unwise to trust the memory of an old man, but the fact remains that it was in 1800–1 that Duncan McGillivray and Thompson himself made their much-discussed expeditions into the mountains from Rocky Mountain House, on the upper waters of the North Saskatchewan River. And it is interesting to note that Mackenzie himself in 1802 referred to these expeditions as "an attempt ... to penetrate in a more southerly direction than I did to the River Columbia ..."[13] But the decisive step was taken by the Nor'Westers when Simon Fraser was instructed to advance up the Peace River, cross the Rockies, establish trading posts in what is now the interior of British Columbia, and endeavour to trace the Columbia River to its mouth.

INTRODUCTION

Three Years of Explorations

Fraser's fame related chiefly to the brief period of three years, from the autumn of 1805 to August of 1808, in which he carried out these instructions. Fortunately this is also much the best documented part of his career. In the pages that follow will be found the journals that he kept during his most important journeys of exploration in 1806 and 1808, and a series of letters written in the winter if 1806–7 that in great part fills the gap between the journals.

Harriet Fraser, the explorer's daughter, believed that the decision to extend their trade to the country beyond the Rockies was made by the partners of the North West Company in the summer of 1805. She was convinced that Simon Fraser attended the annual rendezvous that year at Fort William, received his instructions there, and left for the West in August. There are some inherent improbabilities in this story, but we know that in his later years Fraser discussed his travels with Harriet, and her version should stand until disproven on good authority.

We do know for certain that in the autumn of 1805 Fraser led a party of about twenty men up the Peace River and established a post at Rocky Mountain Portage, at the foot of the turbulent Peace River Canyon. This was intended to be both a trading post and an advance supply base from which he could set off to cross the Rocky Mountains with a minimum of delay. With Fraser were two clerks, John Stuart and James McDougall. Stuart was an exceptionally able and reliable man, and was to serve as Fraser's second-in-command throughout the adventurous three years that lay ahead. McDougall is a lesser character, but he carried out important preliminary explorations on several occasions, and deserves more notice than he has received. Chief amongst Fraser's voyageurs and engagés was one La Malice, whose prominence is difficult to explain, and who showed himself again and again to be a shifty and unreliable character, entirely worthy of his name.

Having set most of his men to work on the building of Rocky Mountain Portage House, Fraser left Stuart in charge and pushed on with McDougall and La Malice to explore the upper reaches of the Peace River. In so doing he was following in the footsteps of his famous predecessor Sir Alexander Mackenzie, and, like Mackenzie, when he reached Finlay Forks he turned to the left and followed the Parsnip River. A few days later he entered the smaller Pack River, which Mackenzie had failed to notice, and this led him to a lake known for a time as Trout Lake, but eventually named McLeod Lake. The natives thereabouts, which Fraser refers to as the Big Men, were a band of the Sekani Indians. They were friendly, and Fraser decided that the lake would be a good site for a trading post. On its shores he built Trout Lake Post, later Fort McLeod, the first permanent settlement west of the Rocky Mountains in what is now British Columbia. Leaving La Malice and two men to winter at the new post and trade with the Indians, Fraser and the rest of the party returned to Rocky Mountain Portage House.

A rough journal kept by John Stuart from December 20, 1805, to February 28, 1806,[14] enables us to follow events at the portage. Little of note occurred. Fraser and McDougall spent Christmas at Dunvegan, the important post farther down the Peace River, where consultations were held with Archibald Norman McLeod, a senior partner in the North West Company. Friction developed between La Malice and his men at Trout Lake Post; the men finally left him and found their way, through bitter winter weather, to Rocky Mountain Portage. McDougall was sent to investigate, and found that La Malice himself had also abandoned the post and the Company's property there, and La Malice eventually turned up at Rocky Mountain Portage.

INTRODUCTION

Fraser's own journal begins in April of 1806, when preparations for a long journey of exploration to the West were in full swing. By that time James McDougall had made a notable reconnaissance trip from McLeod Lake into the lands to the West occupied by the Carrier Indians. He reached the "Carriers' Lake" — a form of reference that has led some to suppose that he went only as far as the body of water known today as Carrier Lake; but it is clear that Stuart Lake was meant, a much larger and more important lake in the very heart of the Carrier country.

To reach this lake, and establish a post on its shores, was to be the first objective of Fraser's own journey. At first sight it is difficult to understand why he did not proceed directly overland to Stuart Lake from McLeod Lake, as McDougall had done. The trip had taken only three days and a half, whereas Fraser was to follow a long, difficult, and roundabout water route that took him more than a month to cover. The explanation is that his primary objective was to explore the Columbia River (as the Fraser was then thought to be) to the sea. As a first step, he would examine again the portion of the river that Alexander Mackenzie had followed in 1793. McDougall had ascertained from the Indians that Stuart Lake drained into the Fraser through a river of some sort, and Simon Fraser's plan, which he duly carried out, was to follow the Fraser until he reached this tributary (which turned out to be a combination of the Nechako River and its own tributary, the Stuart River) and then ascend it to Stuart Lake.

In making his preparations, Fraser was beset with great difficulties. John Stuart, his invaluable clerk, was the only competent canoe-builder at Rocky Mountain Portage, and he was too busy with other duties to devote much time to the work. As a consequence, the three canoes in which the exploring party finally set out were a sorry lot, constantly in need of repair, and the cause of innumerable delays along the way. The best of them was a veteran craft in which Fraser had travelled all the way from Lac La Pluie the previous year, and which he had used again in the autumn on his first journey to McLeod Lake. But even this soon began to disintegrate, and new canoes had to be built before the party could proceed beyond the Pack River.

The men available were on the whole an unsatisfactory lot. Few of them were capable canoe-men, and the majority suffered from physical ailments of one kind or another. Because La Malice was an experienced traveller, Fraser felt that it was essential to take him with him, and, true to his name, he turned out to be the most troublesome of the entire crew.

Fraser, Stuart, and La Malice each took charge of a canoe, and each had a crew of three voyageurs. The names of these nine men happen to have come down to us and they deserve to be recorded here: Bazile, Ménard, La Londe, La Garde, St. Pierre, Saucier, Wananshish, Gagnon and Gervais Rivard. At the Pack River two new canoes were substituted for the original three, and a voyageur named Blais, from Fort McLeod, took the place of Saucier, who was too ill to travel farther.

Break-up was late on the Peace River in the spring of 1806; it was not until May 20 that the river was sufficiently clear of ice to permit a start to be made from Rocky Mountain Portage. By the 28th Fraser was at Finlay Forks, and on June 5 the canoes entered the Pack River. Because it was necessary to build new canoes there, the party did not get on its way again until June 23. A week later Fraser was approaching the height of land that divides the watersheds of the Arctic and Pacific Oceans. His route here lay through three little lakes, now appropriately named Arctic, Portage and Pacific, and these led him to the narrow, shallow and turbulent stream that Mackenzie called the Bad River (the present James Creek). The name was apt and descriptive, for the little river, filled with obstructions and broken by rapids, gave Mackenzie some of the

INTRODUCTION

worst moments of his long journey to the Pacific coast. Fraser had a similar experience; the week he spent descending it was exhausting in the extreme. But it ended at last, and having passed through parts of Herrick Creek and the McGregor River, Fraser came finally, at 10 a.m. on July 10, 1806, to the "Large River ... fine and navigable" that was later to bear his name, but which at the time he hoped and believed was the upper part of the Columbia. The Fraser was still in freshet, and its current carried the party along so swiftly that they were able to encamp next day at the mouth of the Nechako River.

Thus far Fraser had been following in Mackenzie's footsteps; the rest of his journey was a venture into the unknown. The Nechako is broken by rapids, and ascending it proved to be a tedious process. To make matters worse, a Carrier Indian who accompanied the party, and who was supposed to act as a guide, knew so little about the country that Fraser concluded finally that he had probably never seen it before. On July 18, when Fraser's journal breaks off abruptly, the party was still four days distant from the Stuart River. Ascending it, they reached Stuart Lake on the 26th.

There Fraser was greeted by Toeyen, a Carrier Indian who had met James McDougall when he was in the vicinity earlier in the year. McDougall had told Toeyen that a party of white men would be coming to found a trading post, and had given him a piece of red cloth as a means of identification. Years later Father A.G. Morice, who had worked amongst the Carriers as a missionary, heard from them their own account of Fraser's arrival. The version printed in *Morice's History of the Northern Interior of British Columbia*[15] reads as follows:

> The 26th of July, 1806, was a rather windy day on what the Indians then called Lake Na'kal, the surface of which was being ploughed into deep

furrows. The soap-berries were ripening, and most of 'Kwah's [the Indian chief's] people were camped at the mouth of Beaver Creek, to the south-west of the present Fort St. James, when what appeared to them two immense canoes were descried struggling against the wind, around a point which separated them from the outlet of the lake.

Immediately great alarm arises in the crowd of natives. As such large canoes have never plied on Carrier waters, there is hardly a doubt that they must contain Toeyen's friends, the wonderful strangers from "the country beyond the horizon" he had been told to expect back. Meanwhile, the strange crafts are heading for Beaver Creek, and lo! a song the like of which has never been heard in this part of the world strikes the native ear. What can that mean? Might not this be a war party, after all?

"No," declares Toeyen, who, donning his red piece of cloth as an apron, seizes a tiny spruce bark canoe lying on the beach and fearlessly paddles away. On, on he goes, tossed about by the great waves, until he meets the strangers, who, recognizing him by his badge, bid him come on board. His fellow-tribesmen, now seeing in the distance his own little canoe floating tenantless, take fright.

"They have already killed him," they exclaim. "Ready, ye warriors; away with the women!"

At this cry, which flies from mouth to mouth, the men seize their bows and arrows,

INTRODUCTION

and the women and children seek shelter in the woods. But the curious crafts, which, on coming nearer, prove to be large birch-bark canoes, are now within hearing distance, and Toeyen cries out to the men on shore to be of good cheer and have no fear, as the strangers are animated by the most friendly dispositions. The fugitives are hastily recalled, and Simon Fraser, with John Stuart and his other companions, put ashore in the presence of a crowd of wondering Carriers....

On landing, Fraser's men, to impress the natives with a proper idea of their wonderful resources, fired a volley with their guns, whereupon the whole crowd of Carriers fell prostrate to the ground. To allay their fears and make friends, tobacco was offered them, which, on being tasted, was found too bitter, and thrown away. Then, to show its use, the crew lighted their pipes, and, at the sight of the smoke issuing from their mouths, the people began to whisper that they must come from the land of the ghosts, since they were full of the fire wherewith they had been cremated. Pieces of soap were given to the women, who, taking them to be cakes of fat, set upon crunching them, thereby causing foam and bubbles in the mouth, which puzzled both actors and bystanders.

All these phenomena, however, were soon explained away, leaving no suspicion in the native mind, but a most pronounced admiration for the foreigners and their wares....

Fraser's letters show that this paints much too rosy a picture of conditions at Stuart Lake. "It is a fine large Lake," he told the Gentlemen Proprietors of the North West Company in his first report, "But since we arrived here, my ideas are far short of what Mr. McDougalls account would lead [one] to expect." His stock of provisions was low; he was very scantily provided with trade goods; the Indians — whom he later characterized as "a large, indolent, thievish set of vagabonds" — were not numerous, and showed little inclination to part with either food or furs. The salmon run was late, and, as it turned out, was not to begin for another six weeks. As a result, the party was soon in a state of semi-starvation.

Fraser nevertheless set his men to work building the post on Stuart Lake that was later to be famous under the name Fort St. James. As soon as he could collect sufficient provisions, he intended to resume his major task — the exploration of the Fraser River — and to follow the main stream to the south at least as far as Mackenzie had done in 1793. As it turned out, lack of provisions made this impracticable. Weary and vexatious weeks were spent in waiting for the salmon run, which in the Carrier country conditioned many things. It became clear at last that Fraser must abandon his plan; "it would have been little short of madness," he explained to the North West Company, "to attempt going down the Columbia [i.e., the Fraser] in a starving state, without an ounce of any kind of provisions."[16]

Instead, he turned to the other task assigned to him — the founding of still another post west of the Rocky Mountains. On August 28 he sent Stuart and two men to visit a lake that he had heard about, and which might be a suitable site. This was Fraser Lake, which Fraser thought lay to the west, but which was actually south of Stuart Lake. After seeing it, Stuart was to meet Fraser at the mouth of the Stuart River, and Fraser left on

INTRODUCTION

September 3 to keep this rendezvous. Stuart's account of Fraser Lake was so favourable that Fraser went to see it, and there he built the future Fort Fraser.

In the last weeks of the year Fraser's plans suffered another major setback. In his letters to the Company he had stressed the fact that reinforcements were essential if the new posts were to become firmly established and profitable. When he returned to Stuart Lake from Fraser Lake on December 18, it was to find that no supplies or additional men had been sent to him; and this, as he explained to McDougall, was "a considerable loss to the Company, and a severe blow to our discoveries."[17] In spite of this, a letter written to Stuart in February 1807 is full of plans and projects, the most important being the building of a supply depot of some sort on the Fraser River at the mouth of the Nechako. Like Rocky Mountain Portage House, this would be both a trading post for the immediate area, and a base from which an exploring expedition could set off down the Fraser with a minimum of delay.

In the autumn of 1807 two canoes carrying men and supplies finally arrived from across the mountains, and Fraser set about carrying his plan into effect. A post, later named Fort George, was established at the mouth of the Nechako, and Hugh Faries, one of the two clerks who had arrived with the supply canoes, was placed in charge of it. Fraser decided that the other clerk, Jules Quesnel, should accompany John Stuart and himself on the expedition down the Fraser River that was planned for the late spring and summer of 1808.

The great journey of 1808 speaks for itself in the pages that follow, but a few observations regarding it are nonetheless called for.

The exploring party was 24 in number: Fraser tells us that it consisted of 19 voyageurs, two Indians, his two clerks (Stuart and Quesnel) and himself. The names of eight of the French-Canadians are mentioned in the journal: La Chapelle, Baptiste, D'Alaire, La

Certe, Waka or Wacca (the nickname of Jean Baptiste Boucher), Bourboné (whose name should probably be spelled Bourbonnais), Gagnier and La Garde. The latter had been with Fraser on his 1806 expedition, and it is possible that Gagnier is the man whose name appears as Gagnon in the earlier journals.

It was a youthful contingent: Fraser was 32 at the time, Stuart was 29, and Quesnel only 22. Both Fraser's assistants were men of character, with important careers ahead of them. John Stuart was to succeed Fraser in 1809 as officer in charge of New Caledonia, and was to retain the post for no less than fifteen years. He became a partner in the North West Company in 1813, and a Chief Factor in the Hudson's Bay Company in 1821, following the amalgamation of the two concerns. Able and highly respected, he seems to have been somewhat reserved and serious-minded; he enjoyed theological discussions, and frequently indulged this bent in the company of friends, notably Daniel Williams Harmon. Stuart retired to his native Scotland in 1839 and died there in 1847.

Jules Maurice Quesnel was one of the thirteen children of Joseph Quesnel, of Montreal, a poet and musician of some note. He left the fur trade in 1811, and eventually became prominent in Quebec political life. He was a member of the Special Council of Lower Canada from 1838 to 1841, and was then appointed to the Legislative Council of the United Province of Canada. He died in Montreal in 1842.

The first entry in the "fair copy" of Fraser's journal is wrongly dated, and this has given rise to some doubt about the expedition's point of departure. The date given in the manuscript (May 22) does not correspond with the day of the week (Saturday). It has usually been assumed that the date was correct; but this would leave five days unaccounted for in the journal, whose second entry is dated Sunday, May 29. If the first entry is corrected to Saturday, May 28, all details fall neatly into line. There is no adequate reason to think that Fort George, which,

INTRODUCTION

as we have seen, was built specially as an advance base for Fraser and his party, was not the spot from which they set out.

The journey down the Fraser was hazardous in the extreme, but one reason for its perilous nature is seldom made clear. The "tremendous gulphs and whirlpools ... ready every moment to swallow a Canoe with all its contents and the people on board" were not only dangerous in themselves; what multiplied the perils was the virtual impossibility, in many places, of getting out of the river to avoid them. Fraser mentions many instances of this in his journal. "The current throughout the day ran with amazing velocity," he wrote on June 5, "and on this and [the] last course our situation was really dangerous, being constantly between steep and high banks where there was no possibility of stopping the canoe, and even could it be stopped, there would be no such thing as going up the hills, so that had we suddenly come upon a cascade or bad Rapid, not to mention falls, it is more than likely that all of us would have perished, which is much to be apprehended." A century and a half later, the men who set out to duplicate Fraser's journey encountered the same difficulty; "in most of the length of the river," they reported, "the greatest single problem is that once you are in it, you cannot get out."[18]

Fraser faced two other major problems that did not trouble his modern successors: uncertainty about the attitude of the Indians along the river, and total lack of information about its course and character.

The Indians, who were surprisingly numerous, were on the whole friendly, and Fraser showed great skill and courage in his dealings with them. But he was well aware that they were a constant hazard, and in spite of appearances he was under no illusions about the grave dangers that surrounded his little party. "Here we are," he wrote at a time when all was outwardly peaceful, "in a strange Country, surrounded with dangers, and difficulties, among numberless tribes of savages, who never [before] saw the face of a white man. Our situation is critical and highly unpleasant; however we shall endeavour to make the best of it; what cannot be cured must be endured."[19]

The great crisis of the journey came in the first days of July, when Fraser reached the delta of the river and there encountered the hostile and aggressive Cowichan Indians. He brought his men safely through the ordeal, but it momentarily shattered their morale, and it took all his eloquence and prestige to give them heart and determination to undertake the long and fatiguing journey back up the river to Fort George.

When he sought information about the river from the Indians, their reports were almost always vague and discouraging. In part this was probably due to a desire to dissuade the travellers from going further, in the hope of gaining gifts and other benefits from their continued presence. But in many instances, though Fraser did not realize it at the time, they spoke the simple truth about the dangers and difficulties that lay ahead. The river was in places unnavigable, especially when in freshet, and this Fraser discovered for himself in due time. The Indians found it easier in many places to travel by land, and they could not be expected to understand that to survey the actual river, and to travel down it whenever humanly possible, was the purpose of Fraser's journey. As it turned out, even Fraser was compelled to travel considerable distance by land. Between Leon Creek, north of Lillooet, near which he cached his canoes, and Yale, at the foot of the Fraser Canyon, the whole party rarely travelled by water. In some places all had to proceed overland; in others some of the party could use canoes, and the rest followed Indian trails along the hills.

The actual distance down the winding course of the river from Fort George to the Strait of Georgia has never been accurately measured, but it is appreciably more than 500 miles. Fraser completed the journey in 36 days (May 28 to July 2), and made

INTRODUCTION

the return trip in one day less (July 3 to August 6). It has been said that he turned back before he actually reached the Strait, but his journal makes it quite clear that this is not so. The Musqueam area, where he made his last recorded landing, extends along the shore beyond the mouth of the North Arm of the Fraser River, and Fraser certainly saw the open Strait and the mountains on Vancouver Island across its waters. Indeed, it is clear that he paddled along the shore for some distance beyond Musqueam, in the direction of Point Grey; and he would have gone farther still had not the hostility of the Indians thereabouts made it prudent to return before nightfall.

Like Mackenzie before him, Fraser completed his great journey in a state of frustration and disappointment. He had discovered a great river and traced it to the sea, but it was not the Columbia, as he and everyone else had assumed, and its character made long stretches of it useless as a travel and supply route for the fur trade. All that was left to comfort Fraser was the realization that he had performed a journey of immense difficulty with speed and efficiency, and without loss of life or serious injury to any of his men. An occasional sentence in his journal suggests that he was aware that, whatever view his hard-headed colleagues in the North West Company might take, his accomplishment was in its way extraordinary. To quote an instance: "I have been for a long period among the Rocky Mountains," he wrote while in the vicinity of Hell's Gate, in the Fraser Canyon, "but have never seen any thing to equal this country, for I cannot find words to describe our situation at times. We had to pass where no human being should venture."[20]

The absence of familiar place-names will strike any reader of the journals and letters who is acquainted with the interior of British Columbia. It is often assumed that Fraser, Stuart and Quesnel made a sort of triumphal progress through the country, naming lakes and rivers and trading posts after themselves as they went their way. The documents in the case show that this is not so. Fraser notes in his 1808 narrative that he has named the Thompson River after David Thompson and the Quesnel River after his third-in-command, Jules Quesnel, and he refers to Carp Lake and the West Road River (the latter a name bestowed by Alexander Mackenzie in 1793); but these are the only present-day names of features west of the Rocky Mountains that appear in his papers. Fort McLeod is referred to as Trout Lake Post, Fort St. James is called Nakazleh, Fort Fraser is Natleh, and Fort George is given no name at all. The Nechako, Stuart and Chilcotin rivers were all named later, and so were Stuart, Fraser and McLeod lakes.

The earliest use of the name New Caledonia, which was applied to the large area in the northern interior of British Columbia in which all these posts, rivers and lakes are located, would seem to have been in 1808. As we shall see, Daniel Williams Harmon refers to New Caledonia in an entry in his journal made at Fort Chipewyan on September 21, 1808. According to family tradition, Fraser chose the name New Caledonia because the country recalled to his mind his mother's descriptions of the Highlands of Scotland.

As Fraser had named the Thompson River, it is fitting that it should have been David Thompson who named the Fraser River. On Sir Alexander Mackenzie's map, printed in his *Voyages* in 1801, the Fraser is called the "Tacoutche Tesse or Columbia River". Some notes by John Stuart indicate that it was sometimes referred to as the Jackanet River.[21] The first entry in the "fair copy" of Fraser's 1808 narrative shows that the name Fraser River was at one time given to the Nechako; but this must have been a purely local usage, and no other reference to it has been noticed.

Thompson first used the name Fraser River on a "rough chart" of what is now Western Canada, prepared in 1813. He had moved to Terrebonne the previous year, and there set about compiling the famous "map for the North West Company" that

INTRODUCTION

was completed in 1814. Some "remarks" dated April 1813, prepared to accompany the preliminary version of the map, include the note: "The River Mr. Fraser followed down to the Sea, I have named after him ..."[22] Other notes by Thompson show that his delineation of the river was based on John Stuart's notes, not on those of Fraser himself. This recalls the fact that although many courses and distances are recorded in the surviving fragment of Fraser's rough journal of 1808, it was Stuart who was charged with the duty of keeping the official log of the expedition. Unfortunately Stuart's survey has long since disappeared.

The search for a supply and travel route from New Caledonia to the Pacific Coast did not end with Fraser's great journey to the sea. The effort was continued by others, notably by John Stuart, who succeeded Fraser as officer in charge of the New Caledonia posts. Eventually a solution was found by linking the explorations of Fraser and Stuart with those carried out by David Thompson in the valley of the Columbia River. In 1811 Thompson descended the Columbia to its mouth and found that, though broken here and there by rapids and falls, it provided a satisfactory route to the Coast. In 1813 Stuart worked out a practicable link between the Columbia and New Caledonia. This followed the Fraser River as far south as the vicinity of Alexandria, and then veered to the southeast and ran overland to Kamloops, at the junction of the North and South Thompson rivers. Thence the route continued on southwards through the Okanagan Valley to the Okanagan River, a tributary of the Columbia. Here the fur brigades took to the water again, and followed the Okanagan and Columbia rivers to the ocean.

Supplies carried by ship from England to the mouth of the Columbia River, and brought inland over this route, first reached the New Caledonia posts in the fall of 1814. Thereafter it was used regularly by the North West Company, and, after the amalgamation of 1821, by the Hudson's Bay Company. A few years later, however, it became clear that permanent British possession of the lower valley of the Columbia was by no means assured, and the search for an alternative supply route farther to the north was therefore resumed. In 1828, Governor George Simpson of the Hudson's Bay Company decided that the Fraser must be re-examined, and he and his party set out to follow the actual course of the river, regardless of obstacles. Simpson enjoyed one great advantage compared with Fraser: he was descending the river in the autumn, when water levels were relatively low, and most of the rapids and whirlpools were much less swift and formidable than during the summer freshet. Because of this, Simpson and his expert crew were able in great part to accomplish their objective: except for occasional short portages they did in fact contrive to travel down the river virtually the whole way. But the experience was a terrifying one, and Simpson emerged from the ordeal with a healthy respect for Fraser and convinced that the river was useless as a travel route. The 1808 expedition, he wrote in his journal, reflected "infinite credit" on both Fraser and Stuart; he described their journey as "an undertaking, compared to which, in my humble opinion, the much talked of and high sounding performances of his Majesty's recent discovery expeditions in the Arctic regions, were excursions of pleasure." As for the river itself, he had this to say: "Frazers River, can no longer be thought of as a practicable communication with the interior; it was never wholly passed by water before, and in all probability never will again: ... and altho we ran all the Rapids in safety, being perfectly light, and having three of the most skilful Bowsmen in the country, whose skill however was of little avail at times, I should consider the passage down, to be certain Death, in nine attempts out of Ten. I shall therefore no longer talk of it as a navigable stream."[23]

Simpson was thus reluctantly compelled to confirm the verdict that Fraser had passed upon the river twenty years before.

INTRODUCTION

What manner of man was Simon Fraser?

His journals furnish less evidence than one would expect, because they are more in the nature of official logbooks than personal diaries. The chief qualities they reveal are the determination with which he pushed on in the face of great difficulties, his physical courage and stamina, and the firmness, tempered with restraint, with which he handled his men. Not even the thoroughly exasperating behaviour of the rascally La Malice made him either lose his temper or act unfairly.

Fraser's fairly frequent and somewhat disparaging references to Sir Alexander Mackenzie roused the ire of H.H. Bancroft, who has few kind words for him in his *History of the Northwest Coast*. "Fraser," Bancroft wrote, "was an illiterate, ill-bred, bickering, fault-finding man, of jealous disposition, ambitious, energetic, with considerable conscience, and in the main holding to honest intentions."[24] And lest the reader should be too impressed with the final phrases, Bancroft hastened to add that no man could be truly honest who was as unjust and blinded by prejudice as he conceived Fraser to be.

This is certainly a badly distorted conception of the man. Much nearer the mark is a character sketch written in 1908 by E.O.S. Scholefield, who had spent long hours studying both Fraser's letters and journals and all available pictures of him. Scholefield saw in him "a well-built active man, with a heavy, almost dour, face, whose distinguishing features are a determined chin, firm, large-lipped mouth, prominent somewhat snubbed nose, light-blue eyes, broad receding brow, overhung with a mass of tousled hair of reddish tinge — a strong, honest face, indeed, but one giving more the idea of determination and physical robustness than of intellectuality or refinement. A man inured to hardship; versed in woodcraft and the lore of the savage; strong in danger; of inconquerable will and energy; unlettered, not polished, it may be, but true to his friends and honourable in his dealings; somewhat eccentric if we judge aright; a man typical of his age and calling. An heroic spirit truly, if cast in the not altogether heroic mould of a fur trader. He stands there a commanding figure."[25]

The Fraser Manuscripts

In the pages that follow first place is given to the narrative describing Fraser's journey to the sea in 1808. This was his great accomplishment, the feat that revealed the full stature of the man, and that won him a secure place in history. The travels described in his earlier journals and letters are of secondary importance; dozens of other fur traders made journeys comparable to them.

Fortunately the 1808 expedition is the best documented episode in Fraser's career. The most important of all available Fraser manuscripts is the complete narrative of his exploration of the Fraser River that is now a treasured possession of the Toronto Public Library. The original document, 55 foolscap pages in length, consists of a day-by-day account of the voyage, based on the notes that Fraser jotted down during the actual journey, but here and there including additional material, presumably added from memory. Narratives of this kind, often referred to somewhat loosely as "fair copies", were prepared by traders who had made important journeys, and forwarded as a report to headquarters. The manuscript is not in Fraser's own handwriting, but of its authenticity there can be no doubt.

Many years ago, within Fraser's lifetime, the narrative came into the possession of Roderick McKenzie, himself a Nor'Wester and a first cousin of Sir Alexander Mackenzie. After his retirement, Roderick purchased the seigniory of Terrebonne near Montreal, and in his later years set about gathering the materials for a history of the fur trade. The history was not written, but the source materials passed into the possession of

INTRODUCTION

McKenzie's son-in-law, the Hon. L.F.R. Masson, who in 1889–90 published many of the more important items in the two volumes entitled *Les Bourgeois de la Compagnie du Nord-Ouest*. Fraser's narrative was included in the first volume. After Senator Masson's death in 1903 his manuscripts were sold, and the Fraser journal migrated to Toronto.

Although complete in essentials, Masson's printed text departed at many points from the original. Scores of small deletions and revisions have been made in the Fraser manuscript in two distinct handwritings, presumably those of Roderick McKenzie and Senator Masson, and before printing the text Masson made some additional changes that do not appear on the original. For these revisions Masson should not be blamed too severely. It was customary at the time to edit manuscripts in this way, and, compared with some other editors, Masson used both his pen and his blue pencil lightly. One well-known editor of the day went so far as to fabricate and supply a whole chapter that was missing from a journal that he was preparing for the press.

In the present edition every effort has been made to reproduce the original text as it was first written. In most instances it was not difficult to read the words that had been struck out or overwritten; uncertainty exists in only a very few places, and these have been indicated. In order to make the narrative as clear and readable as possible, date entries have been made uniform in style, and all sentences have been made to begin with a capital letter and to end with a suitable punctuation mark.

Printed here for the first time, as a companion piece to the 1808 narrative, is the surviving fragment of the rough notes that Fraser jotted down day by day as he descended the Fraser River. The first entry, which is incomplete, is dated May 30; the last, also incomplete, was written on June 10. The importance of this fragment is twofold. First, it gives us a generous sample of the raw material which Fraser used later when he wrote his more polished and carefully composed narrative. Secondly, it includes Fraser's quite detailed record of the courses he followed and the estimated distances that he travelled. The courses are compass readings and are reasonably accurate, when deviation is taken into account; the distances, on the whole, are over-estimated. When the river was twisting and turning sharply, Fraser could judge distances fairly well; on the straighter stretches, it was much harder to estimate speed and distance with much accuracy. In the twelve days covered by the notes, Fraser travelled from the vicinity of Macalister, north of Soda Creek, to a point near Leon Creek, north of Lillooet. His recorded distances total 145 miles, whereas the actual distance cannot be more than 120 miles at the most. But considering the extremely difficult conditions under which many of the observations were made, the general accuracy of his notes is remarkable. When his courses and distances are plotted, and some allowance is made for his over-estimation of the length of the straighter stretches, they are found to conform closely to the actual windings of the river, as the map and course reproduced elsewhere show.

It is unfortunate that the 1808 fragment and the journal describing the expedition into New Caledonia in 1806 are both available only in the form of transcripts. These were secured by Hubert Howe Bancroft in Victoria in 1878, when he visited the city in search of material for his *History of the Northwest Coast* and *History of British Columbia*. The journals had been brought to Victoria by Fraser's son, John, when he came West in 1863 to seek his fortune in the Cariboo. It was John's intention to edit and publish them after he had seen something of the country to which they referred, but his ill-starred career ended in suicide in 1865. We next hear of the journals in the possession of Dr. I.W. Powell, a prominent citizen of Victoria. E.O.S. Scholefield states that John Fraser stayed with Powell, and that they "became intimate. Young Fraser [Scholefield continues] carried with him

INTRODUCTION

wherever he went the manuscript diaries and letters of his father, of whose exploits he was extremely proud. One day he remarked to Dr. Powell that he would like to give him these precious documents as he was afraid that he might lose them in his wanderings. Dr. Powell accordingly took charge of the thick bundle of papers and he held them for many years. Eventually they were returned to the descendants of the explorer in Eastern Canada. ..."[26] As Scholefield knew Dr. Powell personally, and as this account was published in the latter's lifetime, there would seem to be no reason to think that it is not correct.

Mr. Donald C. Fraser, of Fargo, North Dakota, believes that the journals came into the possession of Simon Fraser's granddaughter, Catherine Fraser, of Hamilton, Ontario. According to family tradition she sold them through an Ottawa dealer, but efforts to trace the transaction and the manuscripts have failed.

While we must be eternally grateful to Bancroft for his foresight in securing copies of the journals, it is much to be regretted that the transcripts were not made with more care. They are full of mistakes, many of them so obvious that one suspects that the copyist cannot have even read over what he wrote, let alone compared it with the original. It is apparent that he knew little or nothing about the subject matter of the journals, and his lack of any knowledge of the French language led him astray at many points, particularly in the spelling of proper names. Other mistakes were probably in the original manuscripts, including the erratic use of capital letters, and the long passages in which a single punctuation mark — in one instance the comma, in another the dash, and in a third the semi-colon — is made to serve virtually all purposes.

How these transcripts should be edited for publication was a difficult matter to decide. The problem was made somewhat easier by the fact that an attempt to reproduce the 1806 journal exactly, mistakes and all, was made in 1929, when it was printed in an appendix to the *Report* of the Public Archives of Canada.

Anyone who wishes to see the text in an unvarnished state may consult it there. For the present volume, the transcripts have been considerably revised, but the many changes have been made solely with a view to presenting the journals as Fraser originally wrote them, and to making his meaning clear. There can surely be no virtue in printing *stinted* for *stunted*, *known* for *grown*, *missing* for *misery*, *far back* for *for bark*, *weakened* for *wakened*, and innumerable other mistakes of the same kind, when the context makes it transparently clear that the second word must have been the one that Fraser himself wrote. In addition to these changes, mis-spellings have been corrected occasionally when the mistake obscured the meaning. The names of Fraser's French-Canadian voyageurs are spelled in many different ways in the transcripts. *Gagnon*, for example, also appears as *Gagmen*, *Gagnion* and *Gaymon*. In the text as here printed, one correct French spelling has been adopted for French proper names and used throughout. A single form has also been used for the spelling of names of Indian tribes. As in the narrative, the form of the date entries has been made uniform, and all sentences made to begin with a capital letter and to end with a suitable punctuation mark. Long, involved sentences, of which there are many, have been made more intelligible and more readable by the insertion of commas and an occasional semi-colon.

All eleven of the letters written by Fraser in New Caledonia were seen by Bancroft in Victoria in 1878, and transcripts of them were made for him at that time. Letter-book copies of four of them (those dated December 21, 1806, and January 31, February 1 and February 10, 1807) were presented to The Archives of British Columbia by Catherine Fraser, Simon's grand-daughter, probably in 1908; these are in Fraser's handwriting. What became of the other seven letters is not known. Bancroft's transcripts were printed verbatim in the *Report* of the Public Archives for 1929. In the present volume the text has been edited in much the same way as the transcripts of the journals, but the changes are neither numer-

INTRODUCTION

ous nor important. The letters seem to have been considerably more legible than the journals, and were copied more accurately.

All the miscellaneous papers except one have been reproduced from the originals; the exception is the letter addressed to Lord Selkirk in 1816, which is taken from a transcript. The original was destroyed by fire at St. Mary's Isle in 1940. Except for trifling changes in punctuation, the text given follows that of all these documents exactly.

There can be no doubt that Fraser hoped some day to publish his journals of the 1808 voyage of discovery. The example of Alexander Mackenzie, who had printed his book and gained a title, had made a great impression on him, as it doubtless did upon other Nor'Westers. If they could not hope to find a field-marshal's baton in their knapsacks, it was perhaps not beyond the bounds of possibility that they might have in their *cassette* a journal that could be printed and attract the attention of officialdom. Bancroft contends that Fraser was jealous of Mackenzie, and perhaps he was. Following in Mackenzie's footsteps, as he did so frequently, he must often have had him in mind. It is interesting to note that Mackenzie's journal of his voyage to the Pacific, and Fraser's narrative of his exploration of the Fraser River, both begin with the same phrase. "Having made every necessary preparation," Mackenzie wrote, "I left Fort Chipewyan, to proceed up the Peace River." "Having made every necessary preparation for a long voyage," Fraser wrote, "we embarked at 5 o'clock A.M."

Even before he made his journey to the sea, Fraser was concerned that his journals should be rewritten and presented in proper style. In February 1807 he sent his journal of his travels in the previous year to John Stuart, with the suggestion that it be revised. It was, he admitted, "exceedingly ill wrote, worse worded and not well spelt. But then," he added, "I know you can make a good Journal of it, if you expunge some parts and add to others and make it out in a manner you think most proper."[27] Bancroft

57

must have been amused by this suggestion, for he had a singularly low opinion of Stuart's literary ability and considered that Stuart's own journal, kept at Rocky Mountain Portage House in 1805–6, was not only "very badly written" but was "by far the worst specimen of literary composition by a fur-trader" that he had seen, with the possible exception of Fraser's journals.[28]

Through the years Fraser clung to the hope that his journal might be printed. The end of the story is suggested by a letter written on February 4, 1815, by George Keith, one of the Nor'Westers, to Roderick McKenzie, then living in retirement on his seigniory at Terrebonne, "Your mention of Mr. Fraser's journal being in such a state of forwardness rather surprised me," Keith wrote. "A year or two ago, I had an indirect hint of his intentions of publishing it, but I hardly thought it could be moulded in such a manner as to be very interesting to the public. However, this was mere conjecture, for, although my curiosity would probably have been gratified, I did not presume to take the liberty of asking to have a peep at the rough manuscript in his possession."[29]

The journal was thus coming within the orbit of Roderick McKenzie, now busy gathering material for a history of the fur trade. Unable to arrange for publication himself, Fraser no doubt eventually turned over his manuscript in the hope that McKenzie could include it in his projected history. But the history was never written, and Fraser's narrative did not see the light until 27 years after his own death and 81 years after the great journey that it describes.

Later Years

Some months after the great voyage down the Fraser, Jules Quesnel described the expedition in a letter to his friend Joseph Maurice Lamothe, of Montreal:

INTRODUCTION

Now I must tell you that I went exploring this summer with Mr. Simon Fraser and John Stuart, whom I believe you know. We were accompanied by 12 men in three canoes. [We] Went down the river that up until now was thought to be the Columbia but finding it very soon unnavigable, we left our canoes and continued our journey on foot in the most appalling mountains that we could never have crossed if the natives, who received us well, had not helped us. After having passed all these difficult spots, not without much trouble as you can imagine, we found the river once more navigable and all embarked in wooden canoes and continued on our way more comfortably, as far as the place where the river empties into the Pacific Ocean. On our arrival, as we were preparing to continue our journey, the Indians of the region, who are very numerous, opposed our advance and it was by the greatest good luck that we were able to escape from this awkward situation without being obliged to kill and to be killed ourselves. We were well treated by all the other Indians on our return trip and all arrived in excellent health in our New Caledonia. The mouth of this river is in Latitude 49°, nearly three degrees north of the real Columbia. This journey did not meet the needs of the Company and will never be of any advantage to them, this river not being navigable, but we have nothing to reproach ourselves with, having done what we set out to do.[30]

A useless enterprise from the point of view of the Company! Such was the immediate verdict on Fraser's accomplishment; it therefore won him little fame and less reward. As a result, it is almost as difficult to trace his career in the years immediately after the expedition as it is in those before 1805.

After his return to Fort George on August 6, 1808, Fraser evidently left immediately to report at Fort Chipewyan, the headquarters of the Athabaska Department. When he arrived, Daniel Williams Harmon happened to be there, and Harmon jotted down the following note in his journal on September 21: "Ever since my arrival at this place, People from almost every corner of this extensive Department have been flocking in — one of whom is a Mr. Simon Fraser from New Caledonia (on the West side of the Rocky Mountain) who accompanied by Messrs. John Stuart and J. M. Quesnel and a Dozen of Canadians as well as two of the Natives, is just returned from a voyage to the Pacific Ocean...."[31] Harmon was bound for Dunvegan, where he was to spend the next two years. While there, on May 16, 1809, he made a further note about Fraser in his journal: "In the morning Messrs. Simon Fraser & James McDougall &c. arrived in four Canoes — the former Gentleman from the Rocky Mountain Portage & the latter from New Caledonia.... The above mentioned People after having past the most of the Day with me embarked to continue their route to Rainy Lake."[32]

Fraser was bound for the annual gathering of the partners of the North West Company at Fort William. There he was granted a year's furlough (a "rotation", in the parlance of the fur trade, because each of the partners took it in turn). Presumably he spent his leave in Canada visiting his relatives, but no details are available. The summer of 1810 found him back at Fort William, where he was reassigned to the Athabaska Department, and this appointment was renewed in each of the next three years. It has been said that Fraser was in charge of the Department, meaning that he was regarded as the senior partner assigned to it, but this is not so; the senior officer was John McGillivray. In January 1812, writing from "Bear Lake, Mackenzie's River Department", George Keith remarked: "Our friend, Mr. Simon Fraser, is still at the head of affairs in this department."[33] Mackenzie River was a district at this time, not a department, and was regarded as part of Athabaska. Keith's chance remark would indicate that Fraser was in charge of it for several seasons.

In 1814 Fraser was entitled to another furlough. The minutes of the Fort William meetings state that "by permission" his rotation was taken by another partner; but it seems certain nevertheless that Fraser himself also went to Canada, for we have his own statement that in the spring of 1815 he "came up from Montreal in company with Mr. Alexander Mackenzie [nephew of Sir Alexander, the explorer], and went with him as far as Red River."[34]

By 1815, Lord Selkirk's efforts to found a settlement in the Red River country had added new bitterness to the mounting rivalry between the North West Company and the Hudson's Bay Company. The Nor'Westers regarded the colony as a threat to their communications, their pemmican supplies and their general security that could not be tolerated, and which must be wiped out with the least possible delay. Fraser thus found himself involved in violence and intrigue as soon as he arrived in Red River. There is no doubt that the Nor'Westers encouraged the half-breed population of the region to terrorize the settlers, drive away their herds and pillage their crops. Alexander Mackenzie was anxious to cripple the colony further by depriving it of its administrative head; and in June 1815, by violence and threats of further attacks, he induced Governor Miles Macdonell to surrender to him. Mackenzie and Simon Fraser departed on June 22 with Macdonell in their custody, and brought him to Fort William, just as the annual North West rendezvous was assembling, on July 15.

Following the death of Simon McTavish, in 1804, his nephew, William McGillivray, had become the leading Montreal agent or director of the North West Company. In 1815 William's brother Simon represented the agents at Fort William; and the notes Simon wrote day by day in a little red book, now in the Public Archives, reflect the turmoil that existed in the ranks of the Nor'Westers at this time. The Company had recently suffered severe losses in some districts; discontent with the agents was widespread. Although violence could be exciting, it is clear that man of the partners had little liking for the position in which competition with the Hudson's Bay Company and the founding of Selkirk's colony had placed them. The future of the concern seemed very uncertain.

Several of the wintering partners were anxious to retire, and Fraser was one of the number. McGillivray's notes show that this was not the first time that he had tried to leave the North West Company; the matter had evidently been discussed in Montreal, earlier in 1815. "In the afternoon," McGillivray wrote the day after Fraser reached Fort William, "Simon Fraser sent Kenneth [McKenzie] to me to say that he wished to retire if he could get his money a little sooner than it was offered him in the Spring. I said I could not even promise him the terms offered in the Spring for times looked worse, and under existing circumstances we did not wish to lose any Partners." There is a further entry the following day: "Simon Fraser came to me to say he wished to retire and told some long stories of grievances, which I did not understand." McGillivray found the general attitude toward retirement alarming: "There seems a general wish to retire from the Country — some from getting old & tired of it, others from a dread of opposition. Fraser has signified his intention decidedly & only defers it this year in consequence of the state of the Concern if every one goes away."

As this last sentence indicates, McGillivray had won his battle; Fraser had agreed not to desert the North West Company in its difficult hour. He had even agreed to return to Athabaska, but McGillivray's notes show that he did so sorely against his will:

INTRODUCTION

"Mr. S. Fraser demurred about going to Athabasca, but after some altercation with Mr. [A.N.] McLeod in which he was told he must go in, or take the consequences, he finally acquiesced ..."

Having said their say, the wintering partners evidently felt somewhat more cheerful. "A Ball is given ... all is fun & good humour," McGillivray records. But the conclusion of the meetings and the dispersal of the partners to their far-flung districts was clearly a vast relief to him. "At length (thank God) they begin to disperse," he wrote on July 22. "Keith, J[ohn]. McG[illivray], Fraser and McLellan move off."

On the last page of the little notebook McGillivray wrote: "The business of the season had a very stormy aspect at its commencement, but it has subsided into a calm and we part very good friends." But little in the nature of a calm lay ahead for the North West Company. Clashes between its traders and those of the Hudson's Bay Company became more frequent, and Selkirk's Red River settlement, which had managed to survive the attacks made upon it in 1815, continued to be a particularly sore point of contention. Further action against it was planned, and word was evidently passed about that an attack of some sort would take place about the middle of June 1816. Many of the wintering partners were converging on the area at that time, on their way to Rainy Lake and Fort William, but most of them were "judiciously late" in arriving. They hoped that the half-breeds, impatient in nature, would act before their arrival and thereby free them from responsibility for anything that might happen. Nor were they disappointed. On June 19 the half-breeds clashed with a party of the colonists in what is known as the Seven Oaks Massacre, and Robert Semple, the new Governor, and nineteen of his men were killed.

When this tragedy occurred Lord Selkirk was in Canada, en route to Red River, bringing with him a contingent of about a hundred soldier-settlers, many of whom were from the famous de

Meuron regiment. News of the massacre reached him at Sault Ste. Marie, and he determined to press on at once to Fort William and have a reckoning with the North West partners in their stronghold there. He camped near the fort on August 12, and the next day seized it and, in his capacity as a magistrate in the Indian Territories, arrested the partners he found there. The number included William McGillivray, chief agent from Montreal, and Simon Fraser.

In making these arrests, Selkirk had the Seven Oaks Massacre primarily in mind. So far as Fraser is concerned, there is no evidence that he had had any part in the affair. On the contrary, there is good reason to believe that he had long been unhappy about the course of events in the West, and that he wished to have no part in them. It is true that he had helped to bring Governor Miles Macdonell as a prisoner from Red River to Fort William in 1815; but it is also true that within a day of his arrival he was trying to arrange his retirement from the North West Company. As we have seen, Simon McGillivray persuaded him, much against his will, to spend the trading season of 1815–16 in Athabaska, a department far removed from Red River. Three days after his arrest, he addressed to Lord Selkirk a "declaration" in which he professed entire ignorance of the recent events there. "I am not acquainted with the circumstances of the Colonists having gone away," he wrote, "nor the particulars of Governor Semple & several of the people having been destroyed by the Half Breeds; upon my way out from Athabasca in the Spring to the Red River in the latter end of June last, Indians informed me of the fact."[35]

This was probably literally true; but Fraser can hardly have been unaware that a move of some kind against the colony was planned. The rest of his statement relates to the events of 1815, and its air of injured innocence is not too convincing. Certainly it did not convince Selkirk, who sent Fraser and the other arrest-

INTRODUCTION

ed partners to Canada, under escort, in the expectation that they would be put on trial there.

The long journey began inauspiciously. The prisoners left Fort William on August 18. On the 26th one of the canoes capsized in rough weather some miles west of Sault Ste. Marie. Nine of the 21 men on board were drowned, including Kenneth McKenzie, and a second partner, John McLoughlin, nearly suffered a like fate. The survivors travelled on to York (Toronto) and Kingston, and on September 10 arrived in Montreal, where they were all immediately released on bail.

Two years and more passed before they were finally brought to trial in York. The only glimpse we catch of Fraser in this long interval is in May of 1817. In the last days of that month he was one of the partners with William McGillivray when the latter recaptured Fort William and re-established it as the main interior depot of the North West Company.

Fraser was tried with John Siveright, Alexander Mackenzie, Hugh McGillis, John McDonald and John McLoughlin. All were charged with "the crimes of treason and conspiracy, and as accessory to the murder of Robert Semple, Esquire, and to divers other murders, robberies and felonies." The actual trial took place on October 30 and 31, 1818. The proceedings have been printed, but Fraser did not give evidence and references to him are few and uninformative. Selkirk did not succeed in substantiating his charges and all four of the accused were acquitted.[36]

The trial at York was the closing event in Fraser's career in the fur trade. Indeed, he must have retired from the North West Company before it took place, for by 1818 he had settled in the Township of Cornwall, where he was to spend the rest of his long life.

In York, immediately after his acquittal, he submitted two petitions for grants of land to the Lieutenant-Governor of Upper Canada. In the first of these, dated November 2, 1818, he describes himself as "one of the first Settlers in the said Township of Cornwall, where he now resides and where he has Erected Mills and made other improvements." The second petition, dated the next day, relates to a lot in the town of Cornwall. Fraser had made improvements to this property, and was anxious to give it to his sister Isabella. Having discovered that land grants were no longer being made to women, he asked that the lot should be given to his brother Angus. Simon was advised that Angus should petition for the lot himself, and it was duly given to Angus in 1819.

In the vast maze of petitions for land and records of land transfers it has not been possible to trace Simon's properties in complete detail, but the general picture is reasonably clear. We know that under the terms of the order in council passed in 1797, when his mother petitioned for grants to herself and six of her children, he received 200 acres in Osgoode, Carleton County. A second grant of 200 acres was authorized in response to his 1818 petition, but the location of the land given to him is not know. Simon made his home on neither of these properties; he settled in the Township of Cornwall, in Stormont County, where his elder brothers William and Angus had taken up land many years before.

William, as previously noted, made his home at Coteau du Lac, in Lower Canada, and his properties in Cornwall Township were taken over by his sister, Margaret Fraser. Angus, however, not only retained his lands and lived on them for over fifty years, but acquired others in adjacent concessions. In April 1817 Simon Fraser bought two properties in the neighbourhood, one of them from his brother Angus, and to these he added a further 100 acres by purchase in 1819. Margaret, Angus and Simon Fraser between them must then have owned about 500 acres of land in the fifth, sixth and seventh concessions of Cornwall Township, all fronting on the middle branch of the Rivière aux Raisins, and all clustered about the large S-shaped twist in the river a mile or two west of the village of St. Andrews. On this twist there was a dam and the mill-site upon which Simon had built the mills referred to in his 1818 petition for land. They seem to have included a saw-mill and there may have been a grist mill as well. There is a tradition to the effect that the mills were a great convenience to the community, but that they were never a profitable venture. According to another version the mills were burned, and Fraser thereby suffered heavy financial losses.

Most of the family properties gradually came into Simon's possession. Neither Angus nor Margaret Fraser were married, and when Angus died in 1842 he left his lands to Simon. Three years later Simon purchased Margaret's holdings. He later disposed of some of his lands, but the agricultural census of 1861 records that his farm then consisted of 240 acres, mostly in pasture and woodland, and valued at $4,000.

Not long after he settled in Cornwall Township, Simon brought a bride to his new home. She was Catherine, daughter of Captain Allan Macdonell, a well-known military figure and a prominent resident of the Township of Matilda, about 30 miles west of Cornwall. The wedding took place on June 7, 1820, in the Roman Catholic Church at St. Andrews. Simon Fraser was then 44 years old; his bride was 29.

In his own notes on the Fraser family, printed in full in this volume, Fraser states that (in 1846) he had five sons and three daughters. We know that at least one other child died in infancy. Although the Frasers lived near St. Andrews for more than forty years, and raised a relatively large family, no direct descendants seem to be left anywhere in the region, and singularly little is known about their life there. John Graham Harkness, the historian of Stormont County, tells us that he made a "diligent effort" to find out something about Fraser, "but almost without result". All he could discover was that Simon was "said to have conducted a saw mill and to have owned some farm land".[37]

Harriet Fraser, the explorer's eldest daughter, believed that her father "was offered the honor of Knighthood in recognition of his services" after he retired from the North West Company. This offer Fraser declined because "His circumstances did not warrant the acceptance of a title ..."[38] It is of course conceivable that this story is true, but it seems unlikely. The strife and violence that characterized the fur trade at the time Fraser retired continued for several years. This was a matter of considerable concern both to the Canadian and British governments, and it seems improbably that they would wish, at that particular time, to honour a former Nor'Wester whose name had recently been publicly associated, however innocently, with the Seven Oaks Massacre. Moreover, it is easier to believe that the offer was never made than that Fraser could resist an opportunity to place himself on a par with Sir Alexander Mackenzie. Scholefield adds a picturesque detail by recalling the tale that Fraser declined the knighthood because he claimed "that he was the rightful successor to the title and ancestral estates of the Lovats.... He would not accept, so the story goes, any title beneath the title of Lord Lovat in dignity."[39]

The letter written by Fraser in 1840 to his friend the Hon. Donald Æ. MacDonell, Member of the House of Assembly of Upper Canada, gives an interesting glimpse of the explorer at the age of 64. It shows, amongst other things, that Fraser had greatly improved the standard of his own education since he retired from the fur trade. His is the letter of a well-informed citizen, who is following the political events of the day with a lively interest. He thanks MacDonell for sending him details of the debates on the union between Upper and Lower Canada that was then imminent, complains that he and his neighbours have "never had so little information about the Parliament as this session", and comments upon the position of the Roman Catholic Church in relation to the disposal of the Clergy Reserves.

INTRODUCTION

The reference to his appearance before a military medical board at Cornwall prompted a search that has revealed that Fraser served with the Government forces at the time of the Rebellion of 1837–8. When he first joined the militia we do not know, but his most important term of service was in November 1838. After dying down for a time, rebel military activity in Lower Canada suddenly flared up again in the first few days of November, following the proclamation of Robert Nelson as President of the "Republic of Lower Canada" on the 4th of the month. Fraser was serving as Captain in the 1st Regiment of the Stormont Militia, which was commanded by Donald Æ. MacDonell with the rank of Lieutenant-Colonel. The Regiment was ordered to go to the support of the force under Colonel Campbell, which was closing in on the rebels at Beauharnois. It came down the St. Lawrence on the evening of November 7, landed at the mouth of the Salmon River, and marched overland to Dundee, where the men camped for the night. In the darkness Fraser suffered a bad fall which resulted in serious permanent injury to his right knee.

The medical board referred to in the letter to MacDonell was the first of several before which Fraser pleaded his case for a pension in compensation for this injury. A statute of Upper Canada authorized a pension of £20 a year to disabled militiamen, but doubts were expressed as to whether it was intended to apply to the sort of injury Fraser had sustained. "This is a special case", a note on Fraser's docket in the files of the Governor's Civil Secretary reads, "which does not seem to be provided for either by Royal Regulation, or by Statute". As the documents printed elsewhere show, the facts of the matter were finally submitted to the Attorney General, who ruled in Fraser's favour, and his name was placed on the pension list on July 20, 1841.

Not content with this success, Fraser sought to supplement his provincial pension with another from the British Government. Successive commanders of the forces and Governors General were bombarded with petitions and memorials, the last being addressed to Sir Charles Bagot on September 1, 1842. For good measure, Fraser sent Bagot a second petition, addressed to Secretary at War, in London, which he hoped Bagot would recommend and forward if he felt he could take no action himself. Whatever chance Fraser may have had of securing further consideration was lost because he failed to mention in his submission that he was already a pensioner of the Province. The Governor General could not "forbear expressing his surprise" at the omission, stated that it was not in his power to place Fraser's name on the Home Government pension list, and declined to recommend his case to the Home authorities, although he would forward the memorial to the Secretary at War if Fraser so wished. There the matter appears to have ended.

The seriousness of his injury was undoubtedly the reason for Fraser's persistence. In the memorial to Bagot he states that it was "the cause of reducing him from a state of comparative affluence to penuery, owing to his not being capable to attend to his ordinary business". To a farmer and mill owner the injury could indeed be a serious matter, and it was in all probability the basic cause of the relative poverty in which most accounts tell us Fraser passed his later years.

A number of Fraser's colleagues in the North West Company settled in communities not far from St. Andrews, and no doubt he visited with them from time to time. No less than four prominent Nor'Westers lived in Williamstown, Glengarry, not a dozen miles from St. Andrews. They were Duncan Cameron, John McGillivray, Hugh McGillis and David Thompson. John McDonald of Garth, another retired wintering partner, settled at Gray's Creek, in the same County. All lived to ripe old ages, but the time came when McDonald and Fraser found themselves the last survivors. In 1859 they met for what both realized would probably be the last time, and before they parted they drew up the moving declaration print-

INTRODUCTION

ed elsewhere in this volume. "We are the last of the old N[orth]. W[est]. Partners," the statement begins. "We are both aged, we have lived in mutual esteem and friendship, we have done our duty in the stations allotted us without fear or reproach. We have braved many dangers, we have run many risks. We cannot accuse one another of any thing mean & dirty through life, nor [have we] done any disagreeable actions, nor wrong to others ... We part as we have lived in sincere friendship & mutual good will."

The statement is dated August 1, 1859. McDonald died at Gray's Creek in 1860. Fraser lived on for another two years. The Fraser River gold rush in British Columbia in 1858, and the discovery of the rich deposits in the Cariboo in succeeding years, directed world attention for the first time to the river named after him. In February 1862, his son, John Alexander Fraser, sent to the editor of the *Hastings Chronicle*, published in Belleville, a long letter in which he outlined his father's explorations and advanced the claim that "his exertions and enterprise in all probability secured to the British Crown" the rich new province of British Columbia, which promised to surpass "in every element of national greatness even our own Canada." Simon Fraser was by now 86 years old, but his mind was evidently still clear and alert. The son refers to an Indian ceremony Fraser had witnessed at Stuart Lake in 1806, and notes that "after the lapse of more than half a century" it was "as fresh in his mind as if it occurred yesterday". But Simon's days were now numbered, and little more than six months later, on August 18, 1862 (not on April 19, as is usually stated), the old explorer died. His wife, Catherine, died the following day without having been told of his passing, and both were buried in a single grave in the Roman Catholic cemetery at St. Andrews on August 21.

The obituary that appeared in the Cornwall *Freeholder* shows that his neighbours had some appreciation of the man and his accomplishments. "In Mr. Fraser," it declared, "the country loses not only one of its most respectable and honored residents, but one of the most illustrious men who ever settled within its borders. One of the few survivors of the fine old 'North Westers', Mr. Fraser's name, as the discoverer, and first explorer of the golden stream which bears his name, will be remembered with honor long after the most of his Provincial contemporaries have been forgotten."[40]

Family and Fame

Parish and census records relating to St. Andrews are both incomplete, but it has been possible to learn a good deal about Fraser's children. He himself states in his notes on his family that he had five sons and three daughters. Fraser meant that he had eight children living at the time he wrote the notes, in 1846; we know that there was at least one other child, a daughter, who presumably died in infancy.

The eldest of the children was Simon William, who was born on April 16, 1821. He left home as a young man and went to Albany, New York. Six other children seem to have arrived in the eight years between 1826 and 1833. Catherine Harriet, who was destined to be the last survivor of the family, was born on June 14, 1827. Both she and her sister Margery indulged in the feminine caprice of giving incorrect ages to the census taker (Harriet professed to be only 19 in 1851 and still only 25 in 1861), but as Harriet gave her correct age in 1871 it may perhaps be assumed that her sister did the same. The 1871 entry gives Margery's age as 45, which implies that she was born in 1826. Helen, the small daughter who must have died in infancy, was baptized on January 25, 1829. We know that Roderick, the second son, was born on July 1, 1830, but we must depend on the ages given in the census records for the birth dates of the remaining children. James Ambrose was probably born in 1831, and John Alexander followed

INTRODUCTION

in 1833. Then, after a lapse of some years, Allan (incorrectly referred to as Angus in the census) was born in 1840, and Isabella, last of the nine children, in 1842.

John, the fourth son, seems to have been the pride and joy of the family. He received a good education, qualified as a civil engineer, and (in his own words) "had several years experience in Canada as a practical Railway Engineer". After his father's death, as we have seen, he decided to seek his fortune in British Columbia, and it is interesting to find that Governor James Douglas received letters of introduction (now preserved in the Archives in Victoria) written on his behalf by Lord Monck, then Governor General of Canada, and the Duke of Newcastle, Secretary of State for the Colonies. Both letters had been written at the request of John A. Macdonald, Premier of Canada. It is intriguing to find John Alexander Macdonald recommending John Alexander Fraser to the attention of these high personages, but unfortunately there is nothing in the Macdonald Papers that throws any light on the relations between the two. In all probability, Macdonald was merely obliging a Member of the Assembly who knew the Fraser family — possibly John Sandfield Macdonald, who was then representing Cornwall in the House.

When he arrived in British Columbia, John Fraser applied for admission as a "sworn surveyor" and on April 3, 1864, he published a professional card in the New Westminster *British Columbian*, offering his services as a mining engineer and surveyor.

This card was dated from Camerontown, on Williams Creek, the richest and most famous stream in the Cariboo gold-fields. Later Fraser lived on the outskirts of nearby Barkerville. Williams Creek had passed its peak by the time young Fraser arrived, and it is unlikely that there was any great demand for his professional services. He was a friendly, sociable soul, and quickly became a well-known and popular figure in the mining community. Doubtless it was through his many friendships that he became involved in a number of enterprises. None of them seems to have prospered greatly, and by the spring of 1865 Fraser was so worried by his financial difficulties that he became mentally unbalanced. Friends did their best to watch over him, but on May 20 he eluded them and committed suicide by cutting his throat. Long years afterwards Harry Jones, one of the last surviving pioneers of the great days of the Cariboo, who reached Fraser's cabin just after he died, described the scene. One sentence recalls Macbeth: "I never thought there was so much blood in the body of a person before."[41]

In view of his Catholic upbringing, it is surprising to find that John Fraser was a Freemason. The account of his funeral published in the *British Columbian* states that "His remains were borne to their last resting place by his Masonic brethren and by the largest concourse of friends ever before assembled in Cariboo for such a purpose."[42] The *Cariboo Sentinel* recalled that "his upright and generous disposition had secured for him the esteem of all who knew him."[43]

The reminiscences of Robert Stevenson, a Cariboo pioneer who hailed from Williamstown, Glengarry, only a dozen miles from the Fraser home in St. Andrews, were printed in 1914 by W.W. Walkem. They include an account of Fraser's suicide. Stevenson's memory was not always accurate, and he was a born romancer, but he knew John Fraser personally and his account may throw genuine light on the circumstances of the family. Simon, he tells us, "left a will bequeathing a very large homestead farm to his children, to be equally divided amongst them when the youngest came of age". The newspapers of the day were filled with tales of the fortunes being made in the golden Cariboo, and the Frasers decided to mortgage the farm and to send young John to the goldfields to make their fortune. To begin with, all went well; but his popularity and social activities soon absorbed an undue proportion of his attention. "He was elected president of the Literary Society, the Glee Club and the Library Association. He was also a member

INTRODUCTION

of the Methodist choir. ... Whilst he was doing well in his mining ventures he was neglecting the mortgage which was hanging over the family homestead, and on which his three sisters and two brothers were living." Stevenson attributes his suicide to the arrival of two letters from home, one of which informed him that the mortgage had been foreclosed, and the other announcing that his fiancée had married another man.[44]

At the time of Simon Fraser's death in 1862, four of his children were living at St. Andrews: Margery, Harriet, Roderick and James. The census records show that all four were still there in 1871. Margery died in May 1884, and James seems to have died the same year. Roderick and Harriet lived on at St. Andrews, apparently in straitened circumstances. In June 1887 Harriet petitioned the Governor General in Council, praying that "some recognition of her father's services" might be given "by making provision for the support of his only surviving daughter". Fraser's enterprise in occupying the country west of the Rocky Mountains had gone far, she felt, to secure those territories for the British and for Canada. According to the Victoria *Colonist*, her case was presented to Sir John Macdonald by a delegation consisting of a dozen Senators and Members of Parliament. Macdonald promised to discuss the matter with his colleagues,[45] but nothing was done. In January 1890, Harriet again submitted her petition, this time with better effect. Council decided not only to give Harriet herself an annuity of $250, but to give a second annuity of $150 to her brother Roderick, both grants being "in recognition of the services of their father in exploring the country which now forms the Province of British Columbia".

A note in the Victoria *Colonist*, written by someone who was obviously well informed about affairs in Ottawa, states that the pensions for Harriet and Roderick were secured largely through the influence of Sir Donald Smith (later Lord Strathcona), a nephew of John Stuart, who had gone down the

Fraser River with Harriet's father in 1808, and Harriet's cousin, the Hon. R.W. Scott (later Sir Richard Scott), whose mother was a sister of Mrs. Simon Fraser. Both Smith and Scott were members of the House of Commons at the time.[46]

In 1896 Fraser's other surviving child, Simon William, who had returned to Canada and was then living in Hamilton, also asked for a pension. He explained that he was 75 years old, "in penurious circumstances and through illness and age ... unable to follow any occupation". He felt that "as a matter of justice" he was "surely entitled to the same consideration" as his sister and brother; but no annuity was forthcoming.

Simon William's petition was dated February 1, 1896;[47] he died later the same year. He had been living in Hamilton with two daughters, Catherine and Margaret, who ran a small confectionery shop. His three sons had all gone to the United States. A grandson, Angus Fraser, joined the United States Army, fought in the Philippines in the Spanish-American War, and rose eventually to the rank of General. He became a prominent citizen in North Dakota, where he served as Adjutant General of the National Guard. General Fraser, who died as recently as 1957, took a lively interest in his explorer-ancestor, and had a small collection of his notes and papers. These are now in the possession of the General's grandson, Mr. Donald C. Fraser, of Fargo, N.D., who very kindly made copies available to the writer.

Roderick and Harriet were the last members of the Fraser family to reside at St. Andrews, and both left it in their later years. Roderick moved to Hamilton, and he died there at the home of his niece, Catherine Fraser, on July 1, 1902, his seventy-second birthday. Harriet lived for a time in Ottawa, where she was a frequent visitor in the home of her cousin, the Hon. Richard Scott. After she received her annuity form the Canadian Government she entered the House of Providence, in Toronto, where she lived for the rest of her life. Only a matter of days before her death,

INTRODUCTION

which occurred on August 19, 1907, the province of British Columbia had granted her a pension of $600 a year.[48]

As this indicates, the province was at long last beginning to recognize the important part that Simon Fraser had played in its history and destiny. Fraser himself, in his last years, had hoped that some monetary reward would be given to him after the discovery of gold on the Fraser River and its tributaries. Indeed, it is apparent that he actually expected something of the kind, for in his will he left to his son John Alexander Fraser "any property real or personal, or both, which I may now have or which may hereafter come to me in consequence of my having been the discoverer and explorer of the Fraser River …" But nothing was forthcoming for many long years, and the annuity given to Harriet was prompted by the approaching centenary of the great voyage down the river, which was to be celebrated in 1908.

Two major events marked the occasion. On September 30, 1908, the Premier of British Columbia, the Hon. Richard McBride, unveiled a memorial column at New Westminster. This stood on Albert Crescent, on a commanding site overlooking the Fraser River. A bust of Fraser, executed by the noted Canadian sculptor Louis Hébert, was later mounted on the column and unveiled on October 4, 1911.

The second event that marked the centenary in 1908 was a notable exhibition of historical pictures and relics that was displayed first in New Westminster, and subsequently in Vancouver and Victoria. Most of the items included were the property of the Provincial Archives, which through the years has assembled an interesting collection of Fraser mementoes. They include his sword stick; his pen, seal and sealing-wax; a cup and saucer and three silver spoons that were used in his home; a watch-chain made from his hair; and his mother's writing-desk. Fraser's silk hat (not a beaver hat, as has been stated), another prized possession of the Archives, was brought to British Columbia by his son John, in 1864. John left it for safekeeping with his friend Dr. Powell, in Victoria, and many years after John's death Dr. Powell placed it in the Archives.

The Fraser family seems to have vanished completely from the Township of Cornwall, and the explorer's grave lay untended for many years in the little cemetery at St. Andrews. Eventually the Government of Ontario and the Hudson's Bay Company took an interest in the matter. The former put the cemetery in good order; the latter placed a new marker over Fraser's grave. The gray granite stone bears the following inscription:

> In memory of Simon Fraser, explorer, born in 1776, died 1862. While in the employ of the North West Company he conducted important exploration and pioneer work principally in the area now known as British Columbia, which he helped to secure for the British. He led the first exploring expedition to descend the great river which bears his name, reaching the Gulf of Georgia on July 2, 1808. This monument was erected in 1921 by the Hudson's Bay Company over the grave where he and his wife were buried.

A decade later a further tribute was paid to Fraser when the Historic Sites and Monuments Board of Canada placed a bronze tablet on a stone monument on Marine Drive, Vancouver, near the western boundary of the Musqueam Indian Reserve. This marks the locality in which Fraser landed for the last time at the end of his journey down the Fraser River in 1808.

Finally, in 1958, when the province of British Columbia was celebrating both its own centenary and the 150th anniversary of

FOREWORD

Fraser's journey, his voyage down the river was re-enacted by a picked crew manning three canoes. These were modern northern freight canoes, made to resemble their birch-bark predecessors by the addition of high bows and sterns and a coat of paint. Fraser was impersonated by Richard F. Corless, Jr., a veteran riverman who was familiar with many of the streams Fraser himself had followed, including the Peace and the Parsnip, as well as the Fraser itself. The party left Prince George, the modern city near the site of Fort George, on May 28, 1958, a hundred and fifty years to the day after Fraser's own departure, and every effort was made to adhere to his time-table. Advance arrangements at portages and adequate assistance enabled the three canoes to reach Musqueam on schedule, on July 2. Even with all the help that modern conditions made available, the descent of the river was a notable achievement, and it gave to those concerned with it a new conception of the stature and ability of the pioneer in whose track they were following. Motion pictures were taken at many points, and these bring vividly to life some of the perils and problems met by Fraser in his memorable journey from the Rocky Mountains to the Pacific Ocean.

W. Kaye Lamb

# THE GREAT JOURNEY: EXPLORING THE FRASER RIVER

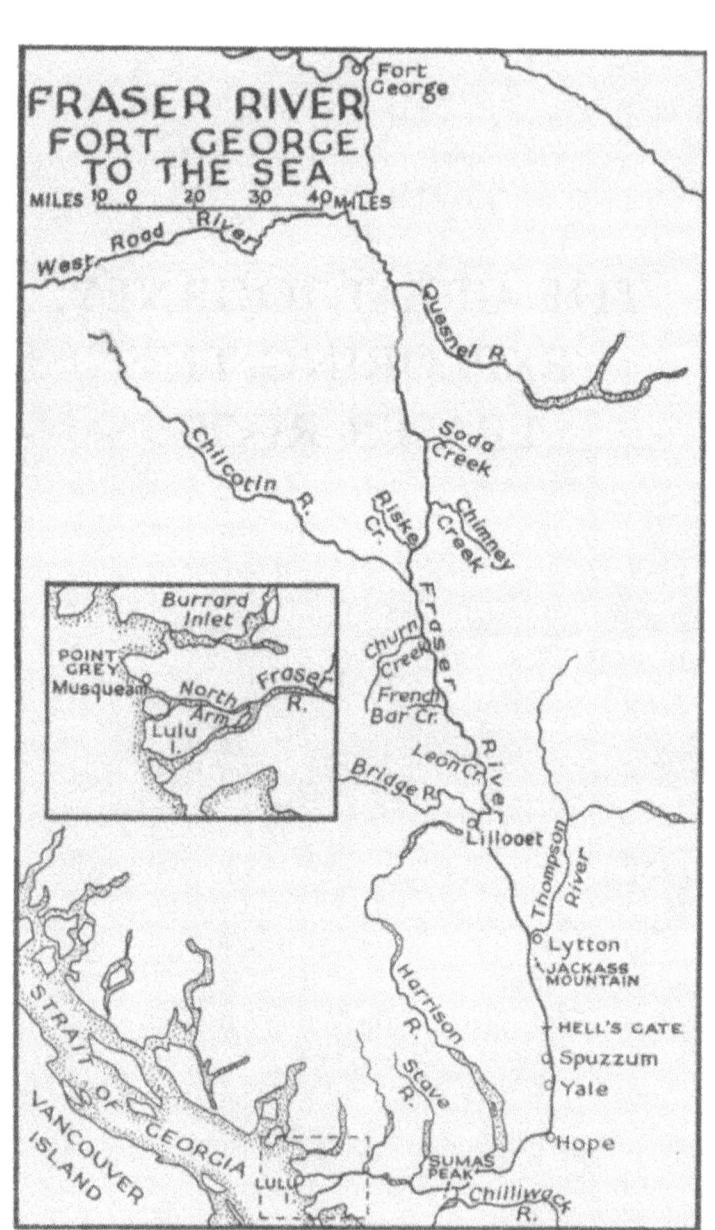

JOURNAL OF A VOYAGE FROM THE ROCKY MOUNTAINS TO THE PACIFIC OCEAN PERFORMED IN THE YEAR 1808

Fort George to the Thompson River

Saturday, May 22 [28], 1808. Having made every necessary preparation for a long voyage, we embarked at 5 o'clock, A.M. in four canoes, at Fraser's River [i.e., at the mouth of the Nechako River].[1] Our crew consisted of nineteen men, two Indians, Mr. Steward [Stuart], Mr. Quesnil [Quesnel], and myself; in all twenty four. At this place [the] Columbia [i.e., the Fraser River] is about 300 yards wide. It overflows its banks, and has a very strong current.

After having proceeded eighteen miles we came to a strong rapid [the Fort George Canyon] which we ran down. One of the canoes came near striking against a precipice which forms the right bank. A little lower down the channel it contracts to about 70 yards, and passes between two rocks.

After running down several considerable rapids, we put a shore at 11 A.M. to breakfast. In the mean[time] Mr. Stewart [Stuart] took a meridian altitude, O.L.L. 115° 9' 45"[2] by artificial Horizon. Error of Sextant 7' 30" +. We saw many fresh tracts [tracks] of Red Deer. Reembarked at one. Fine going; a smooth Current interspersed with small Islands. Several houses & tombs along the left bank.

At 4 P.M. we passed a River [the West Road River] on right 80 yards wide & named it *Bourbonneur*. Here we saw two houses, which our Indians called the summer residence of a Nasquitin

[Nazkoten] Chief. We landed & left marks to let the natives know that we had passed.

Continued our route and encamped at 6. Put our arms in order, gave ammunition to all hands and established a regular watch. We gathered some wild onions for sauce.

Sunday, May 29. Cold morning. We were under way at 4. Went a shore upon an island, and secured [i.e., cached] a bale of salmon for our return.

A little lower [down] the river contracts into a narrow space [the Cottonwood Canyon], and passes violently between high rocks. The canoes, however, being lightened, were run down. Here we put three bales of salmon into *cache*, and carried the rest [over a portage] through a very rugged country. It was late before we had cleared [this obstacle]. We called this place *descharge* [*décharge*] *de la Montagne*.³

Continuing with a strong current in our favour, we passed a small river [the Cottonwood] on our left. Its banks are high, composed of clay and sand; and there is a house near the entrance. Soon after [we] came to another River [the Quesnel]; and we encamped at sun-set.

This afternoon [we] observed several houses of the Nasquitins [Nazkotens]. [They] had a very fine prospect consisting of extensive plains, and behind hills rising upon hills. The trees in this quarter are pine, cypress, birch, hemlock, cedar, juniper &c. At night flashes of lightning were to be seen, [and] loud peals of thunder to be heard accompanied with heavy rain.

Monday, May 30. We embarked at 5 A.M. Experienced a strong current. The country all along is charming, & apparently well inhabited; having seen a large number of houses. At 6 we put to shore at a large house; found a *cache* of fish. After taking a few salmons and leaving the value we secured the rest for the owners. Observed some vestiges of horses at this place. A little below we put a shore again, and left a bale of salmon in *cache*. This

JOURNAL OF A VOYAGE FROM THE ROCKY MOUNTAINS TO THE PACIFIC OCEAN PERFORMED IN THE YEAR 1808

caused some delay. Passed several rapids [in] the afternoon. This country, which is interspersed with meadows and hills, dales & high rocks, has upon the whole a *romantic* but *pleasant* appearance.

Continuing our course expeditiously, on a sudden we perceived some of the Natives on the left shore seemingly in great confusion. We crossed to the right and landed at a large house. Our Indians then called out to the strangers on the opposite shore, informing them that we were *white people* going to the sea.

[From this point to the first sentence of the entry dated June 10, the text is paralleled by the "Second Journal". See pages 131–61.]

A woman of the Atnah nation who happened to be within hearing on our side of the water, came running towards us, speaking as loud as possible, but our interpreter could not understand her — yet she still continued speaking, and endeavoured to supply the deficiency by signs. In this manner she continued, at one time addressing the people on the [other] side, at another directing her discourse to us; in the meantime we crossed [the river]. But we were still on the water when some *couriers* were despatched on horseback with the news [of our arrival] to the next Indians; and we only found a man and a woman with three children of the Atnah nation at the campment; these were alarmed at our strange appearance.

[We] found a young boy, whose mother was of a Tahow-tin [Tauten] nation, who understood a little of the Carrier language; by his means we learned that, in consequence of the couriers just now sent off, many of the natives would make their appearance in that day; and that it would be dangerous for us to proceed before our intentions were publicly known. This information, added to the desire of procuring guides, induced [me] to remain the rest of the day.

In the afternoon, some Toohowtins [Tautens] and Atnaughs [Atnahs] arrived on horse back. They seemed peaceably inclined, and appeared happy to see us, and observed that having heard by their neighbours that white people were to visit their country this season, they had remained near the route on purpose to receive us.

According to the accounts we received here, the river below was but a succession of falls and cascades, which we should find impossible to pass, not only thro the badness of the channel, but also thro the badness of the surrounding country, which was rugged and mountainous. Their opinion, therefore, was that we should discontinue our voyage and remain with them. I remarked that our determination of going on was fixed. They, then, informed us that at the next camp, the great Chief of the Atnaugh [Atnah] had a slave who had been to the sea, who perhaps we might procure as guide.

These Indians had heard of fire-arms, but had never seen any. Seeing our fire-arms, they desired us to explain the manner in which they were used. In compliance we fired several shots, the report of which astonished them to that degree as to [make them] drop off their legs. Upon recovering from their surprise, we made them examine the effect; seeing the marks on the trees, they appeared uneasy, and observed that the Indians in that quarter were good and peaceable people, and would never make use of their arms to annoy white people. Yet, they remarked, that we ought to be on our guard, and act with great caution when we approached villages; for should we surprise the natives they would be apt to mistake us for enemies, and through fear attack us with their arrows. During the above mentioned experiment in firing, we lost our swivel. It had a flaw before, and firing at [this] time, perhaps with an overcharge, [it] broke into pieces, and wounded our gunner. This accident alarmed the Indians, but having convinced them that the injury was of no great consequence, they were reconciled.

The Atnah language has no affinity to any other that I know, and it was by the means of two different interpreters

JOURNAL OF A VOYAGE FROM THE ROCKY MOUNTAINS TO THE PACIFIC OCEAN PERFORMED IN THE YEAR 1808

[that] we were enabled to understand it. The men of this tribe are of a diminutive [size] but of an active appearance. They dress in Skins prepared in the hair; their weapons are bows and arrows neatly finished. The country round consists of plains, well stocked with animals. Some of our men who were out a hunting saw plenty of deer.

Tuesday, May 31. After dressing the gunner's wound and examining the state of our fire-arms, we embarked at 5, accompanied by one of the Toohow-tin [Tauten] Indians as an interpreter for the Atnah language. Aided by several rapids and a continual strong current we soon performed the distance of twelve miles, and arrived at a carrying place [the canyon below Soda Creek]. Here the canoes, being lightened of a half of their lading, were run down. The other half of the lading was carried over by land for two miles through a very uneven country.

The Chief and the Indians, recommended to our attention yesterday, who were encamped on a hill to the left, soon joined us, and presented us with dried salmon and different kind[s] of roots. The last though considered as excellent by the natives, we could not very well relish.

After inquiring repeatedly for the slave, who had a knowledge of the country below, he was at last introduced, and to form an estimate of his capacity, I had two oil cloths[4] spread out for the ground of a chart, upon which I desired him to sketch the country towards the sea. This he readily undertook, but his endeavours soon convinced me that his stock of knowledge was very slender indeed, for his lines were entirely directed by an elderly man, a relative of the Chief. However, in his sketch, we could plainly see a confirmation of the badness of the navigation, and thereby the necessity of leaving [our] canoes, and as much of our baggage as we could spare, in order to prosecute our journey by land.

The Chief who had been an advocate in our cause spoke much in our favour to his own people, and assured us that the next nation were good Indians and would be kind to white strangers. Having given to our new friend a hint that trading posts should be established in his country within a short period, he immediately offered to accompany us all the way, remarking at the same time that he was well known, and that his experience and influence would be of great consequence to the security of our success. Then his brother presented me with a fine beaver skin, and a well dressed deer skin, and then recommended the Chief to our particular protection. I thanked him for his presents, and assured him that every attention should be paid to his relation, and that he should be handsomely rewarded for his trouble on our return. When this ceremony was over, the Chief, his slave, and our Too-how-tin [Tauten] interpreter having got ready, took their departure; but the last was unwilling to proceed, alledging for an excuse that his wife and children would starve in his absence, but notwithstanding this strong argument he was prevailed upon to proceed.

At the lower end of the carrying place we met eighteen men who had come to see us. I shook hands with them; they surveyed us narrowly, but were friendly inclined.

This tribe is extremely fond of smoking, and were very troublesome, constantly plaguing us for our pipes. They make use of, in lieu of tobacco, a kind of weed mixed with fat. The Chief shewed us a Calumet [a long-stemmed pipe] which had found its way from the lower parts of the river.

Left 4 bales of Salmon in charge of the Chief's brother. We embarked and proceeded down a strong current through many bad places, until late in the afternoon when we came to a very long rapid [a canyon near Chimney Creek], which upon visiting we found to be strong and dangerous. It being nearly night we encamped. Blowing a hurricane from the south the whole afternoon, [which] rendered our progress slow, tedious, and often dangerous; at times our canoes were not manageable and within an ace of being dashed to pieces against the rocks, or of filling.

JOURNAL OF A VOYAGE FROM THE ROCKY MOUNTAINS TO THE PACIFIC OCEAN PERFORMED IN THE YEAR 1808

While we were visisting [visiting] the Rapids, we observed some Indians on the opposite side of the river; but they did not observe us. [I] inquired of the Chief, if the Indians were in the habit of running down this rapid: he said no; he conceived that the whirlpools would swallow up or overpower any canoes, or exertions of his nation, but he added, his confidence in our superiority over them was such that he would not hesitate a moment to accompany us wherever we thought proper to venture.

Apprehensive that the old man might regret his undertaking and give us the slip in course of the night, I had his bed made in my tent by way of security. Before he went to rest, he recommended to me to have all our guns and pistols in good order in case of surprise from enemies. "Though the Indians," continued he, "are generally good people, still there may be bad men among them who will go about in the dark."

Wednesday, June 1. This morning at an early hour all hands were ready, and the Natives began to appear, from every quarter, in numbers. Mr. Stuart, six men and myself went again to visit the rapid. We found it about two miles in length, with high & steep banks, which contracted the channel in many places to the breadth of 40 or 50 yards. The immense body of water passing through this narrow space in a turbulent manner, forming numerous gulphs and cascades, and making a tremendous noise, had an awful and forbidden [forbidding] appearance. Nevertheless since it was considered as next to impossible to carry the canoes across the land, on account of the heigth [height] and steepness of the Hills, it was resolved to venture them down this dangerous pass.

Leaving Mr. Stuart and two men at the lower end of the rapid, in order to watch the motions of the Natives, I returned with the other four men to the camp. Immediately upon my arrival I ordered the best five [men] out of the crews into a canoe lightly loaded. This [order] was no sooner given than obeyed; and the canoe in a moment was underway. After passing the first cascade the canoe lost her course, and was drawn to the eddy, where it was whirled about for a considerable time, and seemingly in suspense whether to sink or to swim. The men had no power over her. However it took a favourable turn and by degrees was led from this dangerous vortex again into the stream. It then continued flying from one danger to another, untill the cascade near the last where in spite of every effort, the whirlpools forced it against a projecting rock, which happened to be a low point. Upon this the men debarked, and saved their own lives, and contrived to save the property; for the greatest danger was still a head. Of course to continue on the water would be certain destruction.

During this distressing scene we were on shore, looking on, anxiously concerned; and seeing our poor fellows once more safe gave us as much happiness as to themselves. We hastened to their assistance, but their situation rendered our approach perilous and difficult. The bank was extremely high and steep, and we had to plunge our daggers at intervals into the ground to check our speed as otherwise we might be impelled to slide into the river.

When we joined the party we lost no time, but set to work immediately. We cut steps into the declivity of the hill, fastened a line to the front of the canoe with which some of the men ascended in order to haul it up, while the others supported the canoe upon their arms. In this manner our situation was extremely precarious; our lives hung as it were upon a thread; for failure of the line or a false step of one of the men might have hurled the whole of us into eternity. However we fortunately cleared the bank before dark.

The men who had the rest of the baggage in charge, perceiving from these difficulties, the impossibility of attempting the rapid with safety, began to carry it, and had immense high hills to asscend with heavy loads on their backs.

Numbers of the Natives came to see us in [the] course of the day and remained. They all assured us that the navigation for

JOURNAL OF A VOYAGE FROM THE ROCKY MOUNTAINS
TO THE PACIFIC OCEAN PERFORMED IN THE YEAR 1808

a certain distance below was impractible [impracticable], and advised us to leave our canoes in their charge and proceed on our journey by land to a great river [the Thompson] that flows from the left into this communication. The country they said consisted of plains, and the journey could be performed with horses in four or five days; thence we should have smooth water all the way to the sea.

But going to the sea by an indirect way was not the object of the undertaking. I therefore would not deviate and continued our route according to my original intention.

The Indians seemed pleased in our Company. They carry no arms, and this confidence I suppose was meant as a testimony of their friendship. There is a tribe of *Carriers* among them, who inhabit the banks of a Large River to the right. They call themselves Chilk-hodins [Chilcotins]. About 60 Indians were present on this occasion & as many more were on the opposite side, bawling [to us] to send for them. But as their presence could be of no Service to us we thought it more Suitable to dispense with their company as much as possible.

Thursday, June 2. The river had risen eight feet within these twenty four hours. More Indians arrived. All hands hard at work carrying the baggage, and with the assistance of the Indians and of a line two of the canoes were hauled up the hill. Seeing the difficulty attending this experiment we came to the determination of leaving the other canoes and provisions. Mr. Stuart and some of the men agreed to go by land. But on application to the Indians for the horses they had promised, we received evasive answers, and we passed the rest of the day in anxious suspense.

Friday, June 3. The Indians having deceived me I was under the necessity of deranging my plans of yesterday, and this morning had one more of the canoes taken up the hill, so that all the party may continue by water. We only could procure four horses; these were of service in the carrying place, where the road is excessively bad, being up and down hill, and sometimes along the edge of dangerous declivities, over one of which a horse, with Mr. Stuart's desk, [and] our medicine chest, tumbled, and [some papers and medicines] were lost.[5]

The canoes and the other articles which remained I gave in charge to an Indian, who, we were assured, was an honest good man.

The Indians made us understand that within a couple of days more, we should come to a plentiful country where the Indians were hospitable, but having by this time acquired sufficient acquaintance with the character of our new councillors, we did as we were done by, we gave them civil, but evasive answers, and in all followed the dictates of our own judgment.

This is called the *Atnah Nation*. Their country is well stocked with large animals, and they consequently pay very little attention to fishing. In summer they reside in shades,[6] and their winter quarters which are built under ground, are square below diminishing gradually in size to the top, where there is a small aperture which serves the double purpose of door & chimney, while a post with notches answers for a pair of stairs.

The Atnahs wish to be friendly to strangers but they do not know how. The men are tall and slender, of a serious disposition and inclined to industry. They say they never sing nor dance; but we observed them play at hazard, a [gambling] game well known among the Indians of Athabasca. They besmear their bodies with oil and red earth, and paint their faces in different colours. Their dress is leather. They are great travellers; have been at war beyond the Mountains going by the name of *Rocky Mountains*, where they saw Buffaloes; for seeing our powder horns they knew them to be of that animal.

They informed us that white people had lately passed down the first large river to the left. These we supposed to be some of our friends from the department of *Fort des Prairies*.[7]

JOURNAL OF A VOYAGE FROM THE ROCKY MOUNTAINS TO THE PACIFIC OCEAN PERFORMED IN THE YEAR 1808

Sunday [Saturday], June 4. It was late morning before we got ready. Last night an Indian who seemed to be well acquainted with the River promised to accompany us, but this morning declined, saying he was afraid of the Rapids.

One of the Indians brought us a Pistol which Mr. Quesnel lost yesterday when he was on horse back. This was a piece of honesty we did not expect. Yet all the time we have been at this place though many things were left loose, and scattered in such a manner as to afford the natives plenty of opportunities, nothing went astray. The Atnahs, therefore, are more honest than any other tribe on this side of the Mountains.

These Indians, we remarked, do not burn the dead; but bury them in large tombs, which are of a conical form, about 20 feet [in] diameter, and composed of coarse timber.

At 6 A.M. we were on the water and crossed to the Indians, who were on the opposite sides. Here we observed a precipice of immense heighth [height] a head, which seemed to bar the River. Continued our course with a strong current; ran down several Rapids & Came to a dangerous one, in which the Canoes having shipped much water & being nearly upset, we landed.

Visited the lower part [of the rapid]; having found it strong and full of tremendous Whirlpools we were greatly at a loss how to act. However the nature of our situation left us no choice, for we were under the necessity either to run down the Canoes or to abandon them. The first having been preferred they were unloaded & then manned with five men each. One canoe went first, and having succeeded, the other two immediately followed. The struggle which the men on this trial experienced between the whirlpools and rocks almost exhausted their strength; the canoes were in perpetual danger of sinking or being broken to pieces. It was a desperate undertaking.

After escaping this danger the men returned by land for the baggage. This task was as difficult and dangerous as going by the water, [the men] being obliged to pass on a declivity, which formed the brink of a huge precipice, among loose stones, and gravel that constantly gave way from under their feet. One of them who had lost the path of the others got into a most intricate and perilous situation. With a large package on his back he got so engaged among the rocks that he could neither move forward nor backward, nor yet unload himself without imminent danger. Seeing the poor fellow in this predicament, I crawled to his assistance; but not without great risk, and saved him, however his load dropped off his back over the precipice into the river.

This carrying place, which is two miles long ruined our shoes; and our feet became full of blisters and were very sore with much walking.[8]

Monday [Sunday], June 5. Fine weather. In the night the water lowered about two feet. This was an agreeable circumstance. We were off at 5. Good going; a strong current and many rapids in our favour. At 9, we landed at the head of a dangerous place [the Iron Rapids, between Riske Creek and the Chilcotin River]. The river here, which does not exceed thirty yards in breadth, passes between two precipices, and is turbulent, noisy, and awful to behold! The carrying place is about a mile long; the ground rough; but there is a beaten path. However the men took five horses to transport the baggage across, yet were much harassed with fatigue.

At this place we found a horn of the Sasyan or Rocky Mountain ram. We called this, *Portage de Barrel* [*du Baril*]. Set out and about two miles below passed a small river [the Chilcotin] on the right. The same upon which the Carriers we saw the other day, live. It runs through a fine country abounding with plenty of animals such as orignals [moose], Red Deer, Carriboux [caribou], Beaver &c. The Natives make use of horses.

Soon after we came to a rapid which appearing turbulent, we visited. We then lightened the canoes and run them down the rapid. We experienced great danger; one of the canoes was

JOURNAL OF A VOYAGE FROM THE ROCKY MOUNTAINS TO THE PACIFIC OCEAN PERFORMED IN THE YEAR 1808

sucked into a whirlpool whose force twisted off the stern; but this happening near the bank and the end of the rapid, the men were saved, while the canoe was dragged on shore full of water. The carrying place was along the side of a steep high hill and very bad. The country altogether looks wild.

The rest of the day we had a great run, a strong current, and many rapids, some of them dangerous. We encamped at 7 P.M.[9]

Tuesday [Monday], June 6. Early this morning I dispatched two men to examine the river, but they could not go far. The high hills, the precipices, the difficulty attending *ravines* &c. rendered walking very painful and disagreeable. A pair of shoes does not last a day, and the men have their feet full of thorns.

Embarked at 7. Passed on with great velocity. Observed many shades [shelters] for fishing at the rapids. At 10 arrived at the falls. Here the Old Chief informed us that we should be under the necessity of leaving our canoes. We examined the rapids, and found them impracticable — Cascades and whirlpools hemmed in by huge rocks afford but a dreary prospect to our anxiety. I sent Mr. Quesnel and six men to examine both sides of the river for a carrying place. After an absence of three hours they returned and informed [me] that there was a well beaten track on the opposite side, which was about four miles long, and passed through a wild country. We crossed over and held a consultation, where it was determined to examine again the river before the canoes should be carried. Mr. Quesnel & Mr. Stuart were ordered upon this service for next morning, and we encamped.[10] Some of the men who had been out a hunting saw some animals and wounded one.

Wednesday [Tuesday], June 7. Fine weather. This morning according to our plan of yesterday, the two Gentlemen, accompanied by six men, one of our Indians, the interpreter, and the old chief, set out to examine the state of the river. The men who remained were busy repairing their things. The Mountains in sight are very high and covered with snow. Our Guide says that

95

they are the highest on the communication. The trees here are poplars, and pines. In the evening Cloudy weather, with strong wind, followed with small rain.

Thursday [Wednesday], June 8. Fine weather. Excessive heat all day. Examined our salmon — being our only provisions — and discovered we had not enough for a month. However the Indians say that we shall find plenty from the Natives along the Route.

About 3 A.M. [P.M.] Our party, abating [less] the Chief and the interpreter, returned. They had been at the *Rapid Couverte* [*Rapide Couvert*] — distant about eighteen Miles — and saw but one bad rapid on the way. Going they kept near the river and had great difficulty; but on their return they kept on the top of the hills and had agreeable walking. They saw a band of Indians, with whom our Indians remained for our arrival.

About 6, put our Canoes in the water and conducted them with the line down to the first Cascades; the others were run down though not without danger. Fortunately the water had recently fallen several feet, otherwise we could never have ventured upon these rapids. After two hours paddling down a strong Current we encamped.[11]

Friday [Thursday], June 9. This morning the men put [on] their best cloathes. Our two Indians having only a Beaver Robe and an original [moose] skin, I gave each a blanket and a *braillet* [*brayette*: pair of breeches]. All this was done that we might appear to advantage in the eyes of the new Indians whom we were to find at the *Rapide Couverte* [*Couvert*]. At 7 A.M. our arms and every thing being in due order, we embarked and [a] few hours after arrived at *Rapide Couverte* [*Couvert*].[12] Here [the] channel contracts to about forty yards, and is inclosed by two precipices of great heighth [height], which bending towards each other make it narrower above than below. The water which rolls down this extraordinary passage in tumultuous waves and with great velocity had a tremendous appearance.

JOURNAL OF A VOYAGE FROM THE ROCKY MOUNTAINS TO THE PACIFIC OCEAN PERFORMED IN THE YEAR 1808

It being absolutely impossible to carry the canoes by land, yet sooner than to abandon them, all hands without hesitation embarked, as it were a *corp perdu* [*à corps perdu*: i.e., recklessly] upon the mercy of this Stygian tide. Once engaged the die was cast, and the great difficulty consisted in keeping the canoes in the medium, or *fil d'eau* [current], that is to say, clear of the precipice on one side, and of the gulphs formed by the waves on the other. However, thus skimming along like lightning, the crews cool and determined, followed each other in awful silence. And [when] we arrived at the end we stood gazing on our narrow escape from perdition. After breathing a little, we continued our course to a point where the Indians were encamped. Here we were happy to find our old friends, the Chief and the Interpreter, who immediately joined our party.

The Indians of this place drew a chart of the riverbed which to our view represented it as a dreadful chain of difficulties apparently unsurmountable, and they blamed us for venturing so far with our canoes, & for not going by land as advised by the Old Chief on a former occasion, asserting this communication both by land & by water will in some places be found impracticable to strangers, as we shall have to ascend and descend mountains and precipices by means of rope ladders &c. Here Mr. Stuart had a mer[idian]. alt[itude]. Of O.L.L. 112° 58' 30" art[ificial]. Hor[izo]n.

I prevailed upon another Indian to embark with us as pilot. We then continued our course until late in the evening when our pilot ordered us ashore for the night.[13] This afternoon the rapids were very bad; two in particular were worse, if possible, than any we had hitherto met with, being a continual series of cascades, mixt with rocky fragments and bound by precipices and mountains, that seemed at times to have no end. I scarcely ever saw any thing so dreary, and seldom so dangerous in any country; and at present while I am writing this, whatever way I turn, mountains upon mountains, whose summits are covered with eternal snows, close the gloomy scene.

Our two Atnahs and the Tahow-tin [Tauten] Indians intimated a wish of going a head to the next nation, which they call the Askettihs [the Lillooet Indians were meant]. The distance they say is not more than twenty five Miles, or the same, from here, as the *rapid Couverte* [*Rapide Couvert*]. I told them we should decide upon the point tomorrow, when we would have more knowledge of our situation.

The weather was very hot today and yesterday. The water, as appears by its highest mark has lowered ten feet.

Saturday [Friday], June 10. This morning sent two men to examine the water. At 10 they returned and confirmed the report of the natives that the River was impracticable.

[The "Second Journal" ends at this point.]

In Consequence we immediately set to work, erected a scaffold for the Canoes where we placed them under a shade of branches to screen the gum from the sun, and such other articles as we could not carry along we buried in the Ground. This was done in the presence of the Indians.

Sunday [Saturday], June 11. This morning we made a second *Cache* of such articles as we should absolutely require upon our return. This was done unknown to the natives, for our acquaintance with them was too slight to merit implicit confidence. By 5 A.M. all was ready & each took charge of his own package weighing each about 80 lbs. of indispensable necessaries. The old Chief assured us that we could not suffer for want among the Askettihs, and that we should be there in a Couple of nights. The men hearing this, believed it, thought it a hardship to carry an overplus of provisions, & therefore insisted upon leaving part of their charge. But to this I could not with propriety consent, and we started.

The path which we followed was along the declivity of Mountains, across many ravines, and we experienced a good deal

JOURNAL OF A VOYAGE FROM THE ROCKY MOUNTAINS TO THE PACIFIC OCEAN PERFORMED IN THE YEAR 1808

of fatigue and disagreeable walking: yet, generally speaking, we were much better of [off] than we had reason to expect. At sunset we encamp on the side of a small river. Mr. Stuart and myself still indulging the fond hopes of discovering an opening for making use of canoes went to visit the big river, which we found, as we were taught to expect, impassable. The channel was deep, cut through rocks of immense heighth [height], and forming eddies and gulphs, which it was impossible for canoes even to approach with safety.

Monday [Sunday], June 12. Fine weather, but hot. We passed several long and steep hills this morning. In some parts the road was through a level country but generally full of pointed stones, which annoyed our feet greatly. Here and there a few green spots were observed but few or no trees. About 10 A.M. being tired and thirsty we stopped near a Rock which, from the brushwood at the foot of it, indicated the vicinity of water. Entering this thicket we observed a substance something like *Borax*, which had a saline or sulphurous taste. A hole [was] soon dug, which filled up slowly with this nauseous liquid; some of which, However, we drank.

All at once, and when we least expected a surprise, seven Askittihs [Askettihs] presented themselves before us with their bows and arrows in readiness for attack; they conceived us to be enemies, but upon coming nearer they discovered from our appearance and demeanour their mistake, laid by their weapons, joined us and we shook hands. However we could not understand them. Our Interpreter was a head, but they accompanied us until we had overtaken him. He spoke to them, and they went away, promising to return with provisions, in the evening to our encampment.

We went on and encamped about sunset. Some of the men were displeased at our going so late, being much fatigued, for the road was extremely bad all the afternoon. Soon after our new friends accompanied by our old chief, who had gone a head to the lodges of these people, joined us, and brought different kinds of Roots, wild onions formed into syrope, excellent dried salmon, and some berries. Also a few Beaver skins which were of a reddish colour.

These Indians say that the sea is about ten nights from their village. One of the old men, a very talkative fellow, and we understand a great warrior, had been at the sea; [he] saw *great canoes* [deep-sea ships] and white men [there]. He observed that the chiefs of the white men were well dressed and very proud, for, continued he, getting up and clapping his two hands upon his hips, then strutting about with an air of consequence, "This the way they go."

Tuesday [Monday], June 13. This morning lost sometime in mending our shoes. Fired several shots to show the Natives the effect of our guns. We set out at 5, accompanied by all the Indians and two Horses. Soon after three more horsemen joined our party. I asked [for] one of the horses in order to carry part of our bagage. This the owners declined, and left us. Yesterday our Guides carried our bundles, but today they excused themselves, Saying they were too tired.

Encampt at a considerable river [Bridge River], which flows from the right, and which we called *Shaw's River*.[14] Here we expected to find a band of the natives but we were disappointed; alarmed at our approach, They took to their heels. Some of the others went in search of them.

The country through which we passed this day was the most savage that can be imagined, yet we were always in a beaten path and always in Sight of the river, which, however, we could not approach, its Iron-bound banks having a very forbidden [forbidding] appearance.

Wednesday [Tuesday], June 14. The Indians, who went to look out for those who had run away, returned, and informed us that the fugitives were waiting for our arrival at the next forks.

JOURNAL OF A VOYAGE FROM THE ROCKY MOUNTAINS TO THE PACIFIC OCEAN PERFORMED IN THE YEAR 1808

Last night some of the natives having remarked that we were not white men but enemies in disguise, displeased our Old Chief and a serious altercation took place in consequence. They stated that this tribe were their natural enemies, and that some of his young men had made war upon them in the spring. This he readily admitted, but affirmed that these were foolish young men who had escaped without his knowledge. Seeing the debate getting high, we interposed and the argument immediately ended amicably. Then the Old Chief sent couriers, to inform the natives ahead that we were not enemies [and to tell them] not to be alarmed at our appearance, and to meet us without arms. At the same time he strongly recommended to us to be on our guard.

Having shaved and dressed in our best apparel, we resumed our march, followed by our retinue of yesterday, but recruiting as we went. Halting a little, a stranger, taking up our Interpreter's gun & examining it through curiosity touched the trigger; which one of our men observing just in time, threw up the muzzle as the shot was going off; [he] thus saved the lives of some natives who otherwise would have received the contents. Such a misfortune would have at once put an end to our journey if not to our lives.

When we came to the forks [where the Seton River enters the Fraser], the chief men dressed in their coats of mail advanced to meet us, in order, to know our disposition before we could be admitted into their camp. Our Chief harangued them in his language; they answered him in theirs; and we were obliged to employ three different interpreters, on the occasion to settle the business. These ambassadors are of the Askittih [Askettih] nation; they looked manly, and had really the appearance of warriors. They seemed to speak with fluency; and all was attention marked with signs of applause.[15] Our Chief conveyed our sentiments with great animation. He assured the Askitteh [Askettih] Nation that we were good people and had nothing to do with the quarrels of Indian Nations.

When the conference was over, the Ambassadors returned to their camp, running as fast as their legs could carry them. We immediately followed, and encamped on the right bank opposite the village, being the best position we could find for a defence.[16] The Natives without loss of time began to cross over in wooden canoes, and I had to shake hands with at least one hundred & thirty seven men, while the Old Chief was haranguing them about our good qualities, wishing to persuade some of them to accompany us part of the journey to which several did assent.[17] In the meantime Mr. Stuart and myself spared no pains to impress upon their minds the numberless advantages which all the nations in that quarter would derive from an open communication with the white people.

The Indians brought us plenty of fish, roots, and berries. The Mountains are still high, and covered with snow. The river, we had the pleasure to understand, is navigable from this place.

Thursday [Wednesday], June 15. Bad weather this morning, and we indulged ourselves longer than usual in bed. The *watch* having gone to rest at day light, the other did not pay due attention; and soon after we had the mortification to miss the *Old Chief,* his countryman *the pilot,* and our toohowtin [Tauten] Interpreter. These useful men [had] insinuated more than once their intention of leaving us, being afraid to continue. They behaved well, and I have reason to regret they did not give me an opportunity of paying them for their services. But I hope to meet them again on our return.

Here we are, in a strange Country, surrounded with dangers, and difficulties, among numberless tribes of savages, who never saw the face of a white man. Our situation is critical and highly unpleasant; however we shall endeavour to make the best of it; what cannot be cured, must be endured.

Some of the Indians, who had joined us yesterday forenoon & whom we were happy to acknowledge now as old acquain-

JOURNAL OF A VOYAGE FROM THE ROCKY MOUNTAINS TO THE PACIFIC OCEAN PERFORMED IN THE YEAR 1808

tance, drew at my request a chart of the Country below this to the sea. By this sketch the navigation seems still very bad, and difficult. At some distance to the East appears another large river [the Columbia] which runs parallel to this to the sea.

After obtaining this information we prevailed upon the Indians to ferry us over to the village. They employed but one canoe which made three trips, and took up a considerable time. The village is a fortification of 100 by 24 feet, surrounded with palisades eighteen feet high, slanting inwards, and lined with a shorter row that supports a shade [shelter], covered with bark, and which are the dwellings. This place, we understand, is the metropolis of the Askettih Nation.

With difficulty we procured a canoe. The Indians after bargaining a long while consented to accept of a file, and a kettle in exchange. But of provisions we could only procure thirty dried salmon.

After so long a stay I was impatient to be off; I ordered the canoe to be loaded with heaviest packages. Then Mr. Stuart, one of the men, and two Indians embarked; but the Indians finding the canoe overloaded, put the Frenchman a shore, and continued with Mr. Stuart. I did not relish this arrangement on account of Mr. Stuart, but he thought nothing of it himself, and merely said he would wait for us within a short distance, or at the foot of the first rapid. The other men had to carry their own things, and the ammunition. The last article we considered as too precious to risk out of our sight.

As soon as the canoe had doubled the first point, and disppeared [disappeared], we set off, and walked hard to join our friend. We arrived at the place appointed, but the canoe was not there. Alarmed for Mr. Stuart'[s] safety I continued with augmented speed all along the river side followed by a number of natives; and it was after travelling a distance of ten miles, and coming to an Indian encampment [that] I overtook Mr. Stuart. He could not make himself understood by his conductors, and [was] therefore under the necessity of going on without stopping.

About dark Mr. Quesnel came up with us, and left the men two miles behind encamped.

Some of the Indian[s] in this camp we had seen above. The Askettet's [Askettihs] dress the same as the Atnahs. They are civil but will not part with their provisions without difficulty. They have a variety of roots, some of which taste like potatoes, and are excellent. Their bows and arrows are neat. Their mats are made of different materials, such as rushes, grass, watap [spruce roots], &c. With these mats their shades [shelters] are covered. We observed several European articles among them, particularly a new copper Tea Kettle, and a gun of a large size and which, perhaps, are of a Russian manufacture.

Friday [Thursday], June 16. This morning the men joined us. Of the two canoes which the Indians had, we could obtain but one. It belonged to a sick man, who accepted of medicines in payment. Being in bad order we lost some time in repairing it. Mr. Stuart had a Mer[idian]. Alt[itude]. O.L.L. 124° 59'. Art[ificial]. Horiz[on].

At two we got ready. Mr. Stuart with two Indians went in one canoe, two men went in the other, and I with the rest went by land. Upon our departure, strangers having arrived at the camp, we were called back; to satisfy their curiosity we obeyed, shook hands with them, and then resumed our course.

About two hours after we came up with Mr. Stuart. He waited our arrival to inform us that he had passed through several bad and dangerous rapids on his way from the camp, and that there was a carrying place nearby. Proceeded on to the portage, where we had to carry all for upwards of a mile, and in very bad road.

Here we met some of a neighbouring nation called Hakamaugh [the Thompson Indians] — with these were two of

JOURNAL OF A VOYAGE FROM THE ROCKY MOUNTAINS TO THE PACIFIC OCEAN PERFORMED IN THE YEAR 1808

another Tribe called *Suihonie* [Shoshoni?]; all were exceedingly well dressed in leather, and were on horseback. They have a great quantity of shells and blue beads, and we saw a broken silver broach [brooch], such as the Sauteus [Sauteux, or Saulteaux] wear, among them. They were kind to us, and assisted us at the carrying place with their horses. We put up at the lower end near their camp.

Here we got acquainted with a man of the *Chilkcotin* [Chilcotin] tribe who had left his own country when a boy but still retaining a little of his mother tongue, we made a shift to understand. He observed that he had been at the sea by this communication, where he had seen men like us, who lived in a wooden enclosure upon an Island, and who had tents for the purpose of trading with the Natives in furs. He gave us a good account of the navigation, and he consented to accompany us as pilot. Since the departure of our Tha-how-tin [Tauten] Interpreters, this was the only man with whom we could converse to any advantage.

At this place I saw a shield different from any I had hitherto seen. It was large enough to cover the whole body, composed of splinters of wood like the ribs of stays and neatly inclosed with twine made of hemp.

An Indian, who had been out a hunting, returned with a deer he had killed. We applied for a share of the meat, but he would not part with any. The chief invited us to his quarters; his son, by his orders, served us upon a handsome mat and regaled us with salmon and roots. Our men had some also, and they procured, besides, several Dogs which is always a favourite dish with the Canadian voyagers.

Saturday [Friday], June 17. It was 7 in the morning before we could get ready. Mr. Stuart, three men, and an Indian embarked in the canoes. I and the others went as usual by land, but not before I had satisfied the Indians who assisted Mr. Stuart yesterday, the price of whose labour was a knife. In the forenoon we stopped in a camp on the right side of the river; at the same time sixteen families of Indians appeared on the opposite bank. The Chief to whom we owed the articles of yesterday and who was then our steerman, asked us to unload in order to ferry these people over with the canoes; we could not well refuse this request, and, therefore, we obeyed, and thereby lost some time.

One of the strangers had a sword of a tremendous size, made of sheet iron.

We set off and continued untill sunset, when we encamped. Here a great number of Indians were collected from all quarters through curiosity to see us; we found them civil and friendly. In [the] course of the day while walking I observed many piles of sapin [fir branches] near the road which I took to be tombs, but our young men informed us that they were birth places. Hence it seems that this nation honour the birth as well as the death of their friends with marks of distinction.

Sunday [Saturday], June 18. It rained all night, and this morning the bad weather, added to the trouble attending a concourse of strange Indians, prolonged our stay to 8 A.M. Here we had an eye upon a canoe, but the Indians perceiving our design sent it out of the way.

Our Interpreter, who promised yesterday to conduct us to [the] sea, was either sick or pretended to be so. He would not understand a word and wished to remain. We considered him in the main, of little consequence, for I had reason to doubt the information which he gave us the day before — our own Interpreter having fabricated a little on that occassion.

At 3 P.M. we passed a camp of the natives. These were poor, but generous, for they assisted us. Here we observed a tomb with a canoe upside down upon it, and near it a dog hung upon a tree.

About Sunset we came to a large camp of Indians, where we put up for the night. About the same time Mr. Stuart and his small brigade appeared. Mr. Stuart reported that he had passed

JOURNAL OF A VOYAGE FROM THE ROCKY MOUNTAINS TO THE PACIFIC OCEAN PERFORMED IN THE YEAR 1808

several bad and dangerous rapids in [the] course of the day. Our route also was coarse and fatiguing. The mountains continue to be high, and covered with snow.

The Indians here are a mixture of Askittihs [Lillooets] and Hacamaugh [Thompson Indians]. They gave us a *siffleur* [marmot] which is the first fresh meat we tasted since our departure. Roots are scarce, but the Indians gather a kind of moss, which they make into paste, bake in ovens, and which, tho black, is palatable.

Monday [Sunday], June 19. Rained last night, and there was a fog in the morning. The Hacamaugh [Thompson] Chief went ahead to prepare the way for us. According to his account, he was the greatest man of his nation.

At this place we saw a great number of snails of different colours and which were the first of that kind that I had seen in the Northwest.

At 8 A.M. set out, divided as yesterday. A mile below, the natives ferried us over a large rapid river [the Stein River]. I obtained, for an awl, a passage to the next village, a distance of three miles through strong rapids. The others who went by land met some of the Indians on the way who were happy to see them. This was the village of the Chief who had left us in the morning.[18] We were told here that the road a head was very bad, and consequently we should meet with much difficulty for most part of the way.

The Indians of this village may be about four hundred souls and some of them appear very old; they live among mountains, and enjoy pure air, seem cleanly inclined, and make use of wholesome food. We observed several European articles among them, viz. a copper Tea Kettle, a brass camp kettle, a strip of common blanket, and cloathing such as the Cree women wear. These things, we supposed, were brought from our settlements beyond the Mountains. Indeed the Indians made us understand as much.

After having remained some time in this village, the principal chief invited us over the river. We crossed, and He received us at the water side, where, assisted by several others, he took me by the arms and conducted me in a moment up the hill to the camp where his people were sitting in rows, to the number of twelve hundred; and I had to shake hands with all of them. Then the Great Chief made a long harangue, in course of which he pointed to the sun, to the four quarters of the world and then to us, and then he introduced his father, who was old and blind, and was carried by another man, who also made a harangue of some length. The old [blind] man was placed near us, and with some emotion often stretched out both his hands in order to feel ours.

The Hacamaugh [Thompson Indian] nation are different both in language and manners from their neighbours the Askettels [Askettihs; Lillooets]. They have many chiefs and great men, appear to be good orators, for their manner of delivery is extremely handsome. We had every reason to be thankful for our reception at this place; the Indians shewed us every possible attention and supplied our wants as much as they could. We had salmon, berries, oil and roots in abundance, and our men had six dogs. Our tent was pitched near the camp, and we enjoyed peace and security during our stay.

Thursday [Monday], June 20. The Indians sung and danced all night. Some of our men, who went to see them, were much amused. With some difficulty we obtained two wooden canoes; the Indians, however, made no price, but accepted of our offers. Shortly after a tumult arose in the camp. I was writing in the tent; hearing the noise, I went to the door and observed an elderly man running towards me, but [he] was stopped by some of the others who were making a loud noise. I enquired into the cause; they crowded around me. They [the] chief spoke and all was quiet. I, then, learned that Mr. Quesnel having walked in the direction of a canoe that was at some distance on the beach, the Old man in question, who was the owner, thought he was going to lose it.

JOURNAL OF A VOYAGE FROM THE ROCKY MOUNTAINS TO THE PACIFIC OCEAN PERFORMED IN THE YEAR 1808

This affray over, we prepared for our departure. The Chief pointed out three elderly men who were to accompany us to the next nation. In the mean time, I was presented with berries, roots and oil in abundance. Notwithstanding these tokens of friendship, the impression, which the late disturbance made on my mind, still remained. However kind savages may appear, I know that it is not in their nature to be sincere in their professions to strangers. The respect and attention, which we generally experience, proceed, perhaps, from an idea that we are superior beings, who are not to be overcome; at any rate, it is certain the less familiar we are with one another the better for us.

I showed to the Indians some trading articles and asked for leather, but none was brought. I gave the chief a large knife and an awl, and he expressed his favour in thanks and affability. I gave also a few trinkets to an Indian of a different nation in order that he might show them to his friends.

These forks [the junction of the Fraser and the Thompson rivers] the natives call *Camchin*, and are formed by a large river which is the same spoken of so often by our friend the old chief. From an idea that our friends of the *Fort des Prairies* department are established upon the sources of it, among the mountains, we gave it the name of Thomson's [Thompson's] River.[19]

Thompson River to the Strait of Georgia

About 10 A.M. we embarked. Now all our people were in canoes. Our three new guides, the great chief, a little fellow[20] from whom we received much attention, and some others embarked to keep us company. Aided by heavy rapids and a strong current, we, in a short time, came to a portage. Here the canoes and baggage were carried up a steep hill; the ascent was dangerous—stones and fragments of rocks were continually giv-

109

ing way from our feet and rolling off in succession; from this cause one of our men was much hurt, and a kettle bouncing into the river was lost. The Indians informed us that some years since, at this place, several of their people, having lost their balance from the steps giving way, rolled down to the river and perished, and we saw many graves covered with small stones all over the place.

I have, almost, forgotten to mention that on our arrival at the carrying place, one of our canoes sunk and some things were lost, but the crew was saved, and the canoe recovered.

On the other side of the river, Mr. Stuart, who visited the rapids, observed many kinds of trees different from those we had hitherto seen. He also observed a mineral spring, the water of which was clear and of a strong taste, but the scum was of a greenish colour. The Mountains continue to be high, and their summits covered with snow.

Two Indians from our last encampment overtook us with a piece of Iron which we had forgotten there. We considered this as an extraordinary degree of honesty and attention, particularly in this part of the world. After we had encamped, the chief with his friends went away.

Wednesday [Tuesday], June 21. Early in the morning the men made a trip with two of the canoes and part of the things which they carried more than a mile and returned for the rest. I sent Mr. Quesnel to take charge of the baggage in the absence of the men. About this time Indians appeared on the opposite bank. Our guides harangued them from our side, and all were singing and dancing.

After breakfast the men renewed their work, and Mr. Stuart and I remained in the tent writing. Soon after we were alarmed by the loud bawling of our guides, whom upon looking out we observed running full speed towards where we were, making signs that our people were lost in the rapids. As we could not account for this misfortune we immediately ran over to the bag-

JOURNAL OF A VOYAGE FROM THE ROCKY MOUNTAINS TO THE PACIFIC OCEAN PERFORMED IN THE YEAR 1808

gage where we found Mr. Quesnel all alone. We inquired of him about the men, and at the same time we discovered that three of the canoes were missing, but he had seen none of them nor did he know where they were. On casting our view across the river, we remarked one of the canoes and some of the men ashore there. From this incident we had reason to believe that the others were either a head or perished, and with increased anxiety we directed our speed to the lower end of the rapids.

At the distance of four miles or so, we found one of our men, La Chapelle, who had carried two loads of his own share [of the baggage] that far; he could give us no account of the others, but supposed they were following him with their proportions. We still continued; at last growing fatigued and seeing no appearance of the canoes of which we were in search, we considered it advisable to return and keep along the bank of the river.

We had not proceeded far when we observed one of our men D'Alaire walking slow with a stick in his hand from the bank, and on coming up to him we discovered that he was so wet, so weak, and so exhausted that he could scarcely speak. However after leaning a little while upon his stick and drawing breath, he informed us that unfortunately he and the others finding the carrying place too long and the canoes too heavy, took it upon themselves to venture down by water — that the canoe in which he was happened to be the last in setting out.

"In the first cascade," continued he, "our canoe filled and upset. The foreman and steersman got on the outside, but I, who was in the centre, remained a long while underneath upon the bars [thwarts]. The canoe still drifting was thrown into smooth current, and the other two men, finding an opportunity sprang from their situation into the water and swam ashore. The impulse occasioned by their fall in leaping off raised one side of the canoe above the surface, and I having still my recollection, though I had swallowed a quantity of water, seized the critical moment to disentangle myself, and I gained but not without a struggle the top of the canoe. By this time I found myself again in the middle of the stream. Here I continued astride [the canoe], humouring the tide as well as I could with my body to preserve my balance, and although I scarcely had time to look about me, I had the satisfaction to observe the other two canoes a shore near an eddy, and their crews safe among the rocks. In the second or third cascade (for I cannot remember which) the canoe from a great height plunged into the deep eddy at the foot, and striking with violence against the bottom splitted in two. Here I lost my recollection, which however, I soon recovered and was surprised to find myself on a smooth easy current with only one half of the canoe in my arms. In this condition I continued through several cascades, untill the stream fortunately conducted me into an eddy at the foot of a high and steep rock. Here my strength being exhausted I lost my hold; a large wave washed me from off the wreck among the rocks, and another still larger hoisted me clear on shore, where I remained, as you will readily believe, some time motionless; at length recovering a little of my strength I crawled up among the rocks, but still in danger, and found myself once more safe on firm ground, just as you see."

Here he finished his melancholy tale, and pointed to the place of his landing, which we went to see, and we were lost in astonishment not only at his escape from the waves, but also at his courage and perseverance in effecting a passage up through a place which appeared to us a precipice. Continuing our course along the bank we found that he had drifted three miles among rapids, cascades, whirlpools, &c. all inconceivably dangerous.

Mr. Quesnel being extremely anxious and concerned left his charge and joined us. Two men only remained on shore carrying the baggage, and these were equally ignorant with ourselves of the fate of the others. Some time after upon advancing towards the camp, we picked up all the men on our side of the river. The men

JOURNAL OF A VOYAGE FROM THE ROCKY MOUNTAINS TO THE PACIFIC OCEAN PERFORMED IN THE YEAR 1808

that had landed on the other side, joined us in the evening. They informed us that the Indians assisted to extricate them from their difficulties. Indeed the natives shewed us every possible attention in the midst of our misfortunes on this trying occasion.[21]

Being all safe we had the happiness of encamping together as usual with our baggage. However we lost one of our canoes, and another we found too heavy to be carried such a distance. Our guides asked permission to go and sleep at the Indian Village, which was below the rapids; this was granted on condition that they should return early in the morning.

Mr. Stuart in [the] course of the day saw a snake as thick as his wrist. Small rain in the evening.

Thursday [Wednesday], June 22. Our guides returned as they had promised. Four men were employed in bringing down the canoes by water. They made several portages in course of this undertaking. The rest of the men carried the baggage by land. When this troublesome and fatiguing business was over, we crossed over to the village, where we were received with loud acclamations and generously entertained. The number of men at this place I found to be about 110. The chief of the [Indians at the] forks and our Little Fellow came to us upon our arrival and introduced us to the others.

I sent two men to visit the rapids; but the Indians, knowing our indiscretion yesterday, and dreading a like attempt, voluntarily transported our canoes over land to a little river beyond the rapids. We encamped some distance from the village. The Chief went before to inform the Indians of the next village of our approach. He promised to accompany us until we should have passed all the dangerous places — and the Little Fellow assured us that he would not leave us untill our return.

The Indians having invited us into the village, Mr. Quesnel and some of the men went; the Indians sang and danced and

113

were very civil. They gave the men three dogs. At this time we depended wholly upon the natives for provisions, and they generously furnished us with the best they could procure; but that best was commonly wretched if not disgusting.

Friday [Thursday], June 23. Rained this morning. One of the men was sick. We perceived that one way or other our men were getting out of order. They prefered [preferred] walking to going by water in wooden canoes, particularly after their late sufferings in the rapids. Therefore I embarked in the bow of a canoe myself and went down several rapids.

We met some Indians and waited for the arrival of our people, who had gone by land. Walking was difficult, the country being extremely rough and uneven. Passed a carrying place; one of the men fell and broke his canoe almost to pieces. The natives from below came thus far with two canoes to assist us. They were probably sent by our friends who went a head. In one of the rapids, Mr. Stuart's canoe filled and was nearly lost.

Soon after we came to a camp of the natives where we landed for the night. The number of the Indians here may amount to 170. They call themselves Nailgemugh.[22] We met with a hearty welcome from them; they entertained us with singing, dancing, &c.

The Nailgemugh Nation are better supplied with the necessaries of life than any of those we have hitherto seen. They have robes made of beaver &c. We visited a tomb which was near by the camp. It was built of boards sewed together, and was about four feet square. The top was covered with Cedar bark and loaded with stones. Near it in a scaffold were suspended two canoes, and a pole from which were suspended [word indecipherable], stripes of leather, several baskets &c.

The weather was generally very hot in the day time; but at night, being in the neighbourhood of eternal snows, it was commonly cold.

JOURNAL OF A VOYAGE FROM THE ROCKY MOUNTAINS TO THE PACIFIC OCEAN PERFORMED IN THE YEAR 1808

Saturday [Friday], June 24. This morning traded two canoes for two calico bed gowns. Sent some men to visit the rapids, and set out at 8 A.M. After going a mile we came to a carrying place of 800 yards. Mr. Stuart had a mer[idian]. alt[itude]. 126° 57'.

Continued — passed a small camp of Indians without stopping and came to a discharge [*décharge*] with steep hills at both ends, where we experienced some difficulty in carrying the things. Ran down the canoes; but about the middle of the rapids two of them struck against one another, by which accident one of them lost a piece of its stern, and the steersman his paddle: the canoe in consequence took in much water.

After repairing the damages we continued, and in the evening arrived at an Indian village. The Natives flocked about us, and invited us to pass the night with them. Accepting their invitation we were led to the camp which was at some distance up the hill. The Indians of this encampment were upwards [of] five hundred souls. Our friends, the Chief and the Little Fellow, with some of our acquaintances from above were here. We were well treated, they gave us fresh salmon, hazle nuts, and some other nuts of an excellent quality. The small pox was in the camp, and several of the Natives were marked with it. We fired several shots to shew the Indians the use of our guns. Some of them, through fear, dropped down at the report.

Sunday [Saturday], June 25. Fine weather. The Chief of [the] Camshins [i.e., of the Indians living in the area around the junction of the Thompson and Fraser rivers] returned this morning to his own home, but his people continued with us. This man is the greatest chief we have seen; he behaved towards us uncommonly well. I made him a present of a large silver broach which he immediately fixed on his head, and he was exceedingly well pleased with our attention.

We embarked at 5 A.M. After going a considerable distance, our Indians ordered us a shore, and we made a portage. Here we were obliged to carry up among loose Stones in the face of a steep hill, over a narrow ridge between two precipices. Near the top where the ascent was perfectly perpendicular, one of the Indians climbed to the summit, and with a long pole drew us up, one after another. This took three hours. Then we continued our course up and down, among hills and rocks, and along the steep declivities of mountains, where hanging rocks, and projecting cliffs at the edge of the bank made the passage so small as to render it difficult even for one person to pass sideways at times.

Many of the natives from the last camp, having accompanied us, were of the greatest service to us on these intricate and dangerous occasions. In places where we were obliged to hand our guns from one to another, and where the greatest precaution was required to pass even singly, the Indians went through boldly with loads. About 5 P.M. we encamped at a rapid.

On our arrival this morning [this evening], I dispatched Mr. Stuart and one of the men to examine the rapids. From the place of our encampment we observed the rapids. From the place of our encampment we observed an Indian who was on the opposite side fishing Salmon with a dipping net. Our Indians had a net with which they took five Salmons, which divided among forty persons was little indeed, but better than nothing.

Monday [Sunday], June 26. This morning all hands were employed the same as yesterday. We had to pass over huge rocks, in which we were assisted by the Indians. Soon after [we] met Mr. Stuart and the man. They reported that the navigation was absolutely impracticable. That evening they [had] slept on the top of a mountain in sight of our smoke.

As for the road by land we scarcely could make our way in some parts even with our guns. I have been for a long period among the Rocky Mountains, but have never seen any thing equal to this country, for I cannot find words to describe our sit-

JOURNAL OF A VOYAGE FROM THE ROCKY MOUNTAINS TO THE PACIFIC OCEAN PERFORMED IN THE YEAR 1808

uation at times. We had to pass where no human being should venture. Yet in those places there is a regular footpath impressed, or rather indented, by frequent travelling upon the very rocks. And besides this, steps which are formed like a ladder, or the shrouds of a ship, by poles hanging to one another and crossed at certain distances with twigs and withes [tree boughs], suspended from the top to the foot of precipices, and fastened at both ends to stones and trees, furnished a safe and convenient passage to the Natives — but we, who had not the advantages of their experience, were often in imminent danger, when obliged to follow their example.[23]

In the evening we came in sight of a camp of the Natives, and the Chief with some others crossed the river to receive us. We were then ferried over and afterwards kindly treated. These Indians are of the same nation with the last, but some men of a neighbouring nation called achinrow [hereafter usually spelled Ackinroe] were with them.

The Hacamaugh promised us canoes for the next day. But the canoes being above the rapids, some of the young men went for them. It being impossible to bring them by land, or to get them down by water, they were turned adrift and left to the mercy of the current. As there were many shouls [shoals] and rocks the canoes were in the greatest danger of being broken to pieces before they got to the end of the rapids.

Tuesday [Monday], June 27. This morning the Indians entertained us with a specimen of their singing and dancing. We set out at 6 A.M. accompanied as usual by many of the natives, who assisted in carrying part of our baggage. The route we had to follow was as bad as yesterday. At 9 we came to the canoes that were sent adrift. One of them we found broken and the other much damaged. We lost some time in repairing them. Some of the men with the things embarked, and the rest continued by land.

We came to a small camp of Indians consisting [of] about 60 persons. The name of the place is Spazum [Spuzzum], and is the boundary line between the Hacamaugh and Ackinroe Nations.[24] Here as usual we were hospitably entertained, with fresh Salmon boiled and roasted, green and dried berries, oil and onions.

Seeing tombs of a curious construction at the forks [the mouth of Spuzzum Creek] on the opposite [West] side, I asked permission of the Chief to go and pay them a visit. This he readily granted, and he accompanied us himself. These Tombs are superior to any thing of the kind I ever saw among the savages. They are about fifteen feet long and of the form of a chest of drawers. Upon the boards and posts are carved beasts and birds, in a curious but rude manner, yet pretty well proportioned. These monuments must have cost the workmen much time and labour, as they were destitute of proper tools for the execution of such a performance. Around the tombs were deposited all the property of the deceased.

Ready for our departure, our guides observed that we had better pass the night here and that they would accompany us in the morning. Sensible, from experience, that a hint from these people is equal to a command, and that they would not follow, if we Declined, we remained.

Wednesday [Tuesday], June 28. We set out at 5, our things in canoes as yesterday, and we continued by land. After much trouble both by land and water for eight miles, we came to a carrying place, where we were obliged to leave our canoes, and to proceed on foot without our baggage. Some of the Ackinroe Nation, apprised of our approach, came to meet us with roasted Salmon, and we made an excellent meal.

At this place while waiting for some of our people who were behind, I examined a net of a different construction from any I had hitherto seen. It was made of thread of the size of cod lines, the meshes were 16 inches wide, and the net 8 fathoms long. With this the natives catch Deer, and other large animals.

JOURNAL OF A VOYAGE FROM THE ROCKY MOUNTAINS TO THE PACIFIC OCEAN PERFORMED IN THE YEAR 1808

Continued and crossed a small river [Siwash Creek?] on a wooden bridge. Here the main river tumbles from rock to rock between precipices with great violence. At 11 A.M. we arrived at the first village of the Ackinroe nation, where we were received with as much kindness as if we had been their lost relations. Neat mats were spread for our reception, and plenty of Salmon served in wooden dishes was placed before us. The number of people at this place was about 140.

This nation is different in language and manners from the other nations we had passed. They have rugs made from the wool of *Aspai*, or wild goat, and from Dog's hair, which are equally as good as those found in Canada. We observed that the dogs were lately shorn.[25]

We saw few or no christian goods among them, but from their workmanship in wood they must be possessed of good tools at least for that purpose. Having been newly arrived they had not as yet erected their shades [shelters]. They have a gallery of smoked boards upon which they slept. Their bows and arrows are very neat.

At 1 P.M. we renewed our march, the natives still carrying part of our baggage. At the first point we observed a remarkable cavern in a rock which upon visiting we found to be 50 feet deep by 35 wide. A little above it is an excellent house 46 by 23 feet, and constructed like American frame houses. The planks are 3 or 4 inches thick, each passing the adjoining one a couple of inches. The posts, which are very strong, and rudely carved, receive the beam across. The walls are 11 feet high, and covered with a slanting roof. On the opposite side of the river, there is a considerable village with houses similar to the one upon this side.

About 4 P.M. arrived to [at] a camp containing about 150 souls. Here we had plenty of Salmon cooked by means of hot stones in wooden vessels.

Here we understood that the river was navigable from this place to the sea. We had of course to provide canoes if possible.

We saw a number of new ones, which seemed to have been hollowed with fire, and then polished.

Their [the Indians'] arms consist of bows and arrows, spears and clubs, or horn Powmagans. They had scarcely any leather, so that large animals must be scarce. Their ornaments are the same as the Hacamaugh nation make use of; that is to say, shells of different kinds, shell beads, brass made into pipes hanging from the neck, or across the shoulders, bracelets of large brass wire, and some bracelets of horn. Their hats, which are made of wattap [roots], have broad rims and diminish gradually to the top. Some make use of cedar bark, painted in various colours, resembling ribbands which they fix around their heads. Both sexes are stoutly made, and some of the men are handsome; but I cannot say so much for the women, who seem to be slaves, for in course of their dances, I remarked that the men were pillaging them from one another. Our Little Fellow, on one of these occasions, was presented with another man's wife for a bed fellow.

There is a new tomb at this place supported on carved posts about two feet from the ground. The sculpture is rudely finished, and the posts are covered all over with bright shells, which shine like mercury, but the contents of the tomb emitted a disagreeable stench.

At the bad rock [Lady Franklin Rock], a little distance above the village, where the rapids terminate, the natives informed us, that white people like us came there from below; and they shewed us indented marks which the white people made upon the rocks, but which, by the bye, seemed to us to be natural marks.[26]

In the evening four men went off in canoes to inform the people below of our visit and intentions.

Thursday [Wednesday], June 29. Lost some time this morning in looking out for canoes, but could not procure any. We embarked about 9 A.M. some of us with the Indians and others without, just as best suited the Indians. The river here is wide with

JOURNAL OF A VOYAGE FROM THE ROCKY MOUNTAINS TO THE PACIFIC OCEAN PERFORMED IN THE YEAR 1808

a strong current and some rapids — both sides adorned with fine trees. The mountains are still high and covered with snow.

About 10 passed a village, which is the residence of the last Indians. At 2 P.M. came to a camp on an Island[27] containing about 125 souls. Here we had plenty of Salmon, oil, roots, and raspberries. The natives amused us with dancing. Lost a couple of hours — went on — several of the natives followed us. At 5 we came to another camp of 170 souls. Here the Indians, who favored us with the canoes thus far, left us and went home, and in consequence we were obliged to encamp. The Indians of this place promised to help us on tomorrow. They were extremely civil, in so much as to force us to doubt their sincerity. They gave us plenty of sturgeon, oil, and roots, but which were not of the best quality or flavour.

The Indians in this quarter are fairer than those in the interior. Their heads and faces are extremely flat; their skin and hair of a reddish cast — but this cast, I suppose, is owing to the ingredients with which they besmear their bodies. They make rugs, of Dog's hair, that have stripes of different colours crossing at right angles resembling at a distance Highland plaid. Their fishing nets are of large twine, and have handles [with a length] of 20 feet. Their spears, which are of horn, have also wooden handles of great length.

Here we saw a large copper kettle shaped like a jar, and a large English hatchet stamped *Sargaret with the figure of a crown*. The river at this place is more than two miles broad, and is interspersed with Islands.

Friday [Thursday], June 30. It was [hour omitted] A.M. before we could procure canoes and take our departure. At 11 we came to a camp containing near 400 souls. Here we saw a man from the sea, which they said was so near that we would see it tomorrow. Mr. Stuart took a mer[idian]. alt[itude]. O.L.L. 127° 23'. The Indians of this place seem dirty and have an unpleasant smell; they were surprised at seeing men different from Indians and [were] extremely disagreeable to us through their curiosity and attention.

The Indians, who conducted us during the forenoon, returned [home] with their canoes, which took us some time to replace. It was 2 P.M. before we embarked. Continued our course with a strong current for nine miles, where the river expands into a lake. Here we saw seals, a large river coming in from the left, and a round Mountain a head, which the natives call *shemotch*.[28]

After sunset we encamped upon the right side of the river. At this place the trees are remarkably large, cedars *five fathoms* in circumference, and of proportional heighth [height]. Musketoes [mosquitoes] are in clouds, & we had little or nothing to eat. The Natives always gave us plenty of provisions in their villages, but nothing to carry away. Numbers of them followed us, but they were as destitute of provisions as ourselves. And though they were at a great distance from home, they carried no arms about them. This conduct appeared [to indicate] that they had great confidence either in our goodness, or in their own numbers.

Saturday [Friday], July 1. Foggy weather this morning. Clear at 4 and we embarked. Rugged Mountains all around. The banks of the river are low and well covered with wood; the current is slack.

At 8 A.M. we arrived at a large village. After shaking hands with many, the Chief invited us to his house, and served us with fish and berries; our Indians also were treated with fish, berries, and dried oysters in large troughs. Our Hacamaugh commonly stiled [styled] Little Fellow, so often mentioned here, and who has been highly serviceable to us all along, has assumed an air of consequence from his being of our party; he ranks now with Mr. Stuart, Mr. Quesnel, and myself. The Chief made me a present of a coat of mail to make shoes. For this we may thank our little friend, who also received a present of white shells. I gave the Chief in return a calico gown, for which he was thankful and proud.

JOURNAL OF A VOYAGE FROM THE ROCKY MOUNTAINS TO THE PACIFIC OCEAN PERFORMED IN THE YEAR 1808

The Indians entertained us with songs and dances of various descriptions. The chief stood in the centre of the dance or ring giving directions, while others were beating the drum against the walls of the house, and making a terrible racket — which alarmed our men who were at a distance, and who came to see what caused the noise.

The Indians, who favoured us with a passage to this place, went off with the canoes. We had to look out for others, but none could be procured for any consideration whatever. At last the Chief consented to lend us his large canoe & to accompany us himself on the morrow.

The number of Indians at this place is about 200 who appeared at first view to be fair, but afterwards we discovered that they made use of white paint to alter their appearance. They evinced no kind of surprise or curiosity at seeing us, nor were they afraid of our arms, so that they must have been in the habit of seeing white people.

Their houses are built of cedar planks, and in shape [are] similar to the one already described. The whole range, which is 640 feet long by 60 broad, is under one roof. The front is 18 feet high, and the covering is slanting. All the apartments, which are separated in portions, are square, excepting the Chief's which is 90 feet long. In this room the posts or pillars are nearly 3 feet [in] diameter at the base, and diminish gradually to the top. In one of these posts is an oval opening answering the purpose of a door, thro' which to crawl in and out. Above, on the outside, are carved a human figure large as life, and there are other figure in imitation of beasts and birds. These buildings have no flooring. The fires are in the centre, and the smoke goes out an opening at [the] top.

The tombs at this place are well finished. Dog's hair, which is spun with a distaff and spindle is formed into rugs. There is some red and blue cloth among them. These Indians are not so hospitable as those above; this is probably owing to scarcity of Provisions.

The tide now about 2 1/2 feet. Mr. Stuart had a Mer[idian]. Alt[itude]. O.L.L. 127° 13'. We cast our nets into the water, but took no fish, the current being too strong.

Sunday [Saturday], July 2. This morning we discovered that the natives were given to thieving. They stole a smoking bag belonging to our party, and we could not prevail upon them to restore it. The dogs in course of the night dragged out and damaged many of our things.

I applied to the Chief in consequence of his promise of yesterday for his canoe, but he paid no attention to my request. I, therefore, took the canoe and had it carried to the water side. The Chief got it carried back. We again laid hold of it. He still resisted, and made us understand that he was the greatest of his nation and equal in power to the sun. However as we could not go without [the canoe] we persisted and at last gained our point. The chief and several of the tribe accompanied us. At 11 A.M. arrived at a village where we were received with the usual ceremony of shaking hands, but we were not well entertained. The houses at this place are plain and in two rows. I received two coats of mail in a present which are so good [for] shoes.

The Indians advised us not to advance any further, as the natives of the coast or Islanders were at war with them, being very malicious, and will destroy us. Upon seeing us slight their advice and going to embark, they gathered round our canoe and hauled it out of the water, and then invited us for the first time to the principal house of the village.

Leaving Mr. Quesnel with most of the men to guard the canoe and baggage, Mr. Stuart with two men and myself accepted the invitation. As soon as we were in the house, the Indians began singing and dancing, & making a terrible noise. Mr. Stuart went to see what caused this seeming disturbance; he found that

JOURNAL OF A VOYAGE FROM THE ROCKY MOUNTAINS TO THE PACIFIC OCEAN PERFORMED IN THE YEAR 1808

one of the natives had stolen a Jacket out of the canoe, which upon application to the Chief, was returned, and all was quiet again. Then we made a motion to embark accompanied by the Chief. His friends did not approve of his going, [and] flocked about him, embracing him with tenderness, as if he was never to return. Our followers seeing this scene of apparent distress between the Chief and his friends changed their minds and declined going further. Even our Little Fellow would not embark, saying that he was also afraid of the people at the sea. Then some of them laid violent hands upon the canoe, and insisted upon putting it out of the water. We paid no attention to their arguments, made them desist, and we embarked.

We proceeded on for two miles, and came to a place where the river divides [at New Westminster] into several channels. Seeing a canoe following us we waited for its arrival. One Indian of that canoe embarked with us and conducted us into the right channel [the North Arm of the Fraser River]. In the meantime several Indians from the village followed in canoes, armed with bows and arrows, clubs, spears &c. Singing a war song, beating time with their paddles upon the sides of the canoes, and making signs and gestures highly inimicable. The one that embarked with us became very unruly singing and dancing, and kicking up the dust. We threatened him with the effect of our displeasure and he was quiet.

This was an alarming crisis, but we were not discouraged: confident of our superiority, at least on the water, we continued.

At last we came in sight of a gulph or bay of the sea [the Strait of Georgia]; this the Indians called *Pas-hil-roe*. It runs in a S.W. & N.E. direction. In this bay are several high and rocky Islands whose summits are covered with snow. On the right shore we noticed a village called by the Natives *Misquiame* [Musqueam]; we directed our course towards it. Our turbulent passenger conducted us up a small winding river to a small lake to the village.[29]

Here we landed, and found but a few old men and women; the others fled into the woods upon our approach. The fort is 1500 feet in length and 90 feet in breadth. The houses, which are constructed as those mentioned in other places, are in rows; besides some that are detached. One of the natives conducted us through all the apartments, and then desired us to go away, as otherwise the Indians would attack us.

About this time those that followed us from above arrived. Having spent one hour looking about this place we went to embark, [when] we found the tide had ebbed, and left our canoe on dry land. We had, therefore, to drag it out to the water some distance. The natives no doubt seeing our difficulty, assumed courage, and began to make their appearance from every direction, in their coats of mail, howling like so many wolves, and brandishing their war clubs. At last we got into deep water, and embarked. Our turbulent fellow, who [had] embarked in our canoe before, no sooner found himself on board than he began his former impertinences. He asked for our daggers, for our cloathes, and in fine for every thing we had. Being convinced of his unfriendly disposition, we turned him out and made him and the others, who were closing in upon us, understand, that if they did not keep their distance we would fire upon them.

After this skirmish we continued untill we came opposite the second village.[30] Here our curiosity incited us to go a shore; but reflecting upon the reception we experienced at the first, and the character of the Natives, it was thought neither prudent nor necessary to run any risk, particularly as we had no provisions, and saw no prospect of procuring any in that hostile quarter. We, therefore, turned our course and with the intention of going back to the friendly Indians for a supply, then to return and prosecute our design. When we came opposite the hostile village [Musqueam] the same fellows, who had annoyed us before, advanced to attack us which was echoed by those on shore. In this manner they

JOURNAL OF A VOYAGE FROM THE ROCKY MOUNTAINS TO THE PACIFIC OCEAN PERFORMED IN THE YEAR 1808

approached so near that we were obliged to adopt a threatening position, and we had to push them off with the muzzles of our guns. Perceiving our determination their courage failed, and they gave up the pursuit and crossed to the village. The tide was now in our favour, the evening was fine, and we continued our course with great speed until 11, when we encamped within 6 miles of the Chief's village. The men being extremely tired, went to rest; but they were not long in bed before the tide rushed upon the beds and roused them up.

Return Journey to the Thompson River

Monday [Sunday], July 3. Having been disturbed by the overflowing of the tide, we embarked early and arrived at the Chief's village at 5 A.M. where we found some of the Indians bathing — it is their custom to bathe at this early hour. The others, who were asleep, soon got up and received us at the water side. All seemed surprised to see us again.

About this time our Little Fellow, whom we left yesterday at the village below, made his appearance. He informed us that the Indians after our departure had fixed upon our destruction; that he himself was pillaged, his hands and feet tied, and that they were about to knock him on the head when the Chief of the Ackinroe appeared, released him and secured his escape to this place, where he was now detained as a slave.

This unpleasant recital served to warn us more and more of our danger. Still we were bent upon accomplishing our enterprise, to have a sight of the main [ocean] which was but a short distance from whence we had returned;[31] but unfortunately we could not procure a morsel of provisions, & besides the Chief insisted upon having his canoe restored to him immediately. This demand we were obliged to supress [suppress]. The Chief then invited us to his house. We went, but were not above five minutes absent, before one of the men came running to inform us that the Indians had seized upon the canoe and were pillaging our people. Alarmed at this report we hastened to their assistance. We found that some of the Indians from below having arrived had encouraged the others in these violent proceedings. Sensible from our critical situation that mild measures would be improper and of no service, I pretended to be in a violent passion, spoke loud, with vehement gestures and signs exactly in their own way; and thus peace and tranquility were instantly restored.

From these specimens of the insolence and ill nature of the Natives we saw nothing but dangers and difficulties in our way. We, therefore, relinquished our design and directed our thoughts towards home — but we could not proceed without the canoe, and we had to force it away from the owner leaving a blanket in its place. Thus provided, we pushed off.

Here we missed one of our men G.B. The fellow being afraid had fled into the woods and placed himself behind a range of tombs, where he remained during the greatest part of the time we tarried on shore and it was with difficulty we prevailed upon him to embark. At last we got under way, and had to pull hard against a strong current.

Upon doubling the first point, the Chief with a number of canoes in his suite well manned and armed overtook us and kept in company, singing with unfriendly gestures all the while. Aware of their design we endeavoured to keep them at a proper distance for sometime. At last growing outrageous at our precautions they began to surround [us] and close in, apparently with the intention of seizing upon our canoe and upsetting us. I again had recourse to threats and vehemence of speech and gestures, and which again had the desired effect. The Chief spoke to his party and they all dropped behind, but they still followed and kept us in view.

JOURNAL OF A VOYAGE FROM THE ROCKY MOUNTAINS TO THE PACIFIC OCEAN PERFORMED IN THE YEAR 1808

Soon after a canoe with three men in it from a river on the left shore came to examine us; these after satisfying their curiosity immediately returned. We remarked that one of the crew had a large belt suspended from his neck garnished with locks of human hair.

About dark we observed the war party [that was following us] gain the shore, but we continued all night with a view to get to the next village and to secure provisions before their arrival. The night was dark and the current strong; we pressed on, reached our destination about 8 in the morning.

Here I must again acknowledge my great disappointment in not seeing the *main ocean*, having gone so near it as to be almost within view. For we wished very much to settle the situation by an observation for the longitude. The latitude is 49° nearly, while that of the entrance of the Columbia is 46° 20'. This River, therefore, is not the Columbia. If I had been convinced of this fact where I left my canoes, I would certainly have returned from thence.

Tuesday [Monday], July 4. The people of the village were greatly surprised to see us return, and enquired with impatience if we had been to the Islands, and how we had the good fortune to escape the cruelty of the *Masquiamme* — meaning the nations at the sea shore.

While we were endeavouring to answer these questions, our pursuers of the day before made their appearance. Still bent upon mischief, the leader at landing began to testify his hostile disposition by brandishing his horn club, and by making a violent harangue to the people of the village, who already seemed to be in his favour. He claimed his canoe; seeing a number of canoes scattered about the beach we acquiesced to his demand without hesitation.

After fixing the baggage and placing guards over it, at the request of a chief, Mr. Stuart, Mr. Quesnel and myself accompanied him to his tent; who, as soon as we were seated, offered us

Salmon to eat. We were much flattered with this token of his kindness, but had scarcely begun to partake of his bounty when one of the men came running to the door, exclaiming that the Indians were unruly and proceeding to violence. We hurried out of the tent, and at our appearance all was quiet; yet we could not feel free of alarm seeing the whole village assembled round our baggage, armed with all kinds of hostile weapons and seemingly determined upon mischief.

It was then, that our situation might really be considered as critical. Placed upon a small sandy Island, few in number, without canoes, without provisions, and surrounded by upwards of 700 barbarians. However our resolution did not forsake us. On the contrary all hands were of one mind, ready for action, and fully determined to make our way good at all hazards.

We now applied for canoes in every direction, but could not procure any either for love or money, so that we had to regret the inadvertency committed on our arrival by parting with the one we had before. There being no alternative we had again recourse to the chief, notwithstanding our experience of his illiberality. He asked his price — I consented — he augmented his demand — I again yielded — he still continued to increase his imposition. Feeling highly provoked at the impertinence of his conduct, I exclaimed violently. He then ordered the canoe to be brought.

We immediately prepared to embark, but when we began to load, the Indians crowded about the baggage and attempted to pillage. But as they laid hold upon any of our things we pulled it from them, and had to place ourselves in a posture of defence, and to threaten them with the contents of our pieces before they desisted.

Having got ready we crossed over the river. One of the Indians, who evinced a friendly disposition, followed and gave us some fish. At the same time [we] observed several of the others embarking and steering their course parallel to us along the

JOURNAL OF A VOYAGE FROM THE ROCKY MOUNTAINS TO THE PACIFIC OCEAN PERFORMED IN THE YEAR 1808

other bank. The canoe being leaky and some of the men being in want of paddles, we were obliged to put a shore to repair. This done we went on till 10 P.M. when we encamped upon an Island. In due time the men went to rest. Mr. Stuart and I mounted guard alternately.

Wednesday [Tuesday], July 5. Started early and at 10 A.M. arrived at *Pulagli* village. Here again we found the Chief of the big canoe, with several of his people. Their canoes being small, and consequently more easily managed than ours which was large, gave them the advantage. As we had some reason to suspect that they pressed forward on purpose to renew the quarrel and to be troublesome, and seeing the natives more numerous here than in the last camp, we judged it advisable to avoid them by crossing over to the other side of the river. Then three men followed in a canoe, who favoured us with a paddle and with five large Salmons.

To convey an idea of the effect of our arms to these men, we fired several shots before them — then made them understand that if the chief should pursue us any farther, he should suffer severely for his presumption. They desired us to proceed in peace, and [said] that no one would disturb us for the future.

We continued. About sunset two Indians in a canoe overtook us. We knew them; they invited us to their camp, which was at a small distance on the opposite shore; this we declined. At dark we put up for the night, all wet, the canoe was leaky, but the bank being steep it could not be repaired. We were within sight of the camp, but none of the Indians came near us.

Thursday [Wednesday], July 6. Set out early. Soon after several canoes joined [us]. In these we recognized Blondin, the Chief, that flattered us so much the 29th June — Also the two Indians of the preceeding evening who gave us fish, and who of their own accord assisted us in the rapids. Seeing them so well disposed, I gave them permission to embark in our canoe. They paddled, but were not long on board before they struck up the war song. I imposed their silence. A moment after Blondin got Mr. Quesnel's dagger out of the scabbard, and was hiding it under his robe when he was perceived. Seeing their evil disposition they were instantly put to shore.

Soon after this the other Indians made us signs to follow them; doubting their sincerity we pushed from them and took a different channel. Upon this they doubled their speed. By and by we discovered a large camp of Indians, who soon taught us that they were not assembled there for any good purpose. When we came opposite all were in motion — some were in canoes, others lined the shore, and all were advancing upon us. At last it was with difficulty we could prevent them with the muzzles of our guns from seizing upon the canoe. They, however, contrived to give us such a push with the intention of upsetting us, that our canoe became engaged in the strong current which in spite of all our efforts carried us down the rapids. However we gained the shore at the foot of a high hill, where we tied the canoe to the tree with a line. Here I ordered Mr. Stuart with some of the men to debark in order to keep the Indians in awe. The Indians perceiving our preparations for defence retired, but still kept a head.

I then directed the men, who were on shore, to embark, but Mr. Stuart came to inform me that several of them refused, saying that they were bent upon going by land across the Mountains to the place where we had slept the 24th June. Considering this as a desperate resolution, I debarked and endeavoured to persuade them out of their infatuation; but two of them declared in their own name and in that of others, that their plan was fixed, and that they saw no other way by which they might [save] themselves from immediate destruction, for continuing by water, said they, surrounded by hostile nations, who watched every opportunity to attack and torment them, created in their minds a state of suspicion, which was worse than death.

JOURNAL OF A VOYAGE FROM THE ROCKY MOUNTAINS TO THE PACIFIC OCEAN PERFORMED IN THE YEAR 1808

I remonstrated and threatened by turns. The other gentlemen joined my endeavours in exposing the folly of their undertaking, and the advantages that would accrue to us all by remaining as we had hitherto done in perfect union for our common welfare. After much debate on both sides, our delinquents yielded and we all shook hands, resolving never to separate during the voyage; which resolution was immediately confirmed by the following oath taken on the spot by each of the party: "I solemnly swear before Almighty God that I shall sooner perish than forsake in distress any of our crew during the present voyage." After this ceremony was over all hands dressed in their best apparel, and each took charge of his own bundle.

In [the] mean time some of the peaceable Indians came to pay us a visit. These inherited our superfluities, and it diverted us much to see them dive into the river and scramble about rags, which the men had thrown away as useless.

By this time it was near sun set. We, however, decamped full of spirits, singing and making a great noise. The Indians, who were waiting a head, observing us so cheerful, felt disheartened, kept their distance, and some of them thought proper to paddle down the stream. At dusk we encamped on a small Island below a village.[32] The two young Indians who had been benefited by our scourings encamped with us, but the others did not approach our Island.

Friday [Thursday], July 7. In the morning the residue of the unfriendly Indians, who had passed the night in the vicinity of our Island, directed their course down the current, and we saw nothing of them afterwards.

Our Little Fellow and his Chief who had Slept at the village came over to see us. He informed us that all the people from below were gone away. We crossed over to the village, where we procured a few Salmons and shell fish, which were left there by the above mentioned Indians. The Indians of this village were few in number and very poor.

A couple of leagues further on we came to another village. Here we traded for some fish. By 10 A.M. we came to a portage, where we had to carry most of our things, and had to drag the canoe up by the line. A number of Indians were present. They appeared friendly, and the old man entered into conversation with us. Our Little Fellow informed them of all he knew about us. He spoke particularly of our difficulties — how we resisted the attacks of the tribes below, and explained to them the nature of our big guns, and also of our little guns of which, he said, our pockets were full. As a proof of some of his assertions, we fired several shots. The Indians were astonished.

We renewed our course. Some of our men were rather dull; the thoughts of approaching the passage of the rock probably annoyed them. Below the village of the Rock [the village in the vicinity of Yale, below Lady Franklin Rock] we found some Indians fishing who invited us to the village, But we went to encamp on the opposite shore. While we were landing, our Little Fellow made his appearance as an ambassador from the people of the village who requested our presence among them. I with Mr. Quesnel and six of the men crossed over. The Indians received us with kindness, and we tarried with them a couple of hours, when they carried us back in small canoes. In the evening we observed the Indians fishing. Their nets, that resembled purses, were fixed to the end of long poles, and dragged between two canoes.

Saturday [Friday], July 8. All hands were up early, but before all the necessary arrangements were taken for prosecuting our journey by land, it was past 8. We, then, crossed over to the village. It was here we embarked in canoes the 29th June; and being the end of the navigation, I made [a] present of the canoe and some other little things which we could not conveniently

JOURNAL OF A VOYAGE FROM THE ROCKY MOUNTAINS TO THE PACIFIC OCEAN PERFORMED IN THE YEAR 1808

carry away with us to our Little Fellow, and which he immediately presented to his friends. Then each of us took charge of his own bundle, and we walked into the village.

The Indians did not receive us with the same cordiality they did when we went down. However they spread mats for us, and put stones in the fire to heat in order to prepare us a meal. But this operation required more time than our situation would permit us to spare, and we took our leave, prepared for the worst in as much as we had dangerous places to pass, defiles in which a few men might easily annoy an army with stones. Some of the Indians, who accompanied us and assisted us in carrying our things, pilfered a kettle and my calumet [long-stemmed pipe], but which the Chief ordered to be restored.

About 11 A.M. we arrived at a village where we were kindly treated. Here we missed our kettle a second time, and our Little Fellow informed us that it was stolen. The Indians of the village were alarmed at this incident, thinking no doubt that we would ill use them in consequence. We assured them that the custom of white people was to punish those only who had injured them, and that if we could lay hold on the Indian who took the kettle from us, he should have reason to regret his rapacity. They seemed satisfied at this explanation. I made a few presents to those from whom we experienced friendship. On examining our little baggage we discovered that two or three other articles were missing, which had been taken by the Indians, to whom we had entrusted the baggage at the Rock. This was a lesson not to be forgotten during the remainder of the Journey.

Soon after our departure, at the end of the carrying place, we met two Chiefs in two canoes form the Hacamaugh [Thompson] Nation. They did not expect us, but were so happy to see us return that they lent us their canoes, while they themselves went on foot to the village. These Indians shewed us every possible mark of kindness. Having taken up our quarters with them for the night, they gave us plenty to eat, and entertained us with a variety of songs, dances, &c. during the evening.

Sunday [Saturday], July 9. This being a fine morning we dried our things and at 1 P.M. took our departure. Some of the Indians, who accompanied us, offered to carry part of our baggage; we thanked them for their politeness but could not trust our things out of sight. The Chief of the next village, having heard of our approach, sent two canoes to meet us [in] which we embarked. When we arrived at the village we met with much attention. They gave [us] two excellent dogs which made delicious meals for the men, besides fish and berries in abundance. Here we procured a few articles of curiosity; viz., a blanket of Dog's hair, a matted bag, a wooden comb of curious construction &c. Among these Indians we observed a variety of tools, pieces of Iron and of brass, a bunch of brass keys which were from the crew of a ship that the Indians of the sea had destroyed several years before.

Monday [Saturday], July 10. Set out early. Kept the left side of the river accompanied by several Indians who shewed us the way. The road was inconceivably bad. We had to pass many difficult rocks, defiles and precipices, through which there was a kind of beaten path used by the natives, and made passable by means of scaffolds, bridges and ladders so peculiarly constructed, that it required no small degree of necessity, dexterity and courage in strangers to undertake a passage through such intricacies of apparent danger as we had to encounter on this occasion. For instance we had to ascend precipices by means of ladders composed of two long poles placed upright and parallel with sticks crossways tied with twigs. Upon the end of these others were placed, and so on for any height. Add to this that the ladders were often so slack that the smallest breeze put them in motion — swinging them against the rocks — while the steps were so narrow and irregular leading from scaffold to scaffold, that they could scarcely be traced by the

JOURNAL OF A VOYAGE FROM THE ROCKY MOUNTAINS TO THE PACIFIC OCEAN PERFORMED IN THE YEAR 1808

feet without the greatest care and circumspection; but the most perilous was, when another rock projected over the one you were leaving. The Indians deserve our thanks for their able assistance through these alarming situations.[33]

The descents were still worse. In these places we were under the necessity of trusting all our things to the Indians, even our guns were handed from one to another. Yet they thought nothing of these difficulties, but went up and down these wild places with the same agility as sailors do on board of a ship.

After escaping innumerable perils in [the] course of the day we encamped about sunset. The Indians tried to fish, but caught nothing; they, however, supplied us with plenty of dried fish.

Tuesday [Monday], July 11. Early this morning we continued our route accompanied by our Little Fellow and another Indian. Crossed a rapid river upon a bridge, and soon after got to the end of the portage, where we found three canoes, in which those that were lame embarked; the others continued by land. Some of the Natives from below overtook us, and in the afternoon [we] arrived at the village where we had slept the 24th June. The Indians were happy to see us again, and favoured us with plenty of provisions. I wished to go on without delay, but our Little Fellow aided by the people of the village insisted upon our passing the night with them.

Wednesday [Tuesday], July 12. This morning after procuring a sufficiency of fish we set out. Two canoes having followed, those that were indisposed to walk embarked. The others who went by land had now and then to make use of the canoes as ferry boats in crossing Rivers. At the carrying place where the canoes were left, Mr. Quesnel lost his way and was for some time absent, which caused some alarm. Several men and Indians went in search of him. He, however, found his way to the village, where we were, without their assistance. The weather was excessively hot and the road extremely bad all the day.

Thursday [Wednesday], July 13. Started early accompanied as usual by many of the Indians. Previous to our departure the Chief gave us forty salmons and sent young men along with us to carry them, saying "The Indians above were poor." I returned the Chief's compliment to his satisfaction.

We could not procure canoes, [but] the Indians assured us that the rapids were too strong to use them with advantage. Soon after we left the camp the Indian, who had supplied us with a canoe on our way down, joined our party and offered his services again in like manner; we accepted his offers, which we found useful for many purposes in [the] course of the day.

Passed by a village where the Indians were poor, yet they generously shared with us what little they had. Foul weather — we were wet to the skin. The men being in ill humour some of them would not approach the camp. Such conduct, under the circumstances in which we were, was unpleasant.

Friday [Thursday], July 14. Lost some time waiting for the men who thought proper to remain behind. It was 6 A.M. before they joined the party. I reprimanded them, and they blamed the weather.

At 8 found ourselves above the rapids [in the vicinity of Jackass Mountain] where we escaped perishing the 20th June. An Indian camp on the opposite bank invited us over & we went. Here we found two of the guides we had employed on our way down; and the Indians of their own accord restored a hat, a pair of shoes, and some others articles we had lost in the rapids.

At 2 P.M. arrived at the confluence or forks of Thomson's [Thompson's] River. Two of our men who were behind came up with us accompanied by some Natives. Having been invited we visited a camp which was on elevated ground, where we found Indians from the interior who had a warlike appearance. Crowding round they gazed on us with astonishment. They were called *Swhanemugh*,[34] and spoke a different language from

JOURNAL OF A VOYAGE FROM THE ROCKY MOUNTAINS TO THE PACIFIC OCEAN PERFORMED IN THE YEAR 1808

the tribes in the vicinity. They dress finely in leather, and we understood that their country was well stocked with animals, such as horses, deer, beaver &c. They gave us plenty of fresh salmon, berries, roots &c.

Three or four children, who were unwell, were brought to me by their parents for medical assistance. As I did not think fit to disappoint them, I sent one of the gentlemen for a vial of Turlington. He brought me Laudanum. Considering the one of equal virtue with the other towards a cure, I mixed a few drops of what he brought with water. In this mixture I dipt my finger which I gently applied to the forehead of the sick. Believing no doubt in miracles within a few moments, there were upwards of four score applicants for a touch of my finger; and had we remained any length of time, I have reason to believe the whole camp, which exceeded 1200, would have followed the example. Most of the children were really afflicted with some serious disorder which reduced them to skeletons. The women of this tribe had the neatest dress of any we have seen in this quarter.

The Chief of the Hacamaughs [Thompson Indians], who had been so serviceable to us in going down, was here, but took no notice of us. By this inattention we had reason to suspect his sincerity on former occasions. However the other Indians seemed well disposed towards us. They presented me with an otter belt, and lent us their canoes to cross the river. Still we could perceive something unpleasant in their demeanour; but they had been waiting our arrival for a long time and were now starving. They now and then killed a horse — we saw the hide of one quite fresh hanging upon a tree — and this famine, perhaps, caused the disagreeable gloom which attracted our notice.

Thompson River to Fort George

After leaving those Indians, we continued for the rest of the day until we came opposite a village to which we crossed. The Indians of it we found poor but civil; they regaled us with Dog's flesh.

Saturday [Friday], July 15. Upon our march early with several Indians in our company. Passed two camps in [the] course of the day.

Sunday [Saturday], July 16. This day we passed several camps of Indians. The weather being wet and bad we encamped early with a band of Indians, whose Chief made me a present of a coat of mail to make shoes. We were much in want of this necessary article; continually walking as we were among the worst of roads, our feet were covered with blisters, and some of the men were lame and in perpetual torture.

Monday [Sunday], July 17. I procured this morning several curiosities and satisfied the Chief for his present of the preceeding night. Went off and breakfasted at a place where on the 15th June, I gave medicines to a sick man, who was still there and unwell.

About noon we came to the Fort of [the] Askittih tribes [the Lillooet Indians]. Here the old Atnah Chief & the Toohowtin [Tauten] Interpreter left us on our way down. The Indians received us kindly & requested that we would wait the return of their Chief who had gone to another camp. To this we agreed; and about two hours after the Chief made his appearance accompanied with a numerous suit [suite]. He made us a long and loud speech to which he added the acceptable present of a few coats of mail. He then pressed us to go with him to the other camp. This invitation we had reason to decline. We however, crossed the river, and encamped directly opposite the place which the Chief wished us to visit. The

JOURNAL OF A VOYAGE FROM THE ROCKY MOUNTAINS TO THE PACIFIC OCEAN PERFORMED IN THE YEAR 1808

Indians sent canoes immediately for us; some of us went. The camp consisted of upwards of [a] thousand persons, who being strangers, I shook hands with them all round. The Chief made a harangue & then invited us to his *shade*, where we were treated with great hospitality. At the same time an Indian who was labouring under some disease offered me a pair of shoes in hopes of procuring some relief. When we returned to our encampment we learned that the Indians during our absence had made several trips across the river with invitations to the rest of our party to go and join them.

Tuesday [Monday], July 18. This morning at the earnest request of the Indians, Mr. Stuart & such of the men as wished paid a visit to the camp. Mr. Stuart procured many curiosities, and the men brought back some dogs which, to their palates, proved a delicious dish.

A woman, who had followed our party for those three days past, was left last night at the camp. She however found means to come and join us again, and was the only native in our suit [suite] during this day. The country being extremely rough and the paths numerous, we could not keep together; consequently we lost some time in waiting for those that had deviated from the right path. Encamped near a village, which our Little Fellow went immediately to visit. On his return he informed us that the greatest part of the *cache* which we had left there was destroyed by wild animals, and that for the remainder we were under obligations to the Indians who had secured it for our return.

Wednesday [Tuesday], July 19. The report of the diminution of our *cache* caused a gloominess among the men. Afraid of starving some of them went so far as to insinuate a wish of remaining with the Natives, and one of them dropt behind visibly with that intention; but perceiving that none of the others followed his example, he doubled his pace and in a short time overtook us.

About this time [we] met two of the Atnah nation who were upon their way to the Askitteh Country, and who returning with us gave us some useful information. At sunset we found ourselves at the Foot of the Rock which gave us so much trouble on our way down. Here several natives joined and informed us that a great many more were passing upon the hills. Although there might be no danger, I thought it advisable to run no unnecessary risk; I therefore dispatched Mr. Stuart and two men, by way of precaution, to our canoes which were about three miles distant.

Thursday [Wednesday], July 20. Early in the morning we proceeded on our journey and soon after joined Mr. Stuart, when we had the inexpressible satisfaction of finding our canoes and our *cache* perfectly safe. [This cache was in the vicinity of Leon Creek.] For this good fortune we felt grateful to the Indians who continually attended to their security during our absence. Here we lost no time but set about preparing the canoes for the voyage; but having no materials at hand, one of the canoes, tho' still good, was cut up to repair the other two. While we were employed upon this necessary service, numbers of the Natives called to see us and passed on to the other stages. Our Little Fellow and the two Atnahs accompanied them.

At 3 P.M. all being ready we took our departure. Safe in our canoes we had reason to consider ourselves as once more at home, and notwithstanding the many disagreeable moments which we had experienced, we talked of them as nothing and we felt happy. Encamped at dark.

Friday [Thursday], July 21. Set out early. We had to oppose a strong current, and encountered great difficulties in the rapids. Rain and bad weather rendered our situation very unpleasant. While we were busy in one of the carrying places, several of the natives paid us a visit on horseback, who in measure as their curiosity was satisfied retired. We encamped about dark.

JOURNAL OF A VOYAGE FROM THE ROCKY MOUNTAINS TO THE PACIFIC OCEAN PERFORMED IN THE YEAR 1808

Saturday [Friday], July 22. We were off early. Still a strong current, and many rapids. The waters having greatly abated we had more carrying places now than before. At 8 A.M. we arrived at the *rapid couverte* [*rapide couvert*; French Bar Canyon], which is more than a mile long, & where we were obliged to carry all our baggage over long and steep hills.

Here we found Indians among whom was the old Atnah Chief and his brother, both so overjoyed to see us that they annoyed us with caresses. They assured us that they felt extremely anxious for our safety during our absence, and that they had determined if the Indians of the sea destroyed us to collect their friends and go to revenge us. We could not take these professions for gospel; However we thanked the Chief for his friendship and good intention. At the same time I wished to make him and his friends understand that we were not to be [easily] destroyed, as our nature and our arms were superior to any thing we could meet among the Indians.

When the portage was done we crossed over to the Indian camp. The Chief and his brother embarked and crossed with us. The other Indians made use of a small canoe constructed of pine bark and curiously formed, being narrow at both ends which pointed downwards in the shape of a funnel. The men described it, *un canot puit au bec d'Eturgeons* [*un canot à bec d'esturgeon*; a sturgeon-nosed canoe][35] — it could carry no more than two a time. The Indians of the camp received us with loud acclamations, and made us numerous presents in leather.

Our Little Fellow remained at this camp. He would have accompanied us to the end of the voyage, but the Indians advised him to go and find his friends. I made him a present of some necessary articles, such as pleased him most. The woman also remained, it being the wish of the Chief. We continued our route and encamped at a late hour.

Sunday [Saturday], July 23. Being up I discovered that one end of the canoe had [become] detached from the shore and was already out in the current; the other end was but slightly tied, so that we were very near experiencing an accident [which] would have been of great inconveniency to us, even at this advanced stage of our voyage. We set out as usual early. In [the] course of the day we passed several long and dangerous rapids which caused us much difficulty to ascend. Found a camp of Indians busily employed preparing materials for the Salmon fishery. They behaved to us with great civility. Continued and encamped at our encampment of the 5th June [near Churn Creek].

Monday [Sunday], July 24. We were off early. Hard labour and great exertions, yet we advanced but slowly this day. We observed several Indians on horseback, and many a foot all along the river. Encamped in the evening with a band who were on their way upwards.

Tuesday [Monday], July 25. Arrived early at Chilkoetins [Chilcotin] River. Found the old Chief there. He came the night before from the *Rapide Couverte* [*Couvert*], and rode through the plains beyond the hills which line the water communication. About two hundred natives from different quarters were assembled at this place on purpose to have a peep at us *en passant.* They wished us to delay our departure untill their friends, who were on their way to the camp, should arrive. This wish we could not satisfy. The Indians, however, gave us a plentiful feast made up of venison, onions, Roots &c. They also made us a present of some leather and Beaver skins. After making a suitable acknowledgement for these obligations, we took our departure. The Old Chief with several others in his suit [suite] continued by land to the next stage.

At the *portage de Barril* [*portage du Baril*] the Indians assisted in passing over our baggage, which was of great service to us, the

JOURNAL OF A VOYAGE FROM THE ROCKY MOUNTAINS TO THE PACIFIC OCEAN PERFORMED IN THE YEAR 1808

portage being long and the weather extremely hot. In [the] course of the afternoon we shot a deer on the beach, and encamped soon after.

Wednesday [Tuesday], July 26. Proceeded on as usual, had rain and bad weather. Got to *Portage de Troul* [*Portage du Trou*; presumably the portage around the *Rapide du Trou*] in the afternoon, where we encamped. Here again we found the old Chief with a large assembly of Atnahs and Chilkoetins [Chilcotins]. The latter are from the Westward and came on purpose to have a sight of us, having never seen any white people before. They had the information of our return from the lower parts of the river by messages across the Country. The Chilkoetins [Chilcotins], who are a tribe of the Carriers, and whom we could understand without the assistance of Interpreters, are from the head of a River [the Chilcotin] that falls into this River; they speak of their Country as plentifully stocked with all kinds of animals which are common to the Northwest. They seem to be acquainted with Christian goods, and are if I am not mistaken of a bold, roguish disposition.

Thursday [Wednesday], July 27. We had to ascend some very difficult and dangerous rapids, particularly the one where we were nearly lost the 1st June. Here again one of our canoes narrowly escaped. Hauling it up amongst steep banks and strong cascades, it filled and all our things got wet.

At the end of the carrying place of this rapid [we] found our *cache* of provisions and canoes in the same good order as we left them. After supplying ourselves plentifully I made over the remainder to the Indian who had it in charge. He immediately divided the same among his friends who were greatly in want. Having been in a state of starvation for some time previous to our arrival, they deserve much credit for having abstained from the *cache*.

The things which got wet were spread to the sun, but before they were thoroughly dry we embarked and crossed to the opposite bank. Here we found a dipping net, with which one of our young men tried his skill in fishing, but without success.

Friday [Thursday], July 28. We had to oppose a strong current which greatly fatigued the men. Early in the afternoon we arrived at the village of the Old Chief. He got [there] before [us] as usual, by land. Here ends the Rocky country. All the Portages and bad places being past we had now but plain sailing for the rest of the voyage. The Chief's brother delivered to us four bales of fish which he had in charge.

This being the last village of the Atnah nation the Old Chief did not follow us any further. Having experienced in him kind attention and much service I presented him with a gun, Amms. [ammunition], and some other necessary articles; and to his brother I gave a Poniard.

Saturday [Friday], July 29. This morning after repairing the canoes we took our leave of the Indians at 6. The Atnahs are good people. They expressed their regret at our departure and begged that we would return to their Country as soon as possible to reside among them as traders. This I in a manner promised.

We went on tolerably well for some time, notwithstanding the current we had to oppose. Passed several houses and fisheries, and in the afternoon came to the place [a few miles above Soda Creek] were we saw the first Indians and where we lost our swivel. Here we found a band of Tohootins [Tautens] who received us with kindness. They had some furs but were loath to part with them. These Indians procure their necessaries from the westward, and seem to be well supplied with Iron utensils.

They gave us plenty of salmon which they take in abundance by means of barriers. These barriers form a work of some ingenuity, which is constructed in the manner following. Strong poles are driven into the ground at certain dis-

JOURNAL OF A VOYAGE FROM THE ROCKY MOUNTAINS TO THE PACIFIC OCEAN PERFORMED IN THE YEAR 1808

tances, and these distances are filled with frames made of splinters placed so close that a fish cannot pass between. On the top of these are squared pines for the purpose of walking, and underneath are placed props to support the whole against the force of the current. At the outer farthest end is the gate, and sometimes there are gates in the center, which receive the contrivance that confines the fish. This contrivance is composed of splinters the size of a finger from ten to fifteen feet long and secured by watap [spruce-root] hoops in the form of a cask. The end that is placed below in the current is made inside like a Funnel. Through [this] the fish enter one by one, and cannot find the way back, but remain as in a net.

This Country is mountainous and poor. The Natives generally live on fish, of which they lay by in the summer a sufficiency for the winter, which season they pass in idleness. A few indeed take animals in snares, and when the crust of the snow is strong they run down the deer with dogs — but this is a general custom among Indians.

Sunday [Saturday], July 30. Previous to our arrival at this place two of the Indians had a serious quarrel. The one stabbed the other with a lance which left a bad wound.

Set out at 5. Discovered that one of our *Caches* was destroyed, but it contained only one bale of fish. Observed an Indian in a small canoe. He wished to avoid us, and we had some difficulty to approach him. However with some persuation [persuasion] we prevailed upon him to leave his own canoe and to embark into ours. We were in want of him in order to introduce us to a camp of his friends who were at some distance, and when we came near the camp we sent him a shore to advertise [i.e., to warn] the Indians of our appearance to prevent surprize. In this camp we found several families of the Nasquetin [Nazkoten] Nation. The men received us at the water side armed; being strangers they were doubtful of our intentions, but after having been informed they laid by their weapons and treated us with confidence. Soon after several more made their appearance, coming from all directions, and haranguing at [word illegible]. They had some furs for which they asked a high price. A kind of white shell found along the Sea shore forms the principal medium of exchange among all the Indians to the West of the Rocky Mountains. This is to them what money is to us.

Monday [Sunday], July 31. Passed several camps of Indians in the course of the day. At Sunset [as we were] approaching a camp to put a shore the Indians flew to their arms, put on their coats of Mail, and appeared as mad as furies. However upon proper explanations taking place they altered their tone and received us with kindness.

Tuesday [Monday], August 1. Set out early. Debarked at Quesnel's River where we found some of the natives, from whom we procured some furs, plenty of fish and berries. Continued our route untill sunset.

Wednesday [Tuesday], August 2. Early on the water. Arrived at the Mountain portage [Cottonwood Canyon?]. Some difficulty in the rapids. Found our *cache* safe. Continued and encamped on the left side of the River.

Friday [Wednesday], August 3. Set out as usual. Found a family of Indians busily employed in fishing. They gave us as much Salmon as we wished. In [the] course of the day passed several houses. At one of the camps where we put a shore, the chief, who was considered as a great man, offered us two bear skins in exchange of other articles, and some of his people followed us to our encampment.

Friday [Thursday], August 4. A boy who was a relation of our young [manuscript damaged; one word missing] embarked with us in order to visit his friends. Proceeded on untill night.

Saturday [Friday], August 5. Set out at an early hour. Passed a

JOURNAL OF A VOYAGE FROM THE ROCKY MOUNTAINS TO THE PACIFIC OCEAN PERFORMED IN THE YEAR 1808

Portage and several rapids. Encampt upon the right bank. The men found a large *Fungess* [fungus] which had grown upon a Hemlock tree — it has the same virtue with Rhubarb. The natives use it to dress or whiten their leather.

Sunday [Saturday], August 6. Set out early and at noon arrived at the Fort [Fort George, at the mouth of the Nechako River], where we found Mr. [Hugh] Faries with his two men.

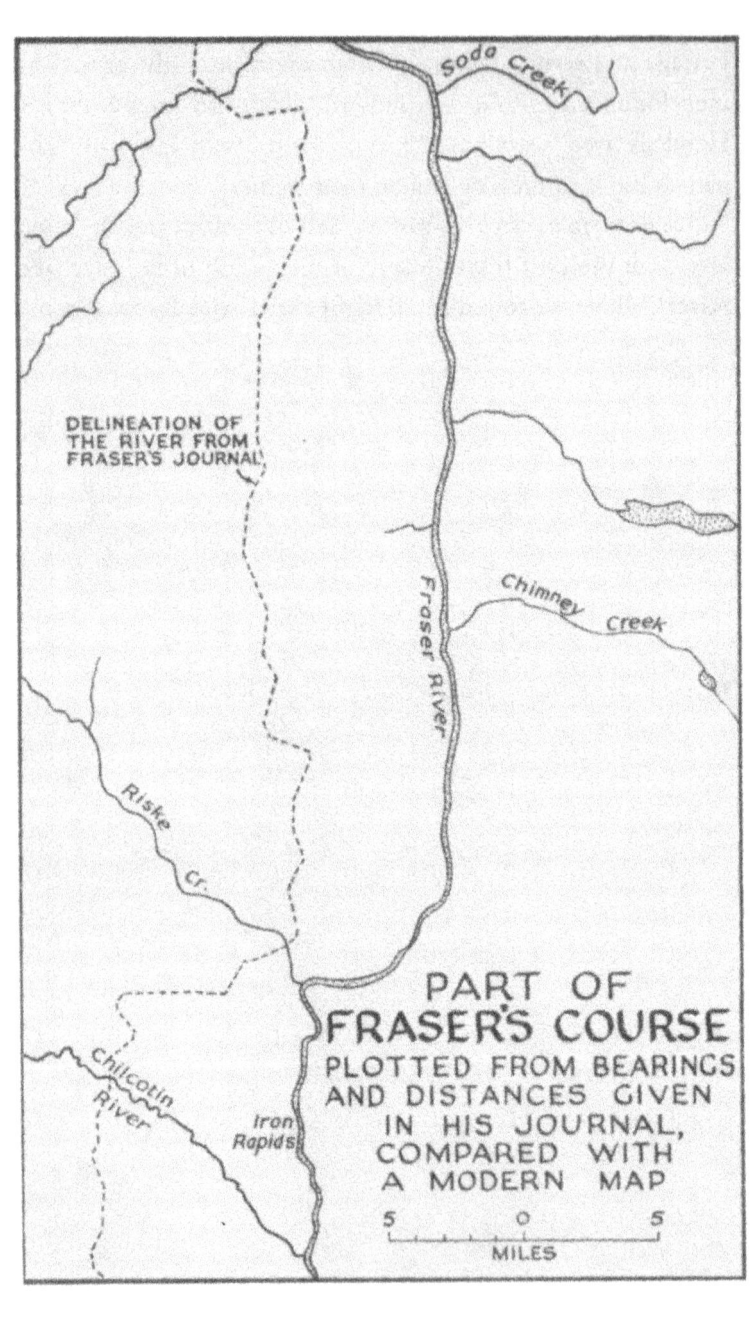

SECOND JOURNAL OF SIMON FRASER FROM MAY 30TH TO JUNE 10TH 1808

[*The surviving text begins abruptly, in the middle of a sentence. When the first entry was written Fraser and his party were a few miles upstream from Soda Creek, probably in the vicinity of Macalister.*]

[M]onday, May 30] ... women of the Atnagh [Atnah] nation who were terrified at our appearance. Their language[s] were mutually unintelligible, but their being a young boy whose mother is of the Tahawtum [Tauten] tribe who understands a little of the Carru [Carrier] language, we understood that they [had] sent courriers before and that several of their relations should be here in the course of the day, and that it might be dangerous for us to proceed before they were apprised of our possible intentions.

This with expectation of procuring guides induced us to remain and encamp with them, and in course of the day, Some Thatawtens [Tautens] and other Atnahs arrived. They all seemed peaceably inclined and even friendly and happy to see us. They say that they kept near the River purposely to see us, they having been informed by some Carriers that we were to come to their lands this summer. One of them (Th. L.)[1] had seen Mr. A.M.K. [Alexander Mackenzie] and even served him as guide, and if we can judge from appearances he has been a little spoiled. However he was of some service to us as it was through his means we were enabled to have any conversation with the others — I mean the Atnahs, whose language has not the least a finity with [that of] any of the different tribes with which I am acquainted. The few of them we saw at this place were of a diminutive size but seemingly very active and in their make more like the Big men[2] than Carriers. They had bows and arrows both extremely well made, which they laid down on coming to us. Most of their bows were of Juniper or Box wood and Ceader and covered with the skin of the rattlesnake, which they say are numerous in this quarter, and their arrows are pointed with stone of the flint kind but dark, and their clothing consisted of dressed leather, leggings and shoes with robes of the Chivirease [chevreuil (deer); i.e., buckskin], Carribo [caribou], Biche [doeskin] and Beaver skins, most of which were dressed in the hair.

They represent the animals as very numerous and the Country in general is Plains, in many places of which there is no wood, and a couple of our men who were hunting saw some Chivirease [chevreuils i.e., deer], tho' surrounded by people in several directions, which proves beyond doubt that they are numerous. And according to their accounts of the River it is little better than a succession of falls and rapids, many of which are impassable and others very dangerous, but all of them said that none of them had been at or even near the sea, and it was their decided opinion that we ought to return back and take the same route Sir A.M.K. [Sir Alexander Mackenzie] did, which however was far from our intentions. And being told that whatever obsticles might impede us [we] were determined to proceed, they informed us that at the first rapid there was a great Chief who had a slave that had been often there [i.e., to the sea], and perhaps might be prevailed on to accompany us, particularly if we promised to come and pass the ensuing winter with them.

All of them had heard of fire arms, but few of them had ever heard the report of a gun and expressed a desire that we should fire ours, to which we complied and fired several guns and pis-

SECOND JOURNAL OF SIMON FRASER
FROM MAY 30TH TO JUNE 10TH 1808

tols, which astonished them much, and on hearing the report they fell flat to the ground, and informed us that all the Indians along this river were quiet and peaceable inclined, and would come to us without an arm in their hands. However, we ought to be prudent and endeavour not to surprise any of them, as in that case they might be tempted to fire through fear.

Those who came to see us from below were on horse back, But tho' animals are plenty and the country in many places clear of wood, they do not use them to hunt, but use them to carry themselves and baggage, which is the chief cause of their not going much in Canoes.

At this place unfortunately we lost our swivil, for firing it to make an impression on the Indians, tho' but moderately loaded, less than three gills [of] powder, it was shattered to pieces and wounded the man that fired it (Gagnier), which accident was perhaps fortunate to us, it being cracked in many places of old. Was it to break amongst a large band of Indians the consequence might be fatal.

Tuesday, May 31. We started at half past five with two Indians on board, it [that] is to say an Atnah and an Thowtern [Tauten] to go where there are several others a short distance below. [I] had no information in addition to what I was informed yesterday. Continued the same course with yesterday 2 miles. A house on the right and Islands near the lower end and a small one on the left. S 70 E 1/2 [mile].³ S 15 E 1 1/2 [miles]. An Isle on the left. S 55 E 1 [mile]. Islands in the right. S 20 E 2 miles. S 70 E 1 mile. S 70 E 1 1/4 [miles]. In this course is a rapid and at the beginning of [the] course is a large Island, in the middle of the river. A white cliff on right. E 1/4 [mile]. N 70 E 2 1/2 [miles]. In the course are rough cliffs of greyish color, on left, and a high but not long one on right divided by [word omitted?] into two, and near [the] end a small Island on left. S 60 E 1/3 [mile]. The hills and banks have a romantic and Grotisk [grotesque] shape. S

30 E 1/2 [mile]. Here we found Indians on the left on very high hills at the head of a strong rapid called La Grand Decharge [Soda Creek Canyon]. All the Indians came to see us near the River and were very friendly to us. They brought us dried Salmon and three different kinds of roots with which they regaled us all.

After having enquired several times for the slave, that knows the Country below [he] at last was introduced to us by the Chiefs desire. I immediately got the two cloths spread out to get a chart of the River drawn by the Slave, which he undertook, but seemingly knew but little of its situation, as he deliniated nothing but what an elderly man, I believe a relation of the Chief, ensigned [indicated]. The chief himself spoke much and paid particular attention to us, and informed us of the Indians being peaceable and that we had nothing to apprehend from them, tho' some of the tribes or nations below were at enmity with them, that they would not hurt white people, but receive them on the Palms of their hands. But notwithstanding, he said that he would accompany us all the way in case that anything might happen to us, that from his age, influence and acquaintance with the country and natives below that he could protect us from any eminant [imminent] danger. Previous to this I inquired if an Indian could be had to accompany us, and I believe that old mans principle reason for accompany [accompanying] us, is that we may return early to establish a Post upon his lands.

All these Indians are fond of smoking tobacco, and they have a kind of weed which they mix with fat, which serves as a substitute for tobacco. The chief produced a pipe which was procured from the lower part of this River.

We lost much time in speaking to the Indians, but got the Canoes ran down the Rapids and part of the loading carried while we were busy getting information and procuring Guides.

Here we left 4 bales of salmon under the care of the Chief's brother, and on our departure he told me to stop till he bring

SECOND JOURNAL OF SIMON FRASER
FROM MAY 30TH TO JUNE 1OTH 1808

[brought] me some leather for making shoes. He returned in about 20 minutes with a large and well dressed buck Deer skin and a Beaver skin, which he made me a present of in recommending me to take good care of the Chief his brother. I told him I would pay particular attention to his brother and [that] he himself would be pleased with me on my return, for his present as well as attention to us all.

All the Indians of this place were very civil to us. They agreed with the others, that animals are plenty and the navigation of the River in many places impracticable. After which we set off, accompanied by the Chief, a slave of his, and our former guide (the latter I now call Interpreter he being the only one we can understand on board), to the lower end of the carrying place afoot.

South 1/2 [mile]. S 30 E 1 mile. The last two courses are a continual strong rapid, and [although] the Canoes were not all half loaded they took water. At the lower end is a Rocky Island and all along, the River is much contracted. Here we met a band of about 18 men that we did not see before. Shook hands with all of them and explained the cause of our passing through their country, which in appearance highly pleased them, after which we embarked and started. S 20 W 1/2 [mile]. Very steep banks on right and a small river [probably Hawks Creek] on left and thick wood on right (small Epenette [épinette; i.e., spruce]); still high sandy banks on left, but in some places wooded. S 30 E 1 1/2 [miles]. Rapids continue and [in] this course is a rocky Island in middle, grotesque banks or pinacles on right. S 5 W 3 1/4 [miles]. In this course is another strong rapid and the banks on right continue until near the end of course. S 20 E 1/3 [mile]. The last course but one may be called continual rapid. There are almost continual banks on both sides of the River and the wood, which is generally cypress, is scanty and but of a small growth, neither does the soil appear to be good, being generally sand on gravel. Near the end of this course is a very steep sandy banks and a rapid, but not strong. S. 20 E 3 1/2 [miles]. S 40 E 1 mile. Near the end of [the] last course is a small River [Williams Lake Creek] on left and the last course is a continual rapid with high banks in left and covered with wood, and the River in most places does not exceed 100 or 120 yards wide. S 10 W 3/4 [mile]. S 1/2 [mile]. Strong rapid and lourneguere[4] all along this course and rocks of blush [bluish] colours on both sides. S 20 E 1 3/4 [miles]. In this course is Rock on left and a rapid and house on right above the hills. S.E. with a rapid and rock on left, while a high [hill] of shape like the side of an old castle, appears a head 2 miles. S 15 E 1 1/4 [miles]. Here is a long and dangerous rapid which [is] called Rapid du Trou from a hole that appears in the perpendicular rock on [the] right side, and we debarked to visit it, and before that was done night came on and we encamped for the night.[5] There is also houses at [the] upper end on the right side.

It blew amazing hard all from the southward which rendered our progress not only tedious but dangerous, for when the wind caught hold of the Canoes in the many whirlpools we passed there was no such thing as managing them, so that every moment we were in danger of going to the bottom, and in many places there was no such thing as hunting on shore. In visiting the rapids we perceived some of the natives on the right shore, but I believe [we] were not observed by them.

Wednesday, June 1. At an early hour this morning all hands were up and soon after the natives appeared in several directions, some of which came to us. However by 5 a.m. Mr. Stuart myself and six men went to visit the rapid again, while the other[s] remained to take care of the baggage and Canoes. We found the rapid to be about 1 1/2 mile long and the rocks on both sides the River contract themselves in some places to either [within] 30 or 40 yards of one another, the immense body of water pass through them in a zig zag and turbulent manner, forming

SECOND JOURNAL OF SIMON FRASER
FROM MAY 30TH TO JUNE 10TH 1808

numerous Gulphs and whirlpools of great depths. However it was deemed impossible to carry the Canoes. It was the general opinion that they ought to be run down. Indeed there was no other alternative than either that or leaving them here.

Mr. Stuart remained at the lower end with Lagarde and Waka, to watch the Natives while the others were running the Canoes down. Tho' they appeared peaceable, it would not be prudent to allow the people to run down the Canoes under such a steep and rocky bank without having a guard above, as it would be in the Indians power to sink them all to the bottom, were they (the Indians) ill inclined, and I returned to the upper end to see the people embark.

Accordingly five of the best men embarked with only about 11 or 12 pieces. They immediately entered the rapid, but the whirlpools below the first Cascade made them wheel about, and they remained a considerable time without being able to move one way or the other, and every moment on the brink of eternity. However by the outmost [utmost] exertions they went down two others, till between that and the fourth, which is the most turbulent [of] the edies and whirlpools, [the current] caught hole [hold] of the canoes and spite of them [i.e., in spite of the efforts of the men] brought it ashore in a moment, and fortunately it was it happened so, or that they were not able to get out again [into the current], for had they got down the fourth cascade it would have been more than likely they would have remained there. Seeing it impossible to go any further, they unloaded upon a small point in a very steep and high and long hill.

Upon my way down to see what had become of the people I met Mr. Stuart coming up, who informed me of their situation, he having seen them from the lower part of the rapids. We went down immediately to the place they were thrown ashore, which we reached with much difficulty on account of the steepness of the banks. I often supported myself by running my dagger into the ground to hold myself by it. Happy we were to find all hands safe after such eminant [imminent] danger.

With much difficulty a road was dug into the hill with a hoe, about the breadth of one foot wide, and a line tied to the bow of the canoe and [it was] brought up an extraordinary bad and long bank. Had any of those that carried the Canoe missed their step, all would have tumbled into the River in spite of those that hauled the line. And when that was effected the baggage was brought up, and by the time the remainder of the Canoes were unloaded night came on.

More of the Natives came to us in the course of the day to [the] number of upwards of forty men, none of which carried arms, and if we may judge from appearance they were very happy to see us, and among them were some from a different tribe that inhabited the banks of a considerable River that falls into this from the right, Some distance below this place. They call themselves Chilk-ho-tins [Chilkotins] and are different from the Atnagh [Atnah] in language and manners, but resemble the Carriers, of which they are a tribe. In both [groups], we saw about sixty men, Indians, on this side of the River, and there were many on the other side of the River that could not cross, and are continually calling out to us to go for them, but as they could not render us [any] service, we have other things to attend to, and besides in the present state of the water it would be dangerous to cross the River at this place.

All agree in saying the navigation of the River is unpracticable, and indeed according to my own ideas in the present state of the water, which has risen 8 [feet] perpendicular in the four and twenty hours that we have been here, it is not possible to proceed in Canoes all along, though in low water the navigation may be practicable. As far as I have been as yet, there are no Falls, and I have ran down stronger [rapids] in appearance. But then the tremendous gulphs and whirlpools which are peculiar [to]

SECOND JOURNAL OF SIMON FRASER
FROM MAY 30TH TO JUNE 10TH 1808

this River is ready every moment to swallow a Canoe with all its contents and the people on board, and the high and perpendicular rocks render it impossible to stop the canoe or get on shore even was it stopped, so that in the present state of the water I pronounce it impracticable.

This rapid did not appear half so strong when visited [viewed] from the top of the hills as what it is. But tho' the navigation is dangerous and difficult by water, the Indians inform us that there is a good road along the River upon the hills all the way to the confluence of another large River [the Thompson] that flow[s] in from the left. From thence the navigation is good to the sea. [They say] that there are Rapids,[6] that the perpendicular rocks terminate, and that they sleep only four nights with horses loaded to go to that Fork.

I could wish that their report be true. Great as the distance is, it would not be more expeditious, but more safe to leave our Canoes here and proceed by the land at once. But it being late, the course we are to take could not be finally determined, and all hands went to bed without placing a watch. All being not only sleepy but tired, and all the Indians having previously retired we apprehended no danger.

Thursday, June 2. More strangers came to our camp and passed the best part of the day with us. The men were employed taking the remainder of the baggage in [and?] a canoe up the hill. On account of the navigation being difficult we leave two Canoes here, which will serve for our return. We also got a cache made to leave part of [our] baggage and provisions in, in order to lighten the two Canoes that continue the route, and besides [some] people will go by land with as many horses as we can procure from the Indians. They do not like either to sell or lend their horses, however we have been promised three, and they are gone for more. The Indians were against our continuing the navigation, on account of their being apprehensive for our safety, but now that we require horses to go by land, they give us encouragement to go by water. We got several charts drawn of the River, But by all it appears bad and some of the men are not willing to go in Canoes. I immagine they have not got the better of the fright they had running down this rapid yesterday, but notwithstanding we shall try it tomorrow.

Thursday [Friday], June 3. The night last past, many of the Indians passed the night at our camp. In the morning I got them to draw another chart of the River, which Mr. Stuart got explained, and took them down in writing, by which the road appears more practicable than by the information they gave us before. Accordingly [I] have changed my plans of yesterday and settled everything to start with three canoes. We took one up the hill this morning for that purpose — in this manner: tied the line to the bow, which was halted [hauled] by one of our men and seven Indians, canoe upside down, and the remainder of the people carried it upon their shoulders. With the help of Messrs. Stuart, Qusnel [Quesnel] and myself it was got up in the same manner as we brought up the other yesterday.

The Indians have amused us this two days past with the promise of bringing us plenty of horses to pass our baggage in the Portage, or to go by land to the large River that falls into this below the Rapids, but they brought only four. But their women passed [i.e., carried past the rapids] about 15 pieces of provisions and etc. The men do not carry, tho' some of them brought pieces up the hill yesterday, and as far as I can judge the women are much accustomed to laborous [laborious] work.

The men in height are generally from five feet six inches to six odd feet and [the] great part of them are above the middle size, but of a slender make, but active like, and as far as I can judge more industrious than the natives this side of the mountains generally are. They are well clothes in leather, which consists of only a robe, a pair of leggings and shoes, with sometimes a cap of an oval make, but more generally a circle of bark

SECOND JOURNAL OF SIMON FRASER
FROM MAY 30TH TO JUNE 1OTH 1808

(Ceder) dyed of different colours tied round their head, and their bodies are besmeard with greace or oil and red earth, while their face is generally painted with different colour.

They seem to run and move about much, and some of them have been across the mountains, as they seem acquainted with Buffalo, for on seeing our powder horns they immediately observed that they were of that animal, and a wounded Buffalo being painted on the stern of D.—[7] they named it, and said that they had seen such on the other side of the mountains, when they were upon a war party. They likewise say that they heard of white people having been down the first large River that flows into this on the left [the Thompson], but whether it had been Capt. Lewis or some of the Fort des Prairie[s] people we cannot determine.[8]

They seem communicative, but whether it be the fault of our interpreter the Thahowteen [Tauten] Indian we have I cannot say, [but] we can learn nothing certain, particularly regarding the River from them, for sometimes they represent [it] entirely impracticable, while in others they say it is navigable tho' there are many rapids and several Portages, one of which [is] two days march long. There [they say] that we will be obliged to leave our Canoes and go afoot, it being impassible on account of the many rapids and the rocks being cut perpendicular on both sides of the River.

[A] great part of the day was employed in getting information, while they brought up an amazing steep bank upwards of 450 feet high, all the baggage, and afterwards made a cache where we will leave anything that we will not be able to take from here. For all along until the evening the Indians represented the River as worse and worse, and from what we had seen of it ourselves it was thought impracticable by water, and the Indians amused us with the hopes of lending a sufficiency of horse to carry everything indespensibly necessary to the confluence of this and the first large River from the left [the Thompson], where the Rapids terminated. But as they brought only four, which would not be sufficient even with what the men could carry of salmon, leaving other necessaries out of the question, for fifteen or twenty days, it was determined to carry the canoes in this Portage and proceed by water at all hazards, for were we only to get down a dozen miles it would be so much gained, and we will then have the same advantage of going by land as now.

This plain few of the men, particularly LaCerte, relished, for the emminant [imminent] danger[s] [there] were in this Rapid renders them diffident and backward to attempt again for a passage by water. However, in consequence of this resolution a road was made same as yesterday in this hill, and in the same manner and by force of people another canoe [was] brought up the hill. By the time this was effected the sun was set, [and] all hands tired.

Many of the natives passed the night with us at our camp, and though no danger was apprehended, a watch was placed. Part of the Indians amused themselves [a] great part of the day at play. Their play of hazard, at least the one they played to day, resembled that of the R[ocky]. M[ountain]. Meadow Indians. By means of a small stick, bone, stone, or anything else of a small size, which under their robe they hide in one of their hands, and afterwards place them in kimboo, while they continue humming a song, which is the only one I observed among them, and either win or lose as their antagonist point[s] out the hand that contain[s] the mark or not.[9]

	Tahotins [Tautens]	Atnagh [Atnah]
Horses	Yezey ygleens	Echeso-kagh-ah
Biche [doe]	Yesey or Yescho	Snach-cul-chegh
Original [i.e., original; elk or moose]	Tunny or Tunnie	Tunnyeh

SECOND JOURNAL OF SIMON FRASER
FROM MAY 30TH TO JUNE 10TH 1808

Chivercan	Yes chea	Y'laugh-keep
Ram or Goat	Sasse-Yhan	S'koe to apes
Wolf	Yes	Manmun Steah
Fox	T'kil-e-chy	S'kal-ape
Carcajoun [carcajou]	Chash-leney	Quel-kuen or Whool-ky
Rabbits	Kugh	Sugh-guey-ech
Mouton	Aspai	Z, whool la-hey
Beaver	Iza	S'Kall-a-u
White Bean	Y'Hass	S'Kam yey
Black Bean	Sasse	S'Kow-lase

The water rose about three or four feet since last night.

June 2 and June 3 continued. Early the morning all hands went to open a road and carry the two canoes to the other end [of the portage] and during the interval, which was long. I spoke again to the Indians about the River and got another chart drawn of it, and particular pains taken to get everything explained, by which it appears [that] the River according to the present accounts [is] not so bad as before represented, which induced me to change my plans of yesterday, which was to proceed with two canoes by water manned by four men each, while Mr. Stuart, accompanied by Mr. Quesnel and the remainder of the people, would continue by land with what horses we could procure here. But neither the Indians like to lend or sell their horses [i.e., But the Indians like neither to lend nor sell their horses], which is perhaps the reason of their giving a different account of the River to what they did yesterday and on former occasions.

But at all events, as we could not procure horses enough to be of much use, and as by that plan we would unavoidably have been obliged to separate Company, it will be more prudent and better to continue all in Canoes, as the third can follow where two can go, with only this exception, that they will not be so well manned and the Bouts [foreman and steersman] of the third [canoe] are novices.

It is true [that] to have two canoes here might be of service on our way back, but to proceed is my present object, and if fortunate enough in that, we will always find out way back, for to gain that end every person will be interested, which perhaps is not so much the case at present.

And in consequence of this last determination another canoe was brought up the hill in the same manner as the one of last night, and the Indians gave a hand to carry the pieces over the Portage, which is bad, constantly on the declevity of a steep hill, amongst rocks and often up and down steep and long hills, and upwards of 3000 paces long. The coarse [course] by water is S 50 E 1 mile, S 5 E 1 1/2 [miles], and here we encamped for the night. The people were much fatigued and well they might.

One of the horses lent us was lead by one of our own men, loaded with two bales of fish and Mr. Stuart's desk, but in passing the declevity of a rock the horse tumbled down the precipice and was near being killed, however receiving no damage excepting breaking Mr. Stuart's desk, losing some papers and medicines.

We left about 1000 salmon in the cache at the upper end of the Portage, a little gum, and watoppe [watap].[10] The Indians wanted us to leave all our fish there, [contending] that it would be loading ourselves to no purpose to take such a quantity of bad salmon with us, [and assuring us] that the natives below would give us plenty of provisions (Askieteghs and Tla-caba-ney's suchanchs and etc.).[11] It is very probably that the natives below have plenty of provisions, but then it cannot be depended upon. I know well from experience what it is to be out of provisions and to depend on such vague report, [and] while we have a salmon remaining, bad as they are, there will be nothing impossible for us to do. They also said that in a couple of days we would

SECOND JOURNAL OF SIMON FRASER
FROM MAY 30TH TO JUNE 10TH 1808

get to places where animals were so plenty [plentiful] that [we] would kill as many as we would require, but no inducements of theirs could make us act contrary to our own ideas.

These Indians, I mean the Atnaghs [Atnahs], appear very friendly, but not of that hospitable disposition that the Carrier Tribes are of. However I asked one of them for a few good salmon, as ours were bad. He soon brought me 20, which were well cured and amazing fat. There is a vast difference between the salmon that are taken here and that which are caught amongst the Carriers. The Atnaghs [Atnahs] does not seem to work the salmon much, as there are plenty of animals upon their lands.

They do not take much pains about their houses, indeed I saw none amongst them that deserve any other name than a shade. They pass the winter in sub terraneous houses or lodges, which are square, with a square hole upon the top for the smoke, by which they go out and in by the assistance of knotches made in a length of wood, which serves for steps.

Sunday [Saturday], June 4. Before everything was ready this morning it was late, however at six o'clock A.M. we were upon the water. Last night another Indian promised to embark with us, on account of his being better acquainted with the Rapids, and lower part of [the] River, than the Old Chief. Accordingly we agreed, but this morning he would not embark, through fear of the Rapids and bad places we had to pass.

Previous to our embarking one of them brought and returned a pistol which Mr. Quesnel lost yesterday on horse back, which is a singular instance of their honesty. Indeed all the time we were in the Portage, tho' many things were loose and that they had many opportunities, we did not perceive that they touched anything.

They differ widely in both customs and manners from any Tribe that I am acquainted with this side of the Rocky mountains. They do not burn their dead, but burry them and arrange their tomb neatly with splintered wood in a conic for, it [that] is to say round about 24 feet circumference below and joining above in the form of a sugar loaf and tied. Their prisoners of war are nominated slaves. The backs of their bows are covered with the skin of the rattlesnake in addition to the usual material. They make fire by friction.

Our first course, S.E. 1/2 [mile]. Here we stopped on right to speak to a band of Indians, some of which we did not see before. On left is a steep bank which is upwards of 8,C [800?] perpendicular feet in height [and] appears in the shape of a pyramid. E 1 1/2 [miles]. In this course are high and steep rocks above the first range of hills, which are fine and varyated [variegated] on both sides, and at [the] end is [a] rocky mountain of considerable elevation. On left the current is amazing strong and full of whirlpools and tremendous to behold. S 20 E to a Rapid and rock on the left 1/4 [mile]. South 1 1/2 [miles]. In this course steep and rough banks of a sand on gravel on left. S. 25 E with a conical rock ahead to a strong Rapid one mile.

Here we debarked to visit, but ran down the Canoes, and it was not necessary to make a portage. There is a fine road and no hills on right. A few pieces were carried to lighten the perserverance [*Perseverance*; the name of one of the canoes]. S.E. to another Rapid but not dangerous — while another conical rock on right appeared ahead 1 mile. S 10 W, to where there is a sub[terranean]. house on left 3/4 [mile], [same course] 1/4 [mile]. S 10 E 1/4 [mile] and both courses a continue [continuation] of Rapid (but safe). Gravel Banks or Debaultee [déboulis; i.e., a slide] on Right, and a rock but not high on left, while the hills on both sides continue broken as it were, and only trees here and there of small growth, generally cyprus with juniper or red cedar, I do not know which. S 40 E 1 1/4 [miles]. In this course is a high and steep [hill or bank] on right with steep banks on left near the end. Rock on right. There are deep holes, through some of which we see day-

SECOND JOURNAL OF SIMON FRASER
FROM MAY 30TH TO JUNE 10TH 1808

light, on the other side. S 10 E 1/3 [mile]. S 20 W, to a Rapid 1/2 [mile]. In this course are some Liard [poplar] and Tremble [aspen]. S.W. one mile. High and steep banks on right with rocks on left and the whole coarse [course] a constant strong Rapid. S.W. a considerable strong Rapid 1 1/4 [miles]. S 10 W 1 1/2 [miles]. There being.[12]

Monday [*Sunday*], *June 5*. Fine weather. We were upon the water at five o'clock in the morning and steered S.W. 1/4 [mile]. S 80 W 1 mile. Strong Rapid along this course. S 55 W 3/4 [mile]. Strong Rapid and steep rock on left in this Co. [course]. S 70 W 2 1/4 [miles]. S 75 W 1/2 [mile]. Banks of a very grotesque shape on right. S 40 W 1/4 [mile]. A small low point on left and a small River [Riske Creek] on right. S 15 E 1/4 [mile]. The hills have a beautiful appearance. S 50 E 1 1/2 [miles]. S 1/4 [mile]. S 35 W 1 [mile]. An ugly Ecove [?] on right of this course. S 20 W 1/4 [mile]. A Rapid. S 15 E 1 [mile]. S 20 E 1/3 [mile]. South one mile. S 15 W 1/2 [mile]. S 20 E 1 [mile]. S 10 E 3/4 [mile]. S 50 E 1 1/4 [miles].

Here we unloaded on the left side of a strong Rapid and carried all the baggage & canoes over a point which has very steep and high banks of about 2/3 of a mile long, and incredible it is to relate the trouble and misery the people had in performing that office. On debarkation we found the horns of that animal the Tahawteen [Tautens] call the Sassian, and the Mayatué of the Crees, or Rocky Mountain Ram. And at this end, when everything was brought over, we tapped our small keg of shrub[13] which induced us to call this Portage de Barriel [Baril] and gave all hands a dram.

The course by water in this Portage is about S 5 E 1/2 [mile], and the rocks contract themselves to within 30 yards of one another, and at [the] lower end is a rocky Island on the left shore. It is terrible to behold the rapidity and turbulency of the immense body of water that passes in this narrow gut, and no less do the numerous Gulphs and whirlpools it forms constantly striking from one rock to another. The rocks are amazing high and craggy, particularly on the right side, and the water in a manner seem to have forced a passage under them and flows out here and there in numerous whirlpools and eddies that surpass any thing of the kind I ever saw before.[14]

In this carrying place, from the time we debarked to our re-embarking again was upwards of four hours. On setting off our first course was S 10 E 1 1/4 [miles]. In this last course are many rocks, particularly on [the] left, but little wood to be seen. S 1 1/4 [miles]. Near [the] end of [this] course is a considerable River Waccans [the Chilcotin River] on right, with an Island at its mouth, and I suppose to see the River[15] which Sir A.M.K. [Sir Alexander Mackenzie] supposed himself to be higher up, and the one he passed in his way across the mountains in his way to the Pacific in 1793.[16] It is likewise the residence of the Chilk-hotins [Chilcotins], a tribe of the Carriers, and by all accounts is very rapidous and full of Chutts [chutes; i.e., falls]. Mossu [moose?], Red Deer, and Chevereau [chevreau],[17] and Beaver are likewise said to be very numerous in that quarter, and the natives have horses.

S.E. 1/3 [mile]. S 80 E 1 2/3 [miles]. In this course is a high bank or Deboullic [déboulis] on left, of a very irregular shape. But there are so many variety [varieties] along this River, that however willing I might be I am not possessed of sufficient abilities to descend [describe] it. At the end of this course is a long and strong but not dangerous rapid, for after visiting it, all the canoes were run down with out any accident, but the drift wood rendered it more dangerous than otherwise it would be. The next course S 40 E 1 1/2 [miles]. In this last course is another Rapid, and afterwards the River turned to S 20 W 1/4 [mile], to another strong Rapid, and there being a strong eddie we turned the canoes against it with a line. Here we debarked to visit the Rapid, in which the current is very swift and violent. The Canoes were run down, the

SECOND JOURNAL OF SIMON FRASER
FROM MAY 30TH TO JUNE 10TH 1808

first at six [i.e., with a crew of six men] and the others at five men each. The road on shore is difficult, it being along the declevity of a steep and high bank, without anything to get hold of. I forced [i.e., overstrained myself] so much in this place to get up a hill that I feel a violent pain in my groins which prevent me from being able to walk any distance. The course by water is S 2/3 [mile] and at [the] end is a very high and steep sandy bank on right with cliffs opposite resembling broken pedestals or chimneys. S 20 E 1/4 [mile]. S.E. 1 1/4 [miles]. S 50 E 1 1/4 [miles]. In this course are ugly sandy banks and hillocks on right and very irregular on right, with but little wood on either except entirely above. S 15 E 3/4 [mile]. S 60 E 1 1/2 [miles]. In this course the hills are less high on right (I mean near the water side). S 10 W 3/4 [mile]. Fine but very irregular on both sides (I mean hills). Here is a strong Rapid but fine going. S 35 E 1 3/4 [miles]. At end of [this course] are fine white rocks, in the shape of well-made pedestals with a head, and at beginning of next [course] S 60 E 1/2 [mile] are curious banks with very irregular pointed heads. All this course is a constant and strong rapid, but the passage nowise dangerous. S 10 E 3/4 [mile]. The banks, tho' continually changing, are such as I am not well able to describe. They are very irregular, grown with short grass, scorched by the sun and very often consists of sand or stone, with but very little wood. Here is another strong Rapid. S 60 E 1/3 [mile]. Still a Rapid. S 50 E 1 1/3 + 1/3 [miles]. S 10 E 1 1/3 [miles]. S.E. 1 mile. In this and last course are strong Rapids. S 5 E 1 [mile]. Very irregular and grotesque banks S.E. 1 [mile], with rocks on both sides perpendicular, and saw Chivereaux [chevreaux; probably meaning goats] on the left. S 1/4 [mile]. S 35 E 1/4 [mile]. S 20 E 1 1/2 [miles]. The rapids, which are constant, are so swift that there is no time to look about. S 50 E 3 [miles]. In this course we encamped on the right shore at half past seven A.M. [P.M.][18]

The current throughout the day ran with amazing velocity,

and on this and [the] last course our situation was really dangerous, being constantly between steep and high banks where there was no possibility of stopping the canoe, and even could it be stopped, there would be no such thing as going up the hills, so that had we suddenly come upon a cascade or bad Rapid, not to mention falls, it is more than likely that all of us would have perished, which is much to be apprehended. In the morning the weather was clear and very warm but afterwards cloudy, and in the afternoon, it blew hard at intervals from the southward.

The berries in this place are much advanced, and we saw wild lint, wormwood, and some other kind of wood and shrubs which we did not know. The water had lowered greatly since yesterday night.

Tuesday [Monday], June 6. Fine weather early in the morning. La Certe and some others were sent to examine the River [so] that we may not suddenly come upon a cascade or dangerous Rapid in this narrow gut, but I believe they did not go far, and indeed the number of hills and precipices render it not only difficult but almost impossible to walk even in the Plains. Upon the top of the hills there are so many thistles that all hands have the sole of their feet full of them, and being almost continually when on shore upon rocks and stones, a pair of shoes does not last a whole day to some of us without piercing.

At 7 o'clock we were upon the water. Continued our course of last night to the end, and afterwards started S 20 E 1/4 [mile]. Here is a small low point, and [a] River [Churn Creek] on right, with irregular sandy banks or hillocks on both sides. S 15 W 1 [mile]. S.E. 1 3/4 [miles]. Near the beginning of this course there is a strong Rapid on right, but safe on left. S 60 E 3/4 [mile], with a steep and craggy rock on right. At the end of this course we saw a Ram on left, and our next course S 30 E 1 1/4 [miles]. S 50 E 1 [mile]. S 20 E 3/4 [mile]. S 70 E 1/4 [mile.] Here is a strong Rapid with rocks on right and our next [course]

SECOND JOURNAL OF SIMON FRASER
FROM MAY 30TH TO JUNE 1OTH 1808

was S 40 E 2 [miles]. Here is a strong Rapid, which we debarked at to visit it (a shade [for] salmon fishery on left), but ran down the canoes. Our next course was S 60 E 1/3 [mile]. N 80 E 1 1/4 [miles]. S 50 E 3/4 [mile], to a rocky point on left and rapid. The next was S 10 W, with a snowclad mountain a head, on right, and our Guide says it is the highest chain of mountains from here to the sea. Two miles. In these two last courses but one there is real Pine Poplar and a small kind of birch, on the chain of mountains last mentioned. Seffleux [*siffleur* is meant; i.e., whistler or marmot] are plenty by our Guides account. S 5 W 1 1/2 mile here, and at last we landed on the right shore.[19]

Found a strong rapid and cascade which we did not venture to run down. Mr. Stuart and myself went immediately to visit it, accompanied by La Certe. The upper end could easily be made, it is [that is] to say, [we could] carry the canoe or take it down with the line, and everything else carried across a short point, but the lower end is bad betwixt steep rocks on both sides, and no possibility to carry.

Soon after Mr. Stuart and myself returned to the Canoes and sent Mr. Quesnel with six men across the opposite side to visit and look for a place to carry, as it appeared to be less steep upon that side of the River. Mr. Quesnel returned in about three hours after, with information that they were entirely across the point below the Rapid upon a well traced road, and that the hills were high and steep to take up the Canoes, and as soon as they were upon the top, that they went down as steep as they went up upon this side all the way to the water side, which Mr. Quesnel reckoned at about four miles distance. After which all hands crossed to the east side and encamped for the night, where we come to the determination, before we would attempt crossing the canoes in this long and difficult Portage, or risk running them down the Rapid, to send [a party] first to visit and examine a considerable distance lower down the River, as the Indians tells us that it is impossible to proceed any further than this with our Canoes, on account of it being a constant succession of Falls and Rapids, and the banks being perpendicular on both sides of the River and no place to stop at, until below the next nation, which they call Askeddey's [Askettihs], but that we would not take more than two days to go there by land loaded.

But as it is my object to determine the practicability of the navigation of this river, tho' it would be much more safe and expeditious to go by land, we shall not leave our canoes as long as there will be any possibility of taking them down by water or land. But should the passage be as bad as the old Chief our guide says it is [and should it] not [be] worth while taking the Canoes any further, I would as soon leave them here as a few miles further down. To ascertain this, Mr. Stuart is settled to go and visit the River far down tomorrow, accompanied by Mr. Quesnel and five of our best men, Wacca, and three of our Indians.

In the course of the afternoon we saw several animals, but those that went after them could not approach any excepting La Garde who wounded a Ram.

Tuesday, June 7. Early in the morning the Gentlemen and men were off to visit the River. I employed the remainder of the people making and mending shoes and [doing] other necessary work. L.G. [La Garde] and Basse [Baptiste?] went after the wounded Ram. They saw but could not overtake it.

Cloudy weather and a shower of rain in the afternoon with strong wind.

Wednesday, June 8. Fine weather and the heat very intense. I got all the salmon properly tied again, which diminishes very fast. We have no more than 2500 remaining, and many of that bad. However our Indian Guides say that we can have more than what will be required, that all the nations below as far as they know have plenty, and that the large salmon (Cace) [Coho?]

SECOND JOURNAL OF SIMON FRASER
FROM MAY 30TH TO JUNE 1OTH 1808

already begin to come up.

Mr. Stuart and all the people returned from below at about 3 o'clock in the afternoon after having been down to the Rapid [Rapide] Couvert, as the Indians call it, about 18 miles distance.

[*Here Fraser interpolates Stuart's report on his examination of the river.*]

The rocks are rugged and steep in many places, which rendered our passage dangerous along the declevity of those Rocks and steep banks, but by perseverance [we] traced the River down all the way to where we returned, and in that distance, tho' the current continued amazing strong all the way, there was but one dangerous Rapid, and in the hills there was a steep rock or bank of considerable elevation and length, resembling an immense pile of natural architecture far surpassing anything that ever entered the idea of mortal man, and in what, though without any regularity, all the different orders seemed to have been combined, which created a pleasing and awful sensation to behold and consider the superiority of Gods works over those formed by the hands of man. But to describe what I have often felt in these romantic and wild regions where nature appears in all its forms is far above my slender abilities even was I possessed of more leasure and materials than I am. To describe everything as it would be worthy of the greatest philosophers and would take up a considerable time without anything else to attend to.

At the Rapid [Rapide] Couvert we perceived Indians, and our Guide and interpreter went to them. They told Mr. Quesnel that they were not of the Atnagh [Atnah] but of the Askedteh [Askettih] nation, and had I been present myself at that time, I would accompany [i.e., I would have accompanied] them, but I was at the water side visiting, and after my joining the others [I] sent down La Certe to the water side to visit a little further, and during that interval two young men came towards us, one of which joined us, and after a short stay begged leave to return. His language was entirely unintelligible to us; however, by the signs he made we understood that our Guide and interpreter were at the tents, and that he himself had killed some mouton and would return to us again with the meat.

I was here again prevented from going to their lodges from having promised La Certe to wait his return, which was late, and we encamped. We remained this morning until 7 A.M., in expectation of some of the natives would join us, but we saw no appearance of any of them, therefore we returned to the Canoes by a different route, for we ascended the hills which are amazing high and long. But once above, the country is even in most places, clear of wood and has a beautiful appearance.

[Here Stuart's narrative ends and Fraser's journal resumes.]

At half-past six P.M. we started to make another piece in Canoes, as the River is navigable as far as the people went down. The Canoes crossed over to the other side of the River and were taken down the first Cascade with the line, and the remainder ran, which was very strong. I myself with Messrs. Stuart, Quesnel and Baptiste went down a foot upon the left shore, by a well beaten path, and instead of four miles, at most [it] is not more than two.

The course by water is about S 15 W 1 1/2 [miles]. Here Mr. Stuart's compass being deranged, I lent him mine. Our next course was S 5 E 1 1/4 [miles]. In these last courses is a large Deboulle [déboulis; slide] on right. S 20 E 2 1/2 [miles]. In this course the rocks are much contracted, and there is a large and long Rapid with many whirlpools, and at end of the Course a deboulle [déboulis] on both sides, with craggy rock hills ahead. S 40 E 1 1/3 [miles]. In this course is another but not strong Rapid. S 30 E 3/4 [mile]. It is here the immense hills of natural architecture

SECOND JOURNAL OF SIMON FRASER
FROM MAY 30TH TO JUNE 10TH 1808

begins, but it is not much seen from the water side. Another Rapid, but not strong in this course S 20 E 1 [mile]. A small revelet [rivulet; probably Lone Cabin Creek], and very craggy on its right, and another stronger Rapid. S 5 E 1 [mile]. At beginning of [this] course, another large Rapid and a large Deboulle [déboulis], with very grotesque banks of irregular shape. S 60 E 1 1/3 [miles]. Fine going and easy to debark on both sides. North 3/4 [mile]. A steep and very craggy rock on right and Deboulle [déboulis] on left, but fine going with a small grave [groove?] on left. S.E. 2/3 [mile]. The River is wide and fine going. E 1 1/3 [miles].

At beginning of this last course we encamped upon the right shore, and the people unloaded and gumed the Canoes.[20] Some of them fired several shots at an Eagle without effect, but they took the young ones out of the nests, which was in the top of a tree. It appears that Kesh [Fish?] comes up, as the tail of one was found in the nest with the leg of mouton.

Berries (Poires) are much advanced, notwithstanding that the mountains are very high and snow to be seen upon them. Wood is scanty all over and stunted, but more pine than any other wood. Plain of small growth, with many different kinds of the willow, elder, and some of the birch specie, and some other I do not know. Thistles of a deminitive growth are so very plenty that no shoes prevents their picking the feet. Wild flax is very plenty, of which the natives manufacture their thread and fishing tackle.

Thursday, June 9. This morning all hands arranged their arms and dressed themselves [in their best clothes], and our two young men, Interpreters, having only a Beaver and Deer skin Robes, I gave them each a blanket and a Brayet [brayette; i.e., breeches] that they may appear decent, and Englishfied amongst the strangers.

It was 7 A.M. when we embarked, and called this place Campment D'Eigle [Campement d'aigle; Eagle Camp]. Started S 55 E 3/4 [mile] from end of camp of last night, the hills of left are low and really fine. S 5 E 1 [mile]. S 70 E 1/2 [mile] + 1/4 [mile].

175

A strong Rapid in this course and very high and grotesque banks of uneven shape. S 35 E 1 1/2 [miles]. S 55 E. A strong Rapid and Rivelet [rivulet; French Bar Creek] on right 1/4 [mile]. S 15 E 3/4 [mile], short. N 50 E, a strong Rapid 1/3 [mile].

Here is an amazing strong Rapid [French Bar Canyon] which is the one called Le Rapid [Rapide] Couvert so long talked of. The rocks contract themselves to within a very short distance of one another, and [this] is the narrowest place we [have] yet passed, and the rocks above project themselves still farther out, and the water between pass[es] with the greatest velocity of any thing I ever saw, and the waves are high, but then the whirlpools and eddies are not so strong as in some places we have passed, but yet according to my ideas [this] is the most dangerous place we hitherto passed. Yet rather than carry the canoes over steep hills, after visiting properly [i.e., after inspecting the river carefully,] the people were allowed to run them [the canoes] down, but the Perseverance [one of the canoes], having remained above while the others were run down, at 6 men each, was partly unloaded and four pieces carried.

The Canoes were fortunately ran down without any accident, but the men had a terrible fright, and us that were at the lower end of the Rapid were in great anxiety waiting the event, which was an awful sight to see, the Canoes wheeling about, and every moment in extreme danger of dashing against the rocks, and from above appeared no longer than Sauteause [Saulteaux] Canoes. Indeed, this Rapid should all ways be a Portage, the rocks are amazing high and perpendicular on both sides, but on the left they are upwards of 1200 feet above the level of the water.

In the last course upon the left side of the River we saw Indians upon the hills, those that Mr. Stuart, and those that were with him, saw the day before yesterday.

The course of this Rapid by water is about S 70 E 1/4 [mile] and S 20 W 3/4 [mile]. From the time of our debarking

SECOND JOURNAL OF SIMON FRASER
FROM MAY 30TH TO JUNE 1OTH 1808

at the upper end till our embarking at the lower end of this Rapid was three hours, and our next course S 30 E 1 [mile], still a Rapid, with a fine low greêve [grève; i.e., sandy beach] on right. Here, on seeing the natives on the left shore, we debarked, and Mr. Stuart had me[ridian]. alt[itude]. 122, 58 1/2 .

The few Indians we saw were of the Atnah nation and with them were our old Guide and Interpreter. These Indians gave a worse description of the River than any we have had yet, for by their Charts it is nothing but a succession of Falls and Rapids surrounded by perpendicular rocks, and they blame us for not leaving our Canoes sooner, when there was a good road by land to the next nation, and say that in spite of what we can do we will be obliged to leave them close by and go by land and the road bad.

Having collected all the information we could, at 1 3/4 P.M. we reembarked, accompanied by another elderly man, exclusive of our former Guide and Interpreter, and steered S 60 E 1/2 [mile]. A strong Batture [sand or gravel bar] on left near beginning of the course, with a very high and rugged rock. S 50 E 1 [mile]. Both this and last course is a rapid, but no wise dangerous, and there is a little wood on both sides. S 70 E with snow on left 2/3 [mile] and two cornical [conical] rocks on right a head of us and near end of course is a small Rivelet [rivulet; Big Bar Creek] on left. N 70 E 1 1/3 [miles]. In this course is a fine beach on left with small shrubs, and no great currents. S 80 E 1/2 [mile]. Here were ducks, the first seen in a long time. [S] 80 E, a very strong Rapid with perpendicular rugged rocks on both sides, 1/2 [mile]. S 60 E 1 1/2 [miles]. In this course the rocks are still more ugly on left, for the mountains are close, [to] the River, and steep, with no interval of even ground to the top. S 55 E 1 1/2 [miles]. Here is another and dangerous Rapid, with rugged rocks on both sides. S 60 E 1/2 [mile]. Still the same rapid, which is amazing strong and full of tremendous whirlpools and Gulphs that surpass anything of which I could form an idea. S 20 E 1/4

[mile]. Still same Rapid. S 35 W 1 1/2 [miles]. E. Course. The Rapid ends but the current continues strong. In this last Rapid much water was taken, the Canoes often wheeled about, and what rendered our situation more dangerous was not to be able to stop or find a place to put ashore on account of rocks.

S.E. 1/4 [mile]. E 2/3 [mile]. Very pretty and long Rapid on right in this course. S.E. 1 1/2 [miles]. In this course are sandy irregular Banks on right, with a strong point on left. Our next course was S 85 E 1 1/3 [miles], and near the beginning of [this] course, a small and rapidous River [Watson Bar Creek] flowed in from the right, and there were several tombs near it, and on that side the hills have a beautiful irregular appearance, but are very ugly and rocky on the opposite [bank]. N 70 E 1 1/4 + 1/4 [miles]. S.E. 1 1/4 [miles]. In this course are sandy banks on right and there are wood on both sides, in this and last course, and the tops of the mountains of both sides are thinly covered. At end of this last course the River is amazing wide and but little current, while there is snow on the mountains on left.

N 70 E 1/4 [mile]. Here is a strong and dangerous Rapid, which however we ran down without any accident, but lost time in visiting [it] and afterwards in gumming the Perseverance, which got hurt on getting a shore at the lower end. The rocks are high on both sides and the Course is S 80 E 1/4 [mile], and S 40 E 1/4 [mile] and there is a good foot path to carry on right, but the hills are steep.

I had some trouble in coming up light, and having gone to one side of the path to see the canoes run down I got my feet full of thistles.

This Rapid is very near as bad as Rapid Couverte [Rapide Couvert]. Our next course was S 55 E 1 1/4 [miles]. S 30 E 1/2 [mile]. In this course are ugly sandy banks on left with extraordinary high and rocky mountains on both sides, particularly on left. S 10 E 3/4 [mile]. Here the River is much contracted, but

SECOND JOURNAL OF SIMON FRASER
FROM MAY 30TH TO JUNE 1OTH 1808

not near so much as in the bad Rapids. The mountains on left is extraordinary high and pointed. S.E. 1 1/4 [miles]. In this course is seemingly very fine, white earth on left and it is all a Rapid, but not dangerous. S 60 E 1 [mile]. In this course a rocky point on the right projecting into the River, which is narrow, and forms a strong Rapid which continues to the end, but is not dangerous, and there is an ugly Deboullé [déboulis; slide] on left with small Epinette [spruce trees] on both sides.

Deboullé [slides] and sandy banks continue on left while we steered S.E. another mile, with a beach of round stones on both sides with some small pines and Epinette [spruce], and in whatever direction I look, whether before or behind, nothing but mountains of a most rugged shape are to be seen. Those on the right indeed near the water side is passible, but [I] never saw any to be compared to those opposite. At end of course was mouton [sheep], at which the people fired several shots without effect, neither did he ever stur while we remained in sight, but on putting ashore he went off.

S 55 E 1/3 [mile]. In [this] course is a small Revelet [rivulet] on Right [Leon Creek], with another almost opposite on left. Here the Rocks contracted themselves in such a manner as to form the appearance of a violent Rapid or cataract, and under these apprehensions we land, I on the left shore, and it being then late we encamped for the night.[21] Our Guide and Interpreter, I mean the two Atnaghs [Atnahs] and the Tahawten [Tauten], absolutely wanted to leave us and go on foot to the next nation, which they called Asked-teys [Askettihs; meaning the Lillooet Indians], and which they represent as at no greater a distance off than the Rpaid [Rapide] Couvert from here. However we prevailed upon them to remain with us till tomorrow morning, that we might determine whether it was really possible to continue in Canoe or not, indeed by all accounts we have had yet this is the last place to where we could possibly go with Canoes, and beyond report says there is no such thing as proceeding either in Canoe or on foot, on account of the narrowness of the River, the strong Rapids and whirlpools between the perpendicular Rocks that come down to the water side, which renders it impossible to stop the canoes or debark were they stopped. But the truth of this will be better known to-morrow, when people will be purposely sent to visit.

The weather was amazing sultry both today and yesterday, and the water from its highest mark has lowered about 9 or 10 feet perpendicular. Had it continued in the state it was seven days ago, we would have been obliged to leave our canoes far from here.

Friday, June 10. Early this morning Lacerte, Bourboné and two others were sent down to visit the River and ascertain the truth of what the Indians told us of it being bad and impossible to continue farther in Canoes or not.

BACKGROUND OF THE GREAT JOURNEY

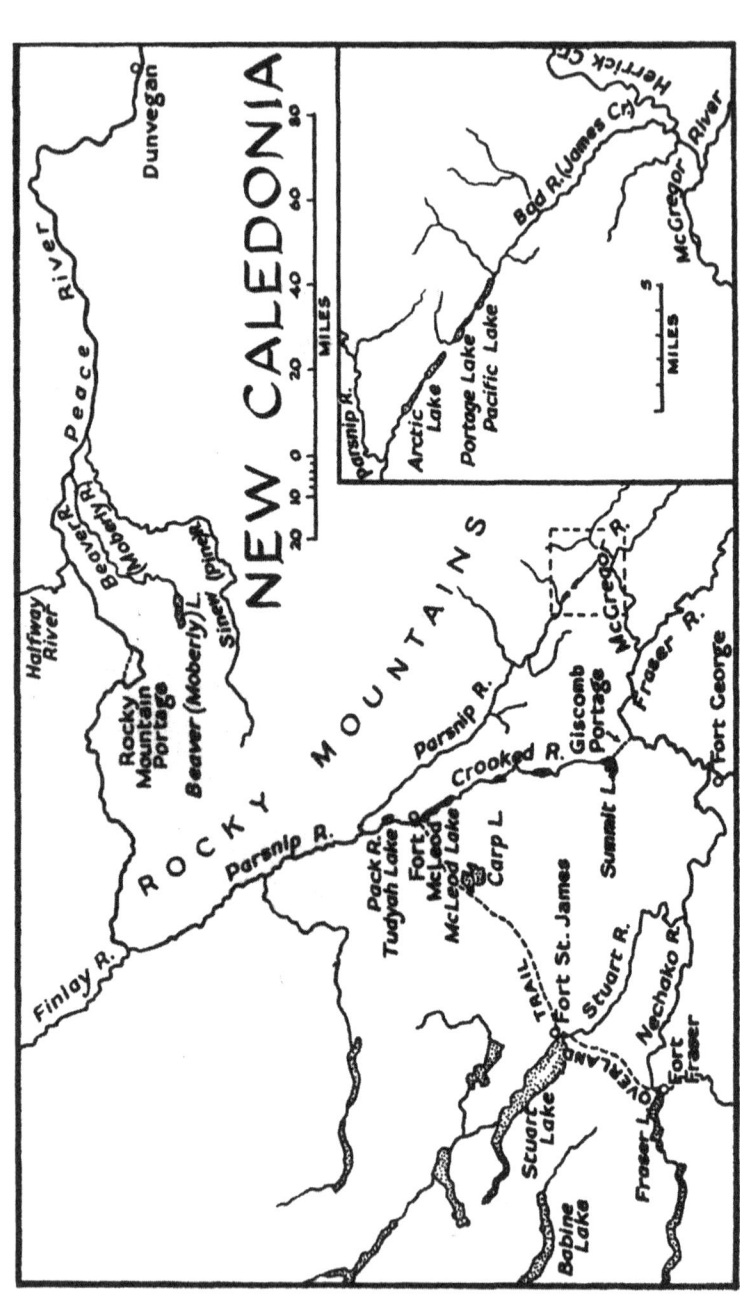

FIRST JOURNAL OF SIMON FRASER FROM APRIL 12TH TO JULY 18TH 1806

[*As in the case of the Second Journal, the surviving text of this earlier journal is incomplete and begins in the middle of a sentence. A remark in a letter written by Fraser in February 1807, suggests that the original manuscript began with an entry dated April 5, 1806.*]

At Rocky Mountain Portage

Saturday, April 12, 1806. ... but as it is here now we will find use for it. We cannot be too well stocked with provisions. About mid-night sent off three men to return to Dunvegan. As it snows too much to walk the whole day, they will march in the night.[1] Gave them as provisions 94 pounds fresh meat.

Sunday, April 13. Fine mild weather. Mr. [John] Stuart and I having wrote to Mr. [Archibald Norman] McLeod, after dark when it began to frease [I] sent off two men with the letters. Gave them 160 pounds fresh meat on account of their having had twelve days [i.e., their being allowed twelve days for the journey, this being the time] that Mr. Stuart had [taken] to bring up himself and baggage [from Dunvegan].

The other two men Bazile and Gervais Rivard remain here, they being intended for the expedition, and were hired for that purpose below, that is if there was not a sufficient number otherwise hired at this place. If there were, they were to go down. But there are only three as yet hired so we will have occasion for them, and they were sent to the Little

Head [the Indian chief] to bring home whatever he may have.

Monday, April 14. Brissère arrived from the Little Head and etc. He brought two Coté de Bouff [*côte de bouef*, meaning here a buffalo-skin bag] full of pounded meat [pemmican] and says the Indians killed 14 [buffalo] cows and are bussy reducing them into Pd. [pounded] meat, and that the Little Head asks some tobacco. Beyson sprained his hand so much that he is not able to make use of it. La Londe arrived from the Beaver Lake [Moberly Lake?][2] and [says] that La Rammée got there only yesterday.

Tuesday, April 15. Made up five bales [of] goods to be sent over the [Rocky Mountain] Portage immediately on the snow.[3] Fine weather.

Wednesday, April 16. Fine mild weather. Early in the morning Beyson and La Londe were sent to the upper end of the Portage. The latter had a piece[4] and the former about one half on account of his having the road to beat and a sore hand besides. After this trip each man will be able to take two pieces.

About 9 A.M. Mr. John McKenvin arrived from the Meadow Indians,[5] after an absence of seventy odd days. He informs us of his having starved much at different times. He accompanied the Indians far off in search of Beaver but though they saw many Beaver Lodges they killed but few on account of the depth of snow, which is from five to six feet deep in the Beaver country. They saw no large animals of any kind, no not even a track, during their long and intricate route until within two days march of the upper end of the Portage. At the place they returned the Indians showed him the place where Trout Lake [McLeod Lake] was and told him it was only three encampments distant from there but he could get no one to accompany him there.

The distance these Indians have to go in search of Beaver and the misery they endure to go there and from there to come here proves this plan to be of little use. Could it be done, it would cer-

FIRST JOURNAL OF SIMON FRASER
FROM APRIL 12TH TO JULY 18TH 1806

tainly be more proper to send them all to Trout Lake, where Beaver is near the Fort, and it is certain they will never work well until they have an establishment formed in the Beaver country.

Mr. McKenvin saw some of the Indians of Trout Lake who had made pretty good hunts and were on their return to Mr. [James] McDougall's [Fort McLeod]. He says that some of them are coming down here but I believe this is a mistake. It is likewise reported that some of the Big Men (Trout Lake Indians)[6] killed one of [the] Carriers last fall on the latters land, which if true may be of some detrement to our expedition.

Argenton, who accompanied our hunters without leave when they went off the 29th of last month to join their relatives, returned with Mr. McKenvin and brought a slave woman, who followed him of her own accord, with her [him]. In order to prevent the Beaver Indians[7] from taking a footing or those of this place, and to prevent others from coming for women, she was taken from him as well as his gun, blanket, axe, Dog, bow, and arrows and etc. and [he was] sent off in that defenseless manner to the Little Head. However he did not go without some reluctance and Mr. Stuart conducting him out of the house and down the hill with a kick. The woman cried most bitterly after his departure and we kept a strict watch over her that she may not escape and go after him.

It is really surprising the attachment these women have to the Beaver Indians with whom they are little better than slaves. For my own part I cannot account for it unless it be that they are well fed, for in every other respect they are certainly much better off with their own relations, who never ill-use them and with whom they are mistress of every thing and yet their [is] scarcely one among them that would not rather go with the Beaver Indians.

Late this evening Gagnon and Saucier, the two men who were [sent] for bark, arrived and brought only two small rolls scarcely worth anything. They say they spoiled upwards of twenty, good bark, on account of its not seasoning well, but it is most probable that they do not know how to season it properly, it being their first experience.

Thursday, April 17. Early this morning Gagnon went over to the other end of the Portage with one piece and Beyson arrived, and La Londe remained there making a cache.

It was Masi de dents de Beghe [?][8] that killed this Indian but it was of no detrement at all to us. I have seen his bones which is well essected [desiccated?]. The Carriers are naturally mild but subject to gusts of passion which often prove fatal to one or the other. One brother thinks nothing of killing another and the others seldom interfere.

Got a *Grille* made to day to dry the split meat that is in the slangard [probably *hangar*, a shed].

In the evening gave Saucier two pieces to take over the Portage that he may start in the night it being then the roads are best. Beyson goes with him to meet the Indians who we expect will soon arrive to get what provisions they may have at the other end of the Portage, as it will save them the trouble of sending it over again.

Friday, April 18. In the course of last night the slave woman deserted and appears to have gone before her relations. About 10 o'clock A.M. Bazile and Gervais Rivard who were at the Little Head arrived. They brought the value of 6 skins Pounded meat 5 ditto dried meat, 4 of grease, and say they left the Indians at La Malices River on their way here. Much about the same time Farcier arrived from the Beaver Lake [Moberly Lake] and says they caught only one white fish and that this is the third day since they ate anything. He returned immediately with 30 pounds of fresh meat for La Rammée with orders to be back tomorrow.

In the morning La Londe came over from the other end of the Portage and returned immediately with two pieces. In the

FIRST JOURNAL OF SIMON FRASER
FROM APRIL 12TH TO JULY 18TH 1806

evening the two, Gervais La Garde [and Gervais Rivard] and Gagnon went off likewise each with two pieces except the latter who had only one on account of his having one of the pieces he got yesterday morning near this end, and that he is to take in passing which will form the same load with the others. Sent word to Beyson to come home in order to be sent to the Little Head with orders to make him hunt.

Saturday, April 19. After breakfast sent Mr. McKenvin to look for the Meadow Indians as we apprehend they will not come to the house [in] time enough and besides the woman that deserted might tell them a parcel of stories and frighten them off. The men who went over [the portage] yesterday returned today excepting La Garde whom McKenvin took with him to the Indians.

Sunday, April 20. Early this morning the two Gervais, La Londe and Saucier went off with two pieces each and Gagnon remained here to wait for Mr. Stuart and myself. Sent Beyson to the Little Heads and etc. to see what they are doing and make them hunt. He had a foot of tobacco for Little Head. About noon [Farcier] arrived from the Beaver Lake [Moberly Lake] and brought a white fish which is all he says they caught. At the same time a boy came from the Little Heads to advertise us of their having killed six Biches [does] two of which are not in *Cache*. Sent Farcier, whom I repremanded for remaining so long at the Beaver Lake, to arrange them as La Pistole, who was there, is gone farther on for two small Red Deer (alias Biche).

Monday, April 21. The men who went over with pieces returned to day. In the morning Beyson and La Pistole arrived with the two Red Deer which weighed 300 pounds, and soon after just as we were at breakfast Little Head, Raquette Relevée etc. arrived. The former being requested to come here was well received, but the others who came without permission were treated in a harsh manner, and Mr. Stuart having previously asked my permission, which was readily granted, to the force of argument added another kind of logic which soon cleared the house, and they took to their heels accompanied by the Little Heads women. At Dunvegan they were forbit [forbidden] to come here, and they promised not to come, but they did not keep to it, [so] it was but right to punish them for their disobedience, and it was more proper to be done by Mr. Stuart, who had a principal hand in settling them below, than any other.

Farcier arrived after putting the two Red Deer last killed in *cache*. He brought home the Rump of one which weighed 60 pounds. Sent La Pistole and Argenton who got his bow and arrows and a gun lent him to go beyond the Grand Fourche [Great Fork] to look for two cows that were put in cache about the middle of January and could not be found since, on account of the road having filled up with snow.

Got five Bags Pemmecan made of 90 pounds each. The Indians being a little composed and returned about sun set. The Little Head began to drink. He and his followers since here about gave [us] 220 pounds Pounded meat, 80 pounds Grease, and about 90 pounds Dried meat, part payment of which they are now drinking.

Authorized Beyson, Bazile and Gagnon to go for bark tomorrow, Gervais and Saucier for the two Red Deer that were last put in cache. La Garde and Farcier to take pieces over the Portage. The former got two pieces and the latter only one and that same he will take over on his back.

Tuesday, April 22. Fine weather. The Little Head and followers went off towards the Beaver Lake [Moberly Lake]. He misbehaved last night for which he was much ashamed to day, and did not dare come into the house.

The people for bark were off early. Gave them 63 pounds of fresh meat. La Londe was sent off with two pieces, with orders to remain at the other end of the Portage and take care of the

FIRST JOURNAL OF SIMON FRASER
FROM APRIL 12TH TO JULY 18TH 1806

property there. Saucier and Gervais arrived in the evening with 450 pounds fresh meat. In the forenoon four Meadow Indians arrived from a band that is near at hand. They say they have no Beaver and brought only the value of a skin of fresh meat each, which they traded for ammunition. They kill plenty of animals, that is Moose and Red Deer, by chasing them with their dogs when the crust [on the snow will carry the weight of the dogs but not that of the moose and deer].

Wednesday, April 23. Fine weather. Ménard arrived with four young men from the Chiefs band. They brought 22 Beaver skins, 2 caracasause [carcajous?] and six Pechause [presumably *pêcheurs* is meant; i.e., fisher] belonging to the chief, which are well dressed. [They] traded the value of two skins. These Indians are not Meadow Indians but of another tribe, and the relations of the chief, who always sides with the Meadow Indians, and who has much authority over them.

We attempted to get some information concerning their country, but they seemed rather stupid, and not much inclined to satisfy our desires, which perhaps is not a little owing to the little knowledge we have of their language, for our interpreters are none of the best. However, we understood that Finlays branch [the Finlay River] does not terminate in the chutes [falls] and Rapids as reported, but with the intervening of some Portages that it is navigable to its source, and from thence there is a Portage about half the length of this, [to] a large lake, called Bear Lake, where the Salmon comes up, and from there is a River that falls into another much larger (according to their Report [larger] than even the Peace River) that glides in northwest direction. In that Lake they say there are plenty of fish, and that the salmon are innumerable, with plenty of Bears and animals of the fur kind there about, but no large animals of any kind. It is from that quarter they get their Iron works and ornaments, but they represent the navigation beyond that Lake as unpracticable, and say there are no other Indians excepting a few of their relations that never saw white people there about, and to get Iron works they must go far beyond it, which they perform in long journeys on foot.

We cannot imagine what River this is by their description, and [judging by] the course it runs it cannot be the Columbia, and I know of no other excepting Cooks, but whatever River it is and wherever they get these, their Iron works and ornaments are such as I have seen with the Carriers. Indeed the Indians of Nakazleh [Stuart Lake] talk of Bear Lake and their account of [the] River that flows from it is conformable with that of the Meadow Indians.[9]

Sent of [off] Ménard immediately to another band of Indians, who have killed 30 Moose Deer, to prevent their throwing away any of the meat, and make them pound and dry it. Gave him six M. [measures] Powder and forty balls to trade. In the afternoon an elderly man arrived and advertised us that he [had] killed an animal in the Stony Islands above the house. Gave him six measures of ammunition as payment and he went of immediately. Saucier and Gervais was busy all day cutting and splitting canoe wood, and after sun set they were sent off to the animal, to prevent its being ate in the course of the night. They will be back with the meat early in the morning. In the forenoon La Garde and Farcier arrived from the upper end of the Portage and returned immediately with two pieces each.

Thursday, April 24. Fine weather. Saucier and Gervais arrived early with 454 pounds [of meat] and the skin. I did not imagine the Moose Deer to be so good at this time of the year as it is, it being really fat.

La Pistole and Argenton arrived and say they could not cross the Grand River to go in search of the cows on account of it being over flown and the Ice broke. Argenton killed a Biche [doe] a short distance this side, and La Pistole put it in a cache. La Rammée, who had been at the Beaver Lake [Moberly Lake]

FIRST JOURNAL OF SIMON FRASER
FROM APRIL 12TH TO JULY 18TH 1806

since the 11th Inst., arrived and says he caught no fish, not knowing where the fishery is, but the Little Head, who he met going there, told him that he would show him where the Indians used to fish. The Little Head sent word several times since his departure [asking] to be excused, but word was always sent him that if he wished to excused, to come and excuse himself personally. Saucier and Gervais were employed about canoe wood. Got a log sawed to make tables for the [fur] *presse.*

Friday, April 25. Early in the morning Saucier and La Rammée were sent to the Beaver Lake [Moberly Lake] to ascertain whether fish can be caught or not. Saucier being a good fisherman and not lazy, I am in hopes of his being successful. Both he and La Garde were both lately hired for the expedition across the mountains. The men who were [sent] for bark arrived and brought only 22 fathoms, which is not very good. The two men that were at the other side of the Portage with pieces arrived also.

Mr. Stuart made a Gabril [?] and they represent it as different from the Columbia, but say it is from that quarter [that] they get [the] most part of their goods, and [that it is] the only place from where they get guns and ammunition. From Nakasleh [Stuart Lake] there is a water communication, with the exception of three Portages, and they positively affirm that white people came there in [the] course of the summer, but as they came on discovery that they had little goods. I have seen a pistol brass mounted with powder and ball which they say they had from them.[10]

Saturday, April 26. This morning four men went for meat and two for more bark and Gervais, who remained here, worked at canoe wood. In the morning [Chief] Little Head arrived, but did not come in the house, but remained lurking about, and as there was little notice taken of him he went off without saying a word to anyone.

Sunday, April 27. Both the men that went for meat and bark arrived. The former brought 770 pounds meat and the latter 20 fathoms bark, but not all good. A little before sun set sent off four men to cross the Portage with seven pieces in sundry articles, our own baggage included. The road begin[s] now to be bad and I believe this will be the last trip with trains [i.e., *traineaux*; sledges]. Indeed we have very few articles more to be sent over [except those] which can't be sent untill we decamp ourselves.

Some time after dark Mr. A.M. Gillivray [Archibald McGillivray] and Gosselin arrived from Dunvegan and brought letters from Messrs. [Archibald Norman] McLeod and J.M. Gillivray [John McGillivray] of Slave Lake, which bring good news from all quarters. Mr. A.M. Gillivray [A. McGillivray] is come up to take charge of this place during the summer.

It appears that J.B. LaFleur, who promised Mr. Stuart to accompany him across the mountains, could not be sent off on any condition. Mallatisse would not come either. Mr. McLeod did all he could to prevail on either the one or the other to come, but nothing short of violence would do. Mr. McLeod writes that had Mallatisse consented to come that he would hire Cardenal for Fort, but now that he will go to Montreal and that Mallatisse will return there.

Monday, April 28. This has been the warmest day we have had yet this season. Sent Beyson to look for a birch tree of good bark that was seen last summer by Le Lo Moilen, but he did not find it. Bazile, Gagnon and Gosselin put up the [fur] press and pulled roots to make two bundles of wattape.

Tuesday, April 29. Fine weather. Beyson gathered some gum, Bazile, Gagnon and Gosselin made bars, wedges and masses for the [fur] press and pulling up [roots] wherewith to make two bundles of wattape.

Wednesday, April 30. Still fine weather. Sent Mr. McKenvin to remain with La Londe at the other side of the Portage and take care of the property there. We do not suspect there is any danger while there is a man there. But as Mr. McKenvin has nothing to

FIRST JOURNAL OF SIMON FRASER
FROM APRIL 12TH TO JULY 18TH 1806

do, and [as] it would be unpardonable if any thing should go wrong while there are so many of us here [I judged it best to send him]. I cannot leave this place myself. It is true that Mr. Stuart would willingly go and prepare everything for embarking, but there being no canoe maker here it falls to his lot to supply the place of one.

The four men that went over last returned. In the afternoon Saucier arrived from the Beaver Lake [Moberly Lake], starving, and says they caught no fish though they changed places several times. He met the Little Head on his way there, and says he asked for tobacco and ammunition.

Thursday, May 1. Cold and cloudy weather. Mr. Stuart began the canoe and the large seams were sound. Bark is bad.

Friday, May 2. Still more cold. Opened the canoe and sewed the *Paiynes* [?].[11] In the morning La Londe, who arrived last night, was sent over again to remain with Mr. McKenvin at the other side of the Portage. While there he has orders to gather gum and return here on the 5th.

Saturday, May 3. Cold with successive showers of snow, sleet and rain, however in the afternoon it cleared up and though still cold, Mr. Stuart put the verangues [varangues; ribs] into the canoe. One half of the verangues were broke [and] he was therefore obliged to make others to replace them. Three young men arrived from the chiefs band. They brought the value of six skins in sundry pieces and one in meat, which they traded and went off immediately. They informed us that the other band of which mention is made before does not intend to come to the Fort, for which reason Beyson was sent off with them to the chiefs band, and there get Indians to guide him to the different bands, with instructions not to return until he brings all the Indians with him.

Sunday, May 4. Weather rather more mild. Early in the morning sent Saucier and Farcier to the Beaver Lake [Moberly Lake] to tell La Rammée and the Little Head to come to the Fort. Sent particular orders to La Rammée to bring the Little

Head to headquarters, and told the others to take the nets out of the water and bring all the fishing tackles here, it being useless to keep people there any longer. Two men have been employed there since the 11th of last month to no purpose. The chief and band arrived in a starving condition. They are poor devils, quite emaciated and paid only 66 skins Beaver Credit and traded one orignal [moose] skin and the value of five skins sundry furs, most part of which furs they brought are very ill dryed, for which they got a severe repremand.

We endeavoured to get some information concerning their lands, but they do not seem willing to communicate any, indeed our Interpreters are not well versed in repeating what they say. Therefore all we could learn from [them] is that they know no better place than this, and that if it is thrown a way that there is no place beyond it that they can go to make up 10 packs, but the furs are so hard and ill dryed that the Packs cannot be well made.

Monday, May 5. Got five of the Packs yesterday untied and remade them again, and after all they are so well as [we] could wish. In the morning La Londe arrived from the other end of the Portage, and soon after the ice moved and broke up in some places, but it soon stopped again and the water rose upwards of 10 feet since yesterday. The ice is amazing strong and thick. Gagnon gummed the canoe inside and Mr. Stuart attempted to *band* it, but was obliged to leave it on account of it being too cold.

Tuesday, May 6. Weather still cold with a strong northerly wind. Gagnon and Gosselin were busyly employed mending the old canoe, and the others employed about canoe wood. At noon La Rammée, Saucier, and Farcier arrived from Beaver Lake [Moberly Lake], and as they caught no fish brought all the fishing tackles. The Lake is still covered with ice and snow. Even the borders is not disolved. They could not persuade the Little Head to come to the Fort. He told them as he was taken no notice of the last time he was here, that he was in doubt whether he would come or not.

FIRST JOURNAL OF SIMON FRASER
FROM APRIL 12TH TO JULY 18TH 1806

By what we could learn from the Indians at different times, an establishment would be well placed on the big River, that falls into the main branch of the Peace River, about half way between this and the Beaver River.[12] This River at its confluence with the Peace River is large and appears to contain a large quantity of water, and the Indians say it is navigable a considerable way up, and that Beaver, Bears, and large animals of all kinds are amazing numerous.

It is thereabout is what may be properly called the Meadow Indians, or as they call themselves *Les Gens du large*, [have their] lands. But it is there likewise they are most subject to be killed by the Beaver Indians of both forks and Fort Vermillion, and on that account they seldom now remain there but nine tenths of the year. But out in the mountains, where there is neither Beaver nor anything else but Badgers, and where they under go great misery, according to their reports there is but a very short distance from that River to a branch of McKenzies River [the Liard] that the *Nakanés* [Kaska Indians} inhabit, with whom they have often intercourse. Most every one of them told us [that] if there was a Fort on the Banks of that Big River, and if the Beaver Indians could be prevented from killing them, that they would make excellent hunts and that it was the only good place they knew.

Wednesday, May 7. Cold weather. Sent Bazile, Gosselin and Saucier to look for and raise more bark in case we should be in want of another canoe, everything is got ready. Should there come more than twenty packs from Trout Lake [Fort McLeod] with these of this place one canoe cannot embark all.

Gagnon and La Rammée mended the old canoe, and the others gathered 32 pounds gum, and pulled up some roots which the women made into Wattape. More Indians arrived and brought a few furs and etc. In the afternoon sent La Londe to the other end of the Portage to remain with Mr. McKenvin and make poles, paddles and etc.

Thursday, May 8. Last night it snowed a little but the weather cleared up this morning, and though we had some showers of rain in the course of day, Mr. Stuart tryed again to band the canoe, but was obliged to give up on account of it being too cold. In the forenoon Beyson arrived with a couple of Indians, and all the band he went for, about thirty men, will be here tomorrow. Ménard is with them. Sent Gagnon and Farcier to the Beaver Lake [Moberly Lake] once more to tell the Little Head to come to the Fort.

Friday, May 9. The weather the same as yesterday. Ménard and the Indians arrived. They had a few skins Beaver Credit, and traded 30 with the value of 80 skins [for] dried provisions, and twenty orignal [moose] skins.

This is the band of Indians that were attacked last summer by the Fort Vermillion Indians, and they did not see the Fort since they were at the Beaver River two years ago, consequently they never saw this place before. Last winter they went down within two or three days march of Beaver River, but were not at the Fort. I repremanded them severely for not coming here last Fall, and asked them the cause of not making a better [hunt], to which they replied that they had made a few furs, but that they lost all when attacked by the Beaver Indians, and that ever since they generally kept in their lurking holes in the mountains, and that they wished to come and see white people in the Fall but did not know where to find them, there being none at Beaver [River],[13] and being told that this place [the post at Rocky Mountain Portage] was abandoned in the Spring and transferred to Finlays branch, they went there but found no one, in consequence of which they thought the white people had abandoned the country, and [they] then returned to their lands, where they were found in the month of March by Indians that had been out on purpose to look for them in the month of February, who informed them of their being a Fort here.

One of them, an old man that calls himself Chief, had a Billet from Chattelen[14] for seventeen skins to be paid here. Mr.

FIRST JOURNAL OF SIMON FRASER
FROM APRIL 12TH TO JULY 18TH 1806

Rocheplane [Rocheblave?] last spring delivered a gun to La Malice to be given him [the Indian chief] as payment, but La Malice took the lock of the gun to mend that of his own, and it remains here useless, therefore I did not pay the Indians, but told him to get payment from those to whom he gave the furs. If ever he will be paid, La Malice of course will pay the gun.

The people who were [sent] for bark arrived with three Rolls. In the evening called all the Indians to the door, to know how many there are of them, which we found to be forty four men, thirty women and seventy nine boys, girls and children, and their is another band near at hand not yet arrived, and there are several gone to work the Beaver, which will form in all of these seen here about 60 men, 40 women and upwards of 100 boys, girls and children. Formerly they say they were much more numerous, but the Beaver Indians war excursions continually deminished them, and the greatest loss generally fall to the share of the women, which added to the number the Beaver and Rocky Mountain Indians continually took from them, may account for the unequal proportion there is between the men and women.

Saturday, May 10. Weather still cold. I am really concerned about the backwardness of the season. The River is yet chock full of ice, and people continually crossing upon it. Made up 560 pounds pounded meat, 76 pounds grease, and 120 pounds dried meat, into bundles to be sent over the Portage to morrow. Another pack was made and the small canoe gummed. Gave the Babith and another Indian each 8 balls and as many shots of powder to go a hunting. They returned in the evening after having killed a Red Deer and wounding several others.

Sunday, May 11. The weather cloudy but rather more warm than usual. In the morning sent Bazile and Gosselin to rise more bark, what there is here already not being of a good quality, and in the evening they returned with 10 fathoms, seemingly pretty good. Two men and three boys were [sent] for and brought the Red

Deer that was killed yesterday. The meat weighed 280 pounds. Ménard and Saucier, the latter of which is sick, was sent over the Portage with the pieces that were made up yesterday. They had 13 young men with them to help them to carry the pieces.

The Indians that were on this side of the River arrived. They brought only 21 skins furs and the value of 6 in provisions. At noon Mr. McKenvin arrived from the other end and says the River is clear of ice above the Portage. Gagnon and Farcier accompanied by a slave boy from the Little Head likewise arrived. They say they could not prevail on the Little Head to come, but that he promised to be here in five nights. Beyson was employed making verangues [varangues; i.e., ribs] for a small canoe, and Mr. Stuart banded the large one, but did not render all the verangues. Gave the Indian boy 4 measures ammunition and 1 1/2 foot tobacco to take to the Little Head, with orders to be here in three nights, and told him likewise that a French man would accompany [him] to morrow morning.

Gave 4 measures ammunition with as many young men to go a hunting to morrow.

Monday, May 12. This morning Mr. McKenvin went to the other end of the Portage to get the men there to split and prepare canoe wood, in case of our being obliged to make one there. The Little Head's slave boy went off early. He slept in the Lodges, and some say he went off with out coming into the house, but other[s] say that he went into where the man that was to accompany him was, but the lazy fellow was still asleep and did not see him.

One of the Meadow Indians says that the Little Head had said that he would not come here until he would be off for above, and all the other[s] for below,[15] which corresponds with the young man's going off without a frenchman, for which reason Mr. McGillivray and Beyson, guided by an Indian, [were sent off] with positive orders to bring the Little Head and all those that are with him here.

FIRST JOURNAL OF SIMON FRASER
FROM APRIL 12TH TO JULY 18TH 1806

Bazile and Bosselin were [sent] for and brought more bark. In the afternoon Ménard and the young men that went over the Portage with him yesterday returned. Gave each of the Indians the value of two skins for their pains, which will render them ready and willing to obey another time. The Pauvres [Pouces?] Coupés Comrade, one of the young men that were a hunting, brought the value of 2 skins [in] fresh meat. The others killed nothing. They are too much afraid to do anything. They have alarms every moment and pretend to see enemies daily. They will not stir from here until the Little Head arrives, [so] that he as well as us may assure them of the peaceable intentions of the Beaver Indians. People are still crossing upon the ice and snow shoes are made use of in the woods.

Tuesday, May 13. In the morning Bazile, Ménard and Gosselin were sent over to the other end of the Portage to remain there some time, and work at canoe wood. They brought over three rolls of bark and a few old puteles [possibly *poutrelles* is meant; i.e., small beams].

Wedneseday, May 14. In the evening Mr. McGillivray and Beyson arrived from the Beaver Lake [Moberly Lake] and informed [me] that Little Head was coming by another route, and soon after he made his appearance, accompanied by his brother, but [he] left his women with the Raquette Relevée &c. beyond the Beaver Lake, which renders it of no service of their coming to the Fort themselves, and it was purposely to bring all that Mr. McGillivray was sent there. The Raquette Relevée and etc. we intended to send down in canoe to Dunvegan, according to Mr. McLeod's desire, and the Little Head was to accompany us in the quality of hunter across the Mountains, but now I am afraid that neither the one or the other can take place. The Indians had a Beaver Robe and about a dozen of skins, but as they told Mr. McGillivray that they would come here themselves, it was not taken from them.

In the morning, although the ice was very bad, the Sauteau crossed when it was at the risk of her life to go after Bazile to the other end of the Portage. She is more like a fury than a woman.

Towards the evening P. Dallaire arrived from Trout Lake [Fort McLeod, on McLeod Lake] with a letter from Mr. [James] McDougall. He left that place the 5th Inst. but was detained a long time along the road by the ice, and had a narrow escape, a bank of ice having fallen into his old Peni [?] canoe and broke it, and from there, about a day's march, he came on foot, and says the ice was not yet broke in many places beyond the Portage. D'Allaire says that when he came off the canoe was not finished, but the Packs [containing the furs to be shipped out from Fort McLeod], 13 in number were made, and Mr. McDougall writes that he went to the Carriers land [lake] and saw about fifty men on the borders of about 3 1/2 days march from Trout [McLeod] Lake, but the distance was long and intricate by water. The above Lake [Stuart Lake], he says, empties its waters into the Columbia by a small River [the Stuart and Nechako rivers], which is reported to be navigable. Fish abounds in the Lake at certain seasons of the year, and animals of the fur kind are plenty, but large animals are scarce. The natives resemble the Ehipewcans [Chipewyans?] in their language and manners.

Thursday, May 15. Fine weather. The ice broke in the course of the night and drifted all this day. In the evening sent off a small canoe with the news to Dunvegan, and Mr. McKenvin, who just arrived from the other end of the Portage, embarked in it as he wished to see Mr. McLeod before he leaves Dunvegan,[16] and Beyson and an Indian goes down to return immediately with a small assortment of trading goods for this place, that the Indians may be supplied with Iron works, Guns and ammunition to be off early in the month of August to work the Beaver. (They promised to make a good spring hunt and to be all here about the beginning of that month.) La Rammée and his spouse likewise

FIRST JOURNAL OF SIMON FRASER
FROM APRIL 12TH TO JULY 18TH 1806

embarked. He being a free man I though[t] it necessary to send him off this first opportunity in order to settle with Mr. McLeod before he leaves Dunvegan.

After their departure Mr. Stuart finished the large canoe, and at dusk the Little Head begged to be allowed to drink a little with a few of the slave Indians, who have some orignal skins to trade, and himself will drink part payment of the provisions that are due to him. He seems very willing to accompany us across the Mountains, but I have no great confidence in him, and do not understand his having [left] his family beyond the Beaver Lake [Moberly Lake], and he seems too submissive and cringing, which makes me thinks that he disembles.

Friday, May 16. The sun shone all day but the weather was rather cold. In the morning the Little Head went away and promised to be back with his family in four nights. Sent a man [La Pistole] with him in order to return to-morrow with some meat and a few furs the Indians have. The slave Indians traded several orignal [moose] skins for ammunition, after which they all decamped, excepting the Babillard and a couple of young men that remained with him to hunt for the Fort during the summer. Gave them but very few credits. As they seldom ever pay, it is a bad custom to give them out many debts. Made up another Pack and got the canoe gummed.

Saturday, May 17. It began to rain in the course of the night last past and did not cease all the day. In the forenoon La Malice and Wananshish arrived from the other end of the Portage. They arrived there late last night with one man, St. Pierre, in a large canoe loaded with 14 Packs [of furs] from Trout Lake [Fort McLeod]. All is well there excepting that they live but very poorly. The Indians told me last Fall [that] there was excellent fishery there in the spring of the year, but very few are caught as yet.

Sent La Malice and D'Allaire back to the other end of the Portage, with as many Indians as we could muster, to bring all the Packs over in one trip tomorrow. Two men, Bazile and D'Allaire, are to remain at the other end of the Portage to mend the old canoe there, that is to say if they can be dispensed with. Hired Wananshish for the term of six years at the rate of 300 livres per annum.

N.B. When La Malice was here in the month of February I told him not to allow any of the women at Trout Lake [McLeod Lake] to embark in the Spring, but D'Allaire brought his with him, and La Malice himself in course of the Winter debauched the woman Blais had, and afterwards prevailed on Mr. McDougall to sell her to him for 300 livres, and she accompanied him here, but [neither] Mr. McDougall nor any other had any such power from me, and I intend that La Malice will not keep her, at least at such a cheap rate. This does not please La Malice and he refuses to accompany us across the Mountains, alledging that by his agreement that he is not obliged to go there or even to winter in any part of the Peace River, and as I had not his engagement I was obliged to take him on his word, and told him that though much in want of him that I would not oblige him to go, since he said it was contrary to his agreement, but that he was answerable for the consequences.

Sunday, May 18. Fine weather. This morning La Pistole, who was sent off with Little Head the day before yesterday, arrived almost out of his *senses*, saying that the day he went off that he followed the Little Head until he got to where there was too much snow for him to keep up with him, and as the Indians had snowshoes they soon left him out of sight, and in endeavouring to follow them in their tracks, their being no snow in some places, he lost himself, and had it not been for a slave boy who met him as he was a hunting, he would not be [would not have been] able to find his way here. I do not vouch for the truth of this story; however, it is certain that the Little Head left him purposely, in order to have it more in his power to absent himself, and not come to

FIRST JOURNAL OF SIMON FRASER
FROM APRIL 12TH TO JULY 18TH 1806

the Fort until after our departure for above, though he promised faithfully to be back in three or four days, which promise I am sure was only to get rid of us with a good grace.

In the evening the people arrived with all the Packs, six frenchmen and eight Indians. Gave each of the latter the value of two skins each [in] ammunition for bringing over each a pack. The Packs were all so ill made and tied with such small cords that we were obliged to set the people immediately about untying them, in order to be made over again, but it being late they only made one up.

Monday, May 19. Cloudy weather and several showers of rain fell in course of the day. Early in the morning set all hands about the Packs and they were finished in the afternoon. The furs [from Fort McLeod] are really fine. They were chiefly killed in the proper season and many of them are superior to any I have seen in Athabasca, being quite black and being well dryed, excepting that they are not all stretched in the proper shape.

D'Allaire arrived from the other end of the Portage early, but as he goes out, [I] hired Ménard to accompany us in his place. D'Allaire was willing to go and would be a useful man, but he made some objections on account of his not being allowed to take his woman with him. Another consideration that induced me to part with him is that there is not any other person here with whom I can trust the canoe that goes down. Its load consists of 28 Packs. St. Pierre, that was here as *boute de canot* [*bout de canot*; bowman or steersman of a canoe] above, was reduced to a middleman, and made to turn off the woman that La Malice allowed him to take last winter at Trout [McLeod] Lake.

Previous to these arrangements I spoke again to La Malice and told him that I was particularly in want of him, and told him to tell [me] in [a] few words what he intended to do. He said he knew himself what he was obliged to do, but that I did not, but [I told him that] if he expected the woman he had would accompany him, whether he went up or down, that he would be mistaken, to which he replied that the woman was sold him and that he considered her as his property; that he was not obliged by his engagement to come to any part of the Peace River, and much less to go farther, but if allowed to keep the woman that he was willing to follow where ever I would lead. I told him that however [much] I might be in want of him that I would not embark the best man in Athabasca on such conditions, that however I might acceed [concede] it as a favor, [but] that I would not oblige myself, and that he had only one choice of two to make, either to accompany me or go to Montreal.

After some reflection he preferred the former, and told me he would go *par plaisir* but not *par obligation*, and he immediately arranged himself to be off to the other end of the Portage. But previous to his departure, I called him in and told him [that], though I would not oblige myself to embark his woman, that now since he was ready to go without [her], I would grant him permission to take her, but not as his property; however that he might keep her as long as he would remain in that quarter and behaved well, provided she was willing to remain with him, after which they both went off to-gether.

Rocky Mountain Portage to McLeod Lake

Tuesday, May 20. Early in the morning took an account of all the property remaining at this place (R.M.P. [Rocky Mountain Portage]), and closed this transactions of the year, and after I had finished writing my public and private letters,[17] we settled the canoe for below to be off at [manned by] five men, and Mr. Stuart and I crossed the River with them after which they departed at 3 P.M.

Previous to our departure all the people that goes above with us crossed the River with the large canoe, previous to its being

FIRST JOURNAL OF SIMON FRASER
FROM APRIL 12TH TO JULY 18TH 1806

loaded, as there are no other large canoe[s] at the Fort to cross [in] after it is off. Mr. A.M. Gillervray [Archibald McGillivray], who has the Fort in charge, remains with only Beysons family until the return of Beyson from Dunvegan, which I expect will be very soon. It was ten oclock at night when we got to the upper end of the Portage. The road is amazing bad and the Portage is at least 14 or 15 miles long.[18]

Wednesday, May 21. Fine weather. Wakened all hand[s] early to prepare the canoes and everything else to be off in the afternoon. But on account of one of the canoes, the one from Trout [McLeod] Lake, being small and our having a quantity of fresh meat over, enough to conduct us to Finlay's branch, we could not embark all on board the two canoes without being too heavily loaded; therefore [I] set La Malice and two others to arrange another canoe that [had] remained here since last summer. La Malice appears to slur it [?] so that we will set off from here with three men & canoe[s].

About sun set Mr. Stuart and I took our departure with two canoes, and encamped at the first point. La Malice will follow tomorrow as soon as the canoe will be arranged. Mr. Stuart['s] canoe made a great deal of water, and is so rood [rude] and ill made that they were every moment in danger of over setting it, for which reason we will be obliged to pass a couple of days at this place to arrange it. It is the worst made that ever I saw and is more like a trough than a canoe, and I am surprised how Mr. McDougall, who was present, would allow such a one to be made. It would be more easy to make a new one than to arrange it.

Mr. Stuart takes the courses and charts of the River.

Thursday, May 22. Fine weather. Early in the morning, part of the people were sent for wood to make verangues [ribs], while the others took all the wood out of the canoe and gummed it properly in side. The bars [thwarts] were likewise taken out, and others were long [more long?], put in their place, after which it was sebarded [?] with verangues not so round as the other[s] that were [there] before, which with properly gumming it outside kept all hands bussy all day so that we could not be off until 9 P.M. However, as we marched late, we came to our first encampment of last Fall,[19] where we put [ashore] for the night. Distance about 7 miles.

Notwithstanding all possible pains were taken to gum and arrange Mr. Stuart's canoe, it still leaks so much water that several things got wet. This is the new canoe that La Malice made at Trout [McLeod] Lake; it is not only ill made but the bark is very bad. I have the canoe I came off with from Lac la Pluie last summer, which is not much better than the other. It was a good canoe, but got much spoiled last fall in the ice at Trout [McLeod] Lake and afterwards going down to the Portage, and I could not get it renewed this spring for the want of a canoe maker. Indeed, Mr. Stuart would have made it, but it was at the upper end of the Portage, and he had too much to do at the Fort to leave it for such a time as would be required to renew the canoe.

Friday, May 23. Fine warm weather. We were obliged to gum both canoes this morning, before we set off, having arrived too late last night to perform that operation. A strong head wind all day. At noon we were obliged to put ashore to gum, the canoes being so leaky that we could not prevent the property from getting wet. Here we lost four hours, and yet we were obliged to put ashore and encamp about an hour before sun set to gum again, in order to be off early in the morning. Little Gervais, who steers Mr. Stuart's canoe, is not able to keep it straight. Indeed, the want of a steerman will greatly retard our progress up this strong current. The water was rather low when we left the Portage but is now rising faster. However, though we seldom make use of the paddles, the bottom being good it is good going by the pole.

FIRST JOURNAL OF SIMON FRASER
FROM APRIL 12TH TO JULY 18TH 1806

Saturday, May 24. We set off early but gummed both the canoes in [the] course of the day. In the afternoon La Malice overtook us and we encamped all together. He has been pretty expeditious. The computed distance of this day is only 12 miles. The canoes are so very bad, and so poorly manned, one of them having a middleman to steer it, that we cannot advance much.

Sunday, May 25. Set off early, and soon after came to the foot of the strongest Rapid we saw yet. The canoes were towed up with the line but one of them struck upon a stem which broke a small hole in the bottom and it took us near an hour to repair it. Afterwards we gummed the three canoes which operation took upwards of two hours. We came to an encamped [encampment] at a little River that falls into the main on the right side and gummed all the canoes again.

Monday, May 26. Fine weather. The sun was up when we left our encampment and shortly after we came to a strong Rapid. The Knight [Sir Alexander Mackenzie] mentions his being obliged to make a Portage of 400 yards to pass it, but if so the water must have been considerable lower than at present, for we found a fine passage along [the] shore on the right, and had the water been higher it would have been still better. We towed up the canoes with the line, but one of them got a little damaged, which took but a short time to repair, but we were afterwards obliged to gum [it], which made us lose a considerable time.

At one of my encampments of last Fall I was surprised to find upwards of a foot of snow in the place of my Tent. The mountains are all covered with snow, but [it] is chiefly disolved near the banks of the River, and it is not a little curious at this late period of the season to see snow drifting on the top of the mountains, which are of no great height, while we are scorching with heat on the banks of the River. We encamped about sun set and gummed all the canoes.

May 26, continued. They [the canoes] are so very bad that though we had upwards of a keg on leaving the Portage that we soon got out of gum and are now obliged to gather for daly use. Here we overtook a band of Meadow Indians who are on their way to the Beaver Country, beyond Finlays branch.

La Malice killed a Rein Deer [a caribou] that was crossing the River; for this we may thank one of the Indians dogs that chased it and brought it to the River side. Previous to our arrival at the Indians we were greatly amused looking at some of the Indians running after the wild sheep, which they call *Aspah*. They are really expert; indeed, running full speed among the perpendicular rocks, which had I not ocular demonstrations I could never believe to have been trained by any creature, either of the human or brute creation, for the rocks appeared to us, which perhaps might be exagerated a little from the distance, to be as steep as a wall and yet, while in pursuit of the sheep, they [the Indians] bounded from one to another with the swiftness of a Roe, and at last killed two in their snares, one of which we traded for ammunition merely for a rarity. They have great resemblance to the European sheep; the wool is almost as fine, perfectly white, and upwards of six inches long, and when fat the Indians represent the flesh as excellent eating. At present that [time?] it is meagre, it is rather tuff, and has a strong musk taste and smell.

Tuesday, May 27. Fine warm weather; the water rises very fast. Indeed it has risen upwards of three feet since we left the Portage, and though the current is amazing strong it is exceedingly good going as yet. We came to and encamped at the last Rapid, which is about 2 miles below the Forks on Finlays branch [i.e., below the junction of the Finlay and Parsnip rivers, which unite to form the Peace River]. La Malice, who was before us, attempted to ascend this Rapid with the pole, but Mr. Stuart, who was the nearest to him, called to him to desist, and

FIRST JOURNAL OF SIMON FRASER
FROM APRIL 12TH TO JULY 18TH 1806

I gave him a set down for risking the property so much where it was [not] necessary.

It was really difficult to come up this Rapid, and we were obliged to take out the load and carry it over a rocky point of 400 yards, and the canoes was taken up light. Had the water been lower we could have gone up easyly loaded, and had it been higher, we could effect the same thing by a safe passage along the right shore, that at present contains only water enough to take up the canoes light. La Malice, who was first up, left his canoe with only the bow of it on shore, and while he was bussy at the lower end it went off and ran down the Rapid. It received however no injury and they went for it with another canoe. I was much displeased with La Malice on this occasion, and as well as his attempting to go up with a full load, and threatened him severely if he was not more careful in the future.

It was after dark before everything was carried to the upper end of the Portage, [and] of course the canoes could not be gummed, which will make us go off late tomorrow. Several of the Indians followed us until within a short distance of our encampment.

We march to day by Mr. Stuarts calculation 19 miles, which is the greatest distance we have done yet in a day. At this place he lost his book of memorandum, having wrapped it up in his cloak and left it on the rock while he went to help the people that were taking up the canoes. The line got entangled in the cloak without anyone perceiving it, and on the men's pulling it the cloak with the contents flew into the River. The cloak was saved but the memorandum perished, and the compass was near sharing the same fate.[20]

Wednesday, May 28. Still fine weather. It was 9 oclock before the canoes could be prepared to be off. In the morning Pouce Coupé's[21] comrade came to us with a couple of Indians that never saw white people before. They are exceedingly well clothed in leather, and though they never were at the Fort, they have guns which they got from their relations. They are the relations of the Meadow Chief but of a different family.

They gave us some information about their lands. What information we got from these Indians is chiefly about Finlay's branch [the Finlay River] and the country beyond it, which is conformable to what we have heard from the other Indians at the Portage. The only additional information we got from them is that there is an immense number of Beaver all along Finlay's branch and the River that falls into it [the Manson River?], and that there are a few caribou about what they call the Bear Lake. They seem to be well acquainted with the Carriers, with whom they live in amity, and from whom I imagine they got the most part of their Iron works and ornaments, at least they are of the same kind. They desired us to be on our guard and beware of the At-tah, which is the name both them and the big men [the McLeod Lake Indians] gives the Atnah tribe, whom they represent as more treacherous than realy wicked, and [who] wood [would] likely if not aware [i.e., if come upon by surprise] shoot their arrows at us.

By what we could understand from these Indians, as well as the others whom we saw at the Portage, nothing can be more erroneous than what Sir A.M.K. [Sir Alexander Mackenzie] reports that it was the near branch[22] of the Peace River he followed. The Indians consider the western branch [the Finlay] always as the main. It is more than twice as large as the eastern branch [the Parsnip] and does not terminate so soon, on the contrary the source of the east branch is comparatively near at hand, of which I will take notice afterwards, but he [Mackenzie] seems to have been ambitious of having traced the Peace River to its source as well as Confluence. This is not the only mistake he seems to have committed, whether designedly or not I cannot say, but this I can affirm, that from the Portage to Finlays branch, and which I contend to be the main branch of the Peace River, we had few of the difficulties he mentions to have encountered. The

FIRST JOURNAL OF SIMON FRASER
FROM APRIL 12TH TO JULY 18TH 1806

navigation is not only safe but as easy as in the lower part of the Peace River, and I have often had more difficulty during the high water coming up there with three men than here. The distance does not appear to be much above ninety or a hundred miles at most,[23] and a canoe well manned might have performed it in three days as the water is now in the long days; and had our canoes been any wise good, even with three men we would have performed it in five, and as for the water, and I am sure we have been as much in it as him, we have not felt it more cold than in other parts of the country, which makes me inclined to believe that he has exaggerated all along, but then he was the first that passed, and it was pardonable in him, and I have not the least desire to detract from his merits. His perseverance was commendable and he succeeded where perhaps many others would have failed.

We traded with the Indians that came with Pouce Coupé's Comrade, and made them a present of 10 balls and a little powder. We informed them of their being a Fort established at Trout [McLeod] Lake, to which place they promised to go in the course of the summer, it being nearer their lands and was [farther] out of reach of their enemies, the Beaver Indians, than the [Rocky Mountain] Portage.

We left the main branch on the west and entered the other on the east [the Parsnip River] at 11 A.M., which is overflown, and the current was so very strong that it was with much difficulty we could advance. No use can be made of the Poles on account of the depth of the water, excepting some times against the banks and drift wood, and the current runs with such velocity that it cannot be stemmed with three paddles, and not easily with four, for we often help them ourselves,[24] and the banks are so thickly interwoven with trees and shrubs that it is seldom they can be approached, so that there is no method left except that of going up by pulling the branches, and the canoes are in continual danger of being broke to pieces by the drift wood.

Killed a swan in the course of the day and encamped late. Having finished the remainder of our fresh meat, gave all hands where with to sup of dried meat. The men very much fatigued, and some of them are very near giving up.

Thursday, May 29. Fine weather. The water still rising and wood continually drifting down the River. My canoe was very near being cut in two. Two of B. [G.] Rivard's dogs were lost, they not being able to follow the canoe. We saw several Beaver in the course of the day, and came to and encamped at sun set upon a bank of gravel opposite my first encampment last Fall in this River, which I consider as a good day, indeed the current was less strong than yesterday. As the men force much [i.e., must exert themselves greatly] in this River we allow them to make three meals a day, and as they eat all together out of the same bag of Pemecan, we put ashore for that purpose, and afterwards it is laid aside and not touched until next meal. This we find to be the best saving way, and the men are better off and better pleased than if they ate a little at every Pipe.[25]

Friday, May 30. Fine weather. We set off at half past 4 A.M., but at the second Pipe a stump seen [ran] through my canoe, which obliged us to put ashore, and we lost two hours to repair and gum it. In the forenoon Mr. Stuarts canoe made so much water that they were obliged to put ashore to gum [it], which operation took up two hours. During that interval Mr. Stuart had an observation for Latitude.

We encountered more misery to day than any day yet, and were obliged to cut several logs and embarass [embarras; i.e., obstructions] to open a Passage. My canoe through the awkwardness of the Bouttes [bowman and steersman] was very much endangered and every soul on board near perishing. In the afternoon we passed a strong Rapid at a point which gave us much trouble to ascend, on account of the Rocks being perpendicular, and no bottom for the poles. We were obliged to

FIRST JOURNAL OF SIMON FRASER
FROM APRIL 12TH TO JULY 18TH 1806

send down the line by tying a stick to it, which was caught by the man in the bow of the canoe, in which manner all the canoes were towed up one after the other with a half load, and the rest of the loads were carried over a Rocky point off about 200 yards. Encamped about 1 1/2 miles above the Rapid on an Island. The computed distance of this day is only 8 1/2 miles, and yet all hands worked hard all day.

Saturday, May 31. Fine weather but rather cold. In the morning at the second pipe my canoe broke upon a stump and it required two hours to mend and gum it, and before noon the same accident happened to Mr. Stuart's and it took up three hours to repair it. We encamped at sun set upon a high bank about 5 miles below the Prairie. This days progress was only 11 miles.

Sunday, June 1. The weather was rather cold in the morning, but afterwards exceeding warm. Indeed I never saw such a changeable climate. At one moment we are shivering with cold, and the next scorching with heat. The water begins to lower and there is but very little wood drifting, but we had the worst going of any day as yet owing to the strength of the current, the depth of the water and the badness of the canoes. In the forenoon La Malice broke his canoe and put ashore to mend it, with the intention of being off immediately, but as soon as the canoe was taken out of the water St. Pierre fainted and remained speechless upward on an hour, which induced La Malice to bond his canoe, thinking to have done before St. Pierre recovered, which made us lose upwards of three hours. My canoe was also gummed and I can say with truth it was much in want of it. Stuart was ahead at the time and we overtook him at the Prairie waiting for us. We came to an encampment after sun set, about 2 miles below River au Nation [Nation River]. The computed distance of today is only 10 miles, which to me appeared very long.

Monday, June 2. Fine day. Exceedingly bad going until we passed the River au Nation, which is a fine navigable River on the right, and so called because the upper part of it is inhabited by some of the big men, though of a different family from those at Trout [McLeod] Lake, after which the current slackened a little.

Here we left one of the canoes and separated its load on the other two, on account of all the men being nearly exhausted with fatigue, and especially La Garde, who steered my canoe since the 26th of last month, has such a sore wrist that he is no more able to. La Malice, who served in that capacity since the Portage, undertakes to steer it to Trout [McLeod] Lake, and I expect to go on better by having all hands on board the two canoes. Hitherto we were not able to embark all in the two canoes, but now that all the fresh meat and three pieces of dried provisions are consumed we will not be much embarassed. Indeed, it is not the load entirely that prevented us leaving a canoe sooner, but considering the crazy state they are in it would be risking our own lives and the property to attempt to load them anywise to come up such strong and rapidious current.

Chiefly by [pulling on] the branches, we came to and encamped opposite a small Island at the distance of 11 miles from our encampment of last night. In the evening the weather was cloudy and all appearances of rain, and before we went to bed it began a small drizzling rain, which continued the most part of the night.

Tuesday, June 3. It rained in the morning, which prevented our setting off until half past 7 A.M. Indeed it did not displease me to have a pretext to indulge the people with a little rest, which they stood much in need of. Several showers fell through the day. At 1 P.M. we put ashore to gum [the canoes], at my third encampment of last year, where we took up two hours. We encamped a little before sun set on account of my canoe being broke in the side, having struck against an embarras [obstruction]. Both canoe[s] have become so heavy and shattered that they cannot be taken out of the water by less than 4 men. Today's distance is 11 1/2 miles.

Wednesday, June 4. Several showers of rain and hail fell in course of the day. All hands were bussy engaged about three hours gumming Mr. Stuart's canoe, which leaked so much that the pieces could not be kept from getting wet. Encamped within an hour of sun set. Distance 15 miles.

Thursday, June 5. Several showers of rain and hail. Notwithstanding we set off early, but about 8 A.M., as our progress was very slow and the current so amazing strong, we unloaded each of the canoes of nine pieces in order to go more expeditiously, and get to the entrance of the small River [the Pack River] to day, and to send down a canoe immediately on our arrival [to bring the pieces left behind]. We encamped at 6 P.M. about 2 miles up the [Pack] River that leads to Trout [McLeod] Lake. Notwithstanding [the fact that] the [Pack] River that leads to this place, Trout Lake [Fort McLeod], is a considerable large and navigable River in all seasons, it does not appear to have been noticed by Sir A.M.K. [Sir Alexander Mackenzie]. As he used to indulge himself sometimes with a little sleep, likely he did not see it, and I can account for many other omissions [in his journal] in no other manner than his being asleep at the time he pretends to have been very exact,[26] but was qualified to make observations and [were I] inclined to find fault with him, I could prove that he seldom or ever paid the attention he pretends to have done, and that many of his remarks were not made by himself but communicated by his men. It is certainly difficult to stem the current of the east branch [the Parsnip River] during the high water, but not near so much as he makes it. There is scarcely a point in it but a canoe with six paddles would go up with ease, and if we had so much difficulty it is not so much owing to the difficulty of the navigation itself as [to] the badness of the canoes and the awkwardness of the Bouts [endmen], particularly steersmen. A canoe well manned might come from Finlays branch to the entrance of the [Pack] River that leads to Trout [McLeod] Lake the fifth day with ease.

On our entering the east branch [the Parsnip] there was a very perceptable change in the climate, and the vegetation was far advanced, whereas as below Finlays branch [on the Peace River] the trees did not begin to bud, I suppose owing to the vicinity [i.e., proximity] of the Mountains, but along this River they are at a great distance and often out of sight. The banks of the River and the country in general appears to be low and in every place marshy, and there is a great deal of Beaver marks all along, and we saw the tracks of large animals in way [many?] places, as likewise [we] observed some jays of a sky color but no other birds that are not common in the Peace River. We likewise saw a vast quantity of the Canadian balsom trees all along. The first we perceived was at Finaly's branch [the Finlay River], and in the vicinity of Trout [McLeod] Lake, which is small[27] but which has a water communication with others more large beyond in a southern direction. There is plenty of hemlock and some of the serven [?] tree, but with the exception for the *Bois picant*[28] we saw no other tree or shrubs except such as are common in the Peace River. The Elder however is more large, there being some of four feet in circumference.

The distance from our last encampment to the little River [the Pack] is computed at 15 miles.

Friday, June 6. It rained all last night and this morning, which prevented our setting off until 8 A.M. We left all the provisions and many other things in cache, and Mr. Stuart and I embarked in one canoe, with four common men and La Malice, with only the goods that will be necessary to be left at Trout Lake [Fort McLeod], and such of our other things as will be required. The

FIRST JOURNAL OF SIMON FRASER
FROM APRIL 12TH TO JULY 18TH 1806

reason of our leaving the remainder of the goods in cache is that we are to return as soon as we can get two canoe[s] made, the Eastern branch [the Parsnip River] being our route to the Carriers, and it has become a work of necessity to get new canoes made, the old ones being so much worn and shattered as not to be able to proceed farther.

The small river [the Pack] is still more hard to ascend than the other, the current being much more strong. On crossing the small Lake [Tudyah Lake], which is upwards of two miles long, we perceived an Indian canoe near the east shore, but it blew too hard for them to come to us and we were in too much hurry to go to them. From there we found several lines set along the River, which had been set in the morning. We visited them all and took two trouts, which made an excellent supper. We encamped upon a bank of gravel about two miles below the Fort, but Mr. Stuart's compass having got wet, it is out of order and he does not take the courses, but the distance from the cache to our encampment may be about 20 miles, of [which] the Small Lake is upwards of 2 miles.

Saturday, June 7. We set off at sun rise but afterwards put ashore to dry ourselves and prepare our arms. And while we were on shore the Montagne de boutte and Little Heads in[29] Tabot Tho' came up with us in two Pine Canoes with their families. It was them we saw yesterday in crossing the Little [Tudyah] Lake. They informed us that Mr. McDougall was at the house alone with only an Indian, and that Blais was gone to the Carp Lake, but that he was expected back to day.

We arrived at the house [Fort McLeod] between 10 and 11 A.M. Mr. McDougall has been anxiously waiting for us these several days. He informed us that several of the Carriers are daily expected here, and that all the Indians of this place are at the Carp Lake, where there are immense numbers of fish of the Carp kind, and that there is no fish caught in this [McLeod]

Lake excepting a very few carp, on account of the water being too high, notwithstanding which we are determined to feed all hands with fish while we remain here making canoes, and for that purpose began immediately to prepare the nets. Mr. Stuart being the most expert hand [at] mending, he mended them all and Saucier and the others set six and the Indians set some also.

Sent La Garde with an Indian in a Pine canoe to the cache near the confluence of the [Pack] River to tell the people that are there what pieces they are to bring up. The Indian is to come up with the people in the large canoe tomorrow, and La Garde is to remain there to take care of the pieces, and that he may not touch the provisions he had the value of 4 measures ammunition to hunt for himself, there being plenty of Gibier [game] there about. Sent likewise Mr. McDougall and Wananshish to the Carp Lake to desire the *Big Men* Indians of this place to come here with loads of fish, and to conduct the Carriers here should they have arrived there. The old Barbein arrived soon after ourselves. He brought a few furs and Carpe.

At Fort McLeod

Sunday, June 8. Fine weather. Bazile, Saucier, and Gagnon employed splitting and bringing canoe wood here and Mr. Stuart and La Malice began to make verangues [canoe ribs]. In the evening the four men from below arrived with the pieces they were ordered to bring, and soon after Mr. McDougall and Blais arrived accompanied by six Carriers, three of which never saw the Fort before. Three big men [McLeod Lake Indians] came also loaded with fish.

Monday, June 9. Weather the same as yesterday. Sent Bazile and St. Pierre to rise bark for two canoes. Blais, Gervais and La Londe to split and bring canoe wood and Gagnon and Ménard [to secure] gum, while Saucier was employed about the nets, but

FIRST JOURNAL OF SIMON FRASER
FROM APRIL 12TH TO JULY 18TH 1806

the meshes being too large, there are but few fish caught in them. However the Indians take a good many in their willow nets, which they share with us.

The remainder of the big men arrived. They brought a few furs and between six and seven hundred dried carpe and a few Roes. Two of the Carriers paid 21 skins Credit as part payment of what they had from Mr. McDougall at the Beaver River [Rocky Mountain Fort], and the others that did not owe traded about 9 dozen skins, and in the afternoon they all excepting one whom we keep us guide went off. They are to return immediately, the distance across land being comparatively short, and meet us with provisions at the Fork of the River that leads to their [Stuart] Lake. We endeavoured to get some information concerning their country and a chart of it, but they are no wise communicative or intelligent. Mr. McDougall was bussily engaged settling the Indians to be off to morrow, that they may go to Carp Lake to dry and bring us more fish.

Thursday [Tuesday], June 10. Still fine weather. All hands employed as yesterday. We took only 20 fish in seven nets, but the Montagne de bout brought us 52. Spoke to him and the Little Heads brother in law [and asked them] to accompany us to the Carriers in the capacity of interpreters, guides, hunters etc. The latter is not much inclined to go but the former is ready and willing.

All the Indians went off, [the] most part of them go to the Carp Lake with orders to be back in five nights with fish. The old Barbin and band are to go towards the Lakes of the height of land [between the upper waters of the Parsnip River and the Fraser River], where they promise to make provisions and wait for us upon the road, where we expect to find them in fifteen days hence. The Little Head brother-in-law and Montagne de bouth fish here abouts. The water is so high that they cannot kill Beaver with Bows and Arrows or spears, and we are so scarce of ammunition that we cannot afford to give them any. The Carriers *Ran*

Chuse who remained there to accompany us to the Columbia asked leave to go to the Carp Lake for two nights, which was granted, and he left his axe and bag as a pledge for his returning.

Wednesday, June 11. Notwithstanding several showers of rain fell, the weather was fine and warm. Only 13 fish in 7 nets. The men finished splitting canoe wood and brought the remainder here. At dusk Bazile and St. Pierre with 40 odd fathoms of bark and birch to make small verangues arrived. Bazile says there are a great many birch trees, but that the birch [bark] of most every one of them is bad.

Thursday, June 12. Several small showers of rain fell in [the] course of the day. Sent Bazile and Blais to procure more dark, their not being a sufficient [amount] of what they brought yesterday good to make two canoes. All the wood is nearly finished, and to morrow we will begin to make one. The woman that St. Pierre had last winter, and which he was made to return at the Portage, accompanied the Barbue, her father.

Friday, June 13. Fine weather. As it was late before everything was ready to begin the canoe, we only laid the bottom and fixed the maitres [gunwales] and entraves [end frames]. Caught only 7 Carp in as many nets. The meshes are so very large and the fish so small that they all pass through the nets. Saucier, who is the fisherman, went to set a couple of nets at the entrance of a small river at about 2 miles of [off] in the Lake.

Saturday, June 14. Fine weather. All hands busyly engaged at the Canoe, but it goes on but slow, Mr. Stuart being the only one that can fix anything. *Ran Chuse* arrived from the Carp Lake and brought a small load of dried fish. He says that while he was there more Carriers arrived from their lands, but as they have no furs do not intend to come here.

At sun set Bazile arrived and brought four or five small Rolls of bark which is very bad. Saucier came with him and brought only 3 trout and 10 Carp, which is all he took in all the

FIRST JOURNAL OF SIMON FRASER
FROM APRIL 12TH TO JULY 18TH 1806

nets. Blais is gone to the other end of the Lake, having sent him in quest of Montagne de bouth, whom we apprehend has disobeyed, and deserted, as he came not these three days with fish.

Sunday, June 15. Fine weather. Early in the morning Blais arrived. He met the Montagne de bouth on his way here, so that he had no intention of absenting himself. Took the canoe off the bed and after putting the timber into it we began the other. 17 fish.

Monday, June 16. Still fine weather. Sowed the large seams of the Canoe, and afterwards opened it, and sowed the Boss and part of the Paigneis.[30] Saucier caught 36 fish in seven nets.

Tuesday, June 17. Still fine weather. Finished sewing the Canoe, and put the timber into it. La Malice, who is sick, kept his bed the most part of the day. He has been complaining for some time, and is under a course of medicine, ever since his arrival, So that he has done little or nothing. Saucier took 25 fish and the Montagne de bouth gave us 16.

Wednesday, June 18. Though the sun shone at intervals it blew a strong northerly wind and the weather was cold. Sewed the small seams of the first canoe and gummed it inside, but in attempting to band [bond?] it, it broke and could not be mended for want of bark. A little before sunset the Little Head's brother in law and Montagne de bout arrived. The former was severely reprimanded for his behaviour and [for] not being willing to accompany us to the Carriers. There was only 11 carpe taken today in all the nets.

Thursday, June 19. Very cold weather. Nothing could be done to the canoes. Sent Bazile, Gervais and St. Pierre for bark to mend the canoe that is broke. Early this morning Blais and Wananshish went to Carp Lake to make all the Indians come to the house with fish. We also perceived that the Little Head's brother in law decamped; he went off early, we suppose [in order] that he might not be compelled to go with us to the Carriers. Only 18 fish in all the nets.

221

Friday, June 20. The weather was cold with showers of rain at intervals. Mr. Stuart mended the canoe that was broke and La Malice began to band [bond?] the other, but [as] he was not doing it to Mr. Stuarts liking he desisted. Bazile and Gervais fell down from a tree yesterday as he was rising bark and hurt himself. He has the Preveties [privates] much swoolen. He has been unwell and complained of a pain in the back ever since we came of [off] from the Portage, which probably proceeds from his having fallen in the Portage the first trip he made with pieces on the snow with trains [traîneaux; sledges].

Saturday, June 21. In the forenoon Blais and Wananshish, with all the Indians (excepting two), loaded with a few dried carp each, amongst them all they [had in] all 300 or 400, arrived. The Little Heads brother in law came back with them, and as he is the most capable Indian to accompany us, I told him that he should absolutely go, and in the evening all the others went off excepting the Montagne de bouth, who goes [with us] also. But previous to their departure I employed the Mosie de dints de Biche,[31] seemingly the best hunter, and who I would take with us in place of Tabah Tha', had not his women been sick. He hunts for Mr. McDougall during the summer.

Finished banding [bonding?] the canoes and scraped them. They are really fine canoes, being large and seemingly the most solid I have seen yet, but then the bark is none of the best.

Sunday, June 22. Fine weather until 2 P.M., when it began to rain, which continued for the remainder of the day. Before the canoes were dry and liehes [?] put upon one of them it was late, so that the last of them was gummed wet.

In the morning a young man arrived with some fish and asked leave to accompany us to the Carriers, which was allow[ed] him on account of the others wishing to have him with them. About 5 PM. the Little Heads brother-in-law, Le Montagne de bouth and the young man went ahead in a small Pine Canoe to

FIRST JOURNAL OF SIMON FRASER
FROM APRIL 12TH TO JULY 18TH 1806

shoot Beaver, and left their women and children to embark with us in the large canoes, but it was almost dusk before the people were done gumming the canoes, so we could not go off.

Fort McLeod to the Nechako River

Monday, June 23. Bad weather. It rained all the forenoon, and as Mr. Stuart had some work of our own to do, we did not set off till the afternoon. Came to the encampment at the *Cache* where we found La Garde, who says that he lived well upon his own hunt all the time he has been here, and the dried provisions do not appear to have been touched.

I left the Post of Trout Lake [Fort McLeod] in charge of Mr. James McDougall with only one man, Saucier, to pass the summer with him, but the man [Saucier] embarked with us to return from the Cache with some Iron works [in order] that the Indians may be supplied early in the Fall with the necessary articles to kill Beaver, so at present he [McDougall] remains all alone.

Spoke to and enquired of Bazile Gervais, who appears still to be sick, if he was able to continue with us, and if not that he would remain here and that Saucier would take his place. He told me that he was not very able, but that he would continue and do his best, but that he feared should he continue and become entirely disabled that he would be reproached, in answer to which I told him that it would be very difficult for us to go up the current with only three men, and that this was the time for him to determine, while we had another man to replace him. But he seemed desirous of continuing, from which I confer [infer] that he is not much hurt, though La Malice told me that he was more so than he pretended to be, however, such as he was, that he would be better than any other we had, so we went to bed without determining whether he would go or remain. The Little Heads brother in law killed a Beaver which he gave us.

Tuesday, June 24. Fine weather. Gave out the loading in the morning, which including the provisions with the mens and our own things, is upwards of 20 pieces [in] each [canoe], after which I enquired of Bazile again if he was able and willing to accompany us, to which he replied that he was not very able, but that he was willing and desirous to continue on, but that I might do as I thought best. I told him therefore that he might continue, the after man, Saucier, being both weak and sickly and scarcely able to perform the duty of a middleman, much less that of a bouth [endman], and [as] Bazile is hired [as a] foreman, I thought it best to put him [take him?], thinking it would be soon well.

So we pushed off down the current until we came to the main river [the Parsnip], and then I steered up a strong and rapidous stream. The water has lowered greatly since we passed here the 6th Inst. Just as we left the little [the Pack] River and entered the large [the Parsnip], my canoe struck on a bank of gravel and gave such a jerk that the foreman fell and hurt his side against the *maitre* [gunwale]. We only came on about two miles when we put ashore to breakfast, and in order to be more saving of the provisions we weighed the Pemican and allowed 3 lb.

In the mean time one of the canoes was taken out of the water to be gummed, and when they were near done, La Malice came and informed us that Bazile was entirely disabled. This surprised and vexed me to see him in such a condition. He ought to have told us in the morning of his being so far gone, he seemed so desirous of accompanying us that instead of being worse I conferred [inferred] that he was not really so ill as he pretended to be, otherwise I would certainly have taken Saucier at once. Immediately ordered six men in one of the canoes to take Bazile with his wife and baggage to where we left Saucier making a Pine Canoe to return to Mr. McDougalls, and there leave him and take Saucier in his place. They were not absent two hours in this errand. On this occasion we lost six hours on

FIRST JOURNAL OF SIMON FRASER
FROM APRIL 12TH TO JULY 18TH 1806

shore gumming, sending back Bazile and bringing Saucier, melting grease that was in bags, and putting it in kegs.

The Carrier and the young man are a head in a small canoe and Tabah Tha' sand Montange de bout with their families are on board our canoes. Came to and encamped late opposite a high sandy bank. Tabah Tha' killed a Beaver and the Montagne caught a fine trout, both of which they gave us. Had fine weather going all day and could use either Paddles or Poles, the bottom being good as we chose.

Wednesday, June 25. Fine weather. We set off early and came on well all day without loosing any time, excepting an hour and a half that was required to weigh the provisions for the people and allowing them time to eat, which they do on shore, and another at noon, that Mr. Stuart took to observe.

We came to and encamped a little before sun set near a small Lake³² that the Indians said abounded with Beaver. They went a hunting but had no success. But they killed one before we encamped.

La Malice paddled only at intervals to day, he being unwell, and in the evening he declared himself disabled and told Mr. Stuart that he was afraid that he was enruptured, but by the medicine he takes (for I never heard of a syringe being used for a rupture) it appears to me that it is the —— disease. But what ever it is he appears to suffer very much and is quite disabled. It is really vexing that he did not inform us of being unwell before he left Trout [McLeod] Lake, as [he] would have been left there rather than be burdened with him along the voyage. Our situation is realy critical with the set of awkward men we have, there not being even a good bouth [endman], and all the bad places are yet to be passed. We could not provide ourselves with better men, there being none of that description at the [Rocky Mountain] Portage excepting one, namely, Grandbois, whom I sent down to Dunvegan with letters the beginning of April, and he remained there.

Here we overtook the Carrier and the young man who were ahead. We will be obliged to embark them, [they] having sent their canoe against a stump. It is quite broke and cannot be used anymore.

Thursday, June 26. The Indians had left some of their paddles at the Lake where they were last night looking for Beaver, and as they were obliged to go for them this morning, it was half past four when we embarked. The current was very strong [the] most part of the day and the water rises a little. We encamped a little before sunset.

Friday, June 27. We set off at an early hour this morning and breakfasted at a considerable large River that flows into the main on the left side. It is better than one half as wide as the one we navigated. After passing this River the current slackened and we went on well, but was obliged to put ashore on account of La Malice, where we lost four hours. As he could not sleep for several nights past, last night Mr. Stuart gave him 30 drops laudnum, and he complains of being worse since, on which account we gave him a vomit.

We were not far gone from this place when we came to a strong current and rapidous place of about 3 miles long, but above the current was slack, and we came on with great expedition, including the Indian women and all there being seven or eight Paddles in each canoe, and a little before sun set we found four young men of the Barbins band exactly where Sir A. McK. [Sir Alexander Mackenzie] found the first Indians upon his expedition in 1793.[33] Here we formed our encampment for the night. These young men informed us that they separated from the old Barbin some time ago, but that he is waiting for us about half a days march farther on. They likewise told us that they killed a bear this morning, the meat of which is yet to the fire, and as their Lodges are near they were going for it early tomorrow. Our hunters killed a Beaver and a couple of Outards [*out-*

FIRST JOURNAL OF SIMON FRASER
FROM APRIL 12TH TO JULY 18TH 1806

ardes; i.e., Canada geese]. La Malice seems very weak and often delerious, and yet he eats as well as the others.

Saturday, June 28. The young men brought the meat of the Bear early, and as it was cut up for to dry by the women it was worth but two skins. Two of the young men embarked with us to accompany us to the old Barbun, and it was past five when we set off.

We did not continue more than a third of a mile when we passed a River half as large as this that flows in upon the left. The current was very slack, and about noon we came to a River that flows in upon the left as large as the one we navigated. There we found the old Barbin in the very identical spot he was found by Mr. Finlay in the summer of 1797. He has been here several days waiting our arrival and has four strangers with him, relations of his that never saw white people before. The old fellow went for them to the Lakes at the height of land, so we can say with justice that he is the author of our seeing them at present. They examined us with great admiration and attention, and seemed quite pleased at meeting us. They say that ever since Mr. Finlay has been in this quarter that they kept hereabouts in hopes of seeing white people. As they promised to go to Trout Lake [Fort McLeod] in [the] course of the summer, and kill plenty of Beaver to take with them, [I] gave them a few articles on credit.

Traded two small Pine Canoes from the old Barbin to send our hunters a head to kill Beaver, there being a vast number from here to the height of land. We got no other provisions than a few small fish from these Indians. Soon after our arrival at the Indians a heavy shower of hail fell, followed by the rain which continued the remainder of the day, which nevertheless did not prevent our setting off as soon as we had done with the Indians. It was 5 P.M. when we left the Indians, and we were accompanied by an elderly man, one of the strangers, and his sons, who returns to his wife and children, which he left at the height of land.

We were not above half an hour gone when La Malice jumped on shore, we being near the bank, and fell down senseless. This obliged us to put ashore and pitch our tents for the night in an abominable bad place, and no wood to make a fire. As it rained we had much trouble to clear a place and unload the canoes, and after that was effected Mr. Stuart returned to the place where we left the Indians with six men and all the nets, in order to set them, in case we should be obliged to remain here tomorrow on account of La Malice. By all appearances if he is really as bad as he pretends he will not live long. We are all really ill of [off], in regard to the men. Saucier is sick, Gagnon complains of his side, Blais of having a pain, and a lump upon his stomach, and Gervais is not well, and La Londe is not able to steer his canoe. Our hunters being ahead, and not knowing that we remain here, [I] sent three men for them in case they might be displeased at their women being here without themselves. They all returned before dark, and came back with an Indian, after he had prepared all the nets and left the men there to set and [take] care of them, with orders to be here early in the morning.

Sunday, June 29. Rainy weather. The men were back early with the nets but no fish; however it was past 7 A.M. before La Malice was ready to be off. About noon we were obliged to put ashore and light a fire to warm La Malice and cook for him. He will not eat nothing but cakes and pemmican boiled up with flour and sweetened with sugar. This made us lose a couple of hours. We encamped about sun set in a bad place, and yet a better place could not be found, on account of the country being low and marshy and over flowed with water.

Monday, June 30. Bad rainy weather, notwithstanding which we set off early and soon passed a considerable River that flows in from the left, close the place called by Sir A.M.K. [Sir Alexander Mackenzie] the Beaver Lodge. About half a mile farther on we passed another River on the right and then put ashore to cook for La Malice.

Soon after we left the main branch, on the left, and entered another small River on the right, the waters of which are very clear and deep. (Sir A.M.K. represents this River as terminating in the mountains near [at] hand, but if the Indians be allowed to know better than him it is not so, for they say that it is navigable much farther and terminates in a small Lake where the *sinew en Baulenne*.[34] In many place[s] this side of Trout [McLeod] Lake the River is shallow, and in the Fall I am of opinion that canoes would not easily pass. This River I cannot understand which hath its source. In its present state it is at least fifty yards wide,[35] and the one we entered is twenty yards [wide]. All the large River[s] that fall in from the left this side of Trout [McLeod] Lake the Indians represent as navigable for their canoes for a considerable distance, and say that they terminate in small Lakes not far from one another near the sources of the different braches of the Sinew River [now the Pine River], where Large animals are very numerous; indeed they represent them as plenty [plentiful] at the distance of less than two days march from this place, and if so it would be an excellent station for a fort, but of this here after.)

The entrance of the first Lake [at the height of land] was stopped with drift wood, but at the expense of some time and trouble we opened a passage into the Lake [Arctic Lake][36] and advanced about a mile and a half, where we found the strange Indian all ready mentioned with his family, and also *Ranchuse* the Carrier, who came ahead with him yesterday. The former seems very intelligent and communicative. He gave us a great deal of information concerning this part of the Country, and drew us a chart of it, at which he seemed very expert, but of all that he told us the only thing worth mentioning is that had he been at Trout [McLeod] Lake, he said he would have shown us a more safe and shorter way to the Columbia [i.e., to the Fraser], by which he said we would have been at the Carriers land ere now, and that there was a Portage of a mile and one half at most from one of the Lakes beyond Trout Lake into a fine navigable River, and no Rapids, that flows into the Columbia [the Fraser].[37]

He gave us a few fresh and a good many dried white fish and a little Bears fat, likewise two drysed [dressed] and one green orignal [moose] skins, for which he got goods. We asked him to accompany us with his family to the next Lake in order to show us the best fishing to the next Lake in order to show us the best fishing place and set his own nets also. He immediately consented, and some of his children embarked on board our canoes, which himself and family soon followed in their small canoes.

We continued to the extremity of the Lake, about three miles, and there unloaded at the height of land, which is one of the finest Portages I ever saw, between six and seven hundred yards long, and perhaps the shortest interval of any between the waters that descend into the northern and southern oceans. On entering the next Lake [Portage Lake], which is about three miles long, we began to glide with the current, and had much trouble in trying to force our way out of it to the next Portage on account of the drift wood. Here we unloaded and the canoes and baggage here, same as in the last Portage. The distance is 160 yards to another Lake [Pacific Lake], not quite so large as the last one, and here we formed our encampment for the night.

Tuesday, July 1. Very rainy bad weather. Notwithstanding all the nets were set. La Malice walked over both the Portages, though we offered to carry him. He is very troublesome in his sickness and called Mr. Stuart to his tent to tell him his mind, as he said, and enquired if either of us owed him a grudge. This he asked, he said, because while at the Portage we disregarded him, and now considered him no more than a dog. Mr. Stuart told

FIRST JOURNAL OF SIMON FRASER
FROM APRIL 12TH TO JULY 18TH 1806

him that if either of us owed him a grudge, or had any thing to say to him, that we would not wait his being in his present weak condition to do it, and that if he had been in better health, since he began the subject himself, he would perhaps tell him his opinion of himself and [his] sickness.

This assertion of his, La Malice, is entirely false. We have been attentive and kind to him. Nothing is more certain than that from the time he declared himself sick he was as well attended and taken care of as if it was one of ourselves [i.e., as if he had been Fraser himself or Stuart], and notwithstanding his complaints he used more than one half of the medicines (god knows good or bad) we possessed, and destroyed more flour and sugar than both of us did since we left the Portage, and yet he threatens to remain upon the beech and not embark, alledging that by agreement he is not obliged to voyage in this part of the country, and not well taken care of. When we prepared to leave him here with a bag of Pemican, exclusive of the other provisions we had, and a man to conduct him down to Trout Lake [Fort McLeod], not one of them would consent to remain unless absolutely compelled, and as he is brutish and appears as if inclined to commit suicide, we did not think it right to compel a man to remain with him, so we will be obliged to take him with us, and attend to him the best way we can, and yet I must owe that he is not very deserving, but it is a duty encumbent on one christian to help another in distress, and we will continue to take care of him more for our own sake than his.

I recollect when St. Pierre fell in a fit the 1st inst. he was abandoned by La Malice, and scarcely drawn out of the water, and when I afterwards reprimanded him for his apparent disregard of his duty as a christian, even if he was indifferent to the feelings of humanity, he told me laughing that as he thought he [St. Pierre] was dying, he left him to die alone, and set about mending his canoe, but now it is his turn to suffer and he complains. He even said he would not embark unless we waited here a couple of days for him to see if he would get better, and that he was not obliged to voyage along any part of the Peace River, much less the waters that descend to the Pacific Ocean, but then he appears sometimes to be delerious and does not seem to know what he says, so in his present situation we must put up with him. It would be both ungenerous and in human to abandon him.

Took up the nets that were set last night but no fish in them, I suppose owing to their being carelessly set late last night by the men. Mr. Stuart arranged them all properly and set them again. The Indians took a few white fish of a good size in their nets.

Wednesday, July 2. Weather same as yesterday. Visited the nets in the morning and took some Trout and some white fish, which were excellent, indeed the trout were of five different kinds, some of which I had never seen before, and the best I ever ate.

On account of La Malice and the badness of the weather we did not set off until late in the afternoon, and before our departure we held a consultation about what we would do with La Malice. As he appears very weak at times, and as he may make us lose much time, we are at a loss whether to leave him here with a man to conduct him to Trout Lake [Fort McLeod], when he gets better, or take him with us, but it was the general opinion to take him with us, so we pushed off and after passing the Lake, which is not quite three miles long, we entered a small River [James Creek][38] between fifteen and twenty yards wide, the current of which ran with great velocity.

The passage from the Lake to the River being choaked up with drift wood, we had some trouble to clear our way. Near the entrance of the River we passed a couple of Beaver dams and soon got to a large tree that laid across the River, and it was with great difficulty that we prevented the canoes from running against it. But we soon cut the tree and continued at the risk of breaking the canoes, and we did not proceed far when they were

FIRST JOURNAL OF SIMON FRASER
FROM APRIL 12TH TO JULY 18TH 1806

so much hurt and leaked so much that we were obliged to put ashore and encamp. All hands were wet to the skin, especially Mr. Stuart and myself, being obliged to sit before the canoes and visit the shore in case the channel might be stopped, and it rained so hard that all our baggage is wet by the rain as well as the leakage of the canoes.

Thursday, July 3. Rained constantly until noon and for the remainder of the day at intervals. Mr. Stuart set off with six men and 11 pieces in one canoe to examine the River as far as the Little Lake. They returned late, after having encountered many obstacles, and broke a large hole in the canoe, which required a considerable time to repair. Our progress will be very slow now, as we will be continuously compelled to put the people of both canoes in one on account of the current and Rapids being too strong to be managed by four men, and none of them adroit. The navigation of the River is very dangerous on account of it being narrow, the current running so swift and many trees and *embaras* [*embarras*; obstructions] laid across.

Friday, July 4. We set off early, with both canoes, as they were but lightly loaded, and continued for about one and one half miles, where we got to the head of a long and strong Rapid, where we put some pieces on shore to be carried to the lower end, and the canoes were continued one after another by six men and one of ourselves, and though they were but lightly loaded it was with much difficulty they were run down, and through the awkwardness of the men mine was run against a large *embaras* in the middle of the River, which broke the bow and smashed all the pieces to the second bar. Fortunately there was not much water in the River and the channel was narrow. All hands jumped out and pulled the wreck on shore before it had time to fill and sink. We lost [the] most part of the day to mend it, and after all the entraves[39] being broken to pieces, and no wood to work at to make another, or a sufficient quantity of bark, it could not be put so well as it was before. This labor always falls to Mr. Stuart's lot, there being no other person that can do it.

While some of the people were employed about the canoe, I sent five men down with the other canoe and seven pieces to the Little Lake,[40] and they returned in the evening, and my canoe being mended, we went down with both and arrived after sun set. The Indians came down on foot through the woods and set their nets. We set one of ours also.

N.B. Yesterday the goods were aired a little but could not be dried properly on account of the rain that fell at intervals.

Saturday, July 5. The weather was cloudy both to day and yesterday. At an early hour this morning I started with six men and twelve pieces, but soon put five of them on shore and continued with the remainder for about 3 miles, and there left them and returned with the canoe. This distance is a continual rapid. We carried [the canoe] across an *Embaras* [obstruction] and cut several trees that were fallen across the River. During my absence Mr. Stuart got all the property properly dried, which it was much in need of, and he returned down with another half load and will return in the morning. Sent all the Indians down on foot in order to lighten our canoes.

There was no fish caught at this place excepting a few jut [that] the Indians caught in their nets and we saw no Beaver along the River. But a Carribue [caribou] crossed the Lake, which nevertheless escaped.

La Malice seems to be better than he was for some time past; likely he will be well when we get out of the River. He begins to find fault with the men and has strength to quarrel and beat his *lady*. I cannot comprehend his sickness; he has always had a good appetite and complains only of a severe pain in his bowels and *privates*.

Sunday, July 6. Cloudy weather with some rain. Mr. Stuart returned at 8 A.M. The water rises fast, for the pieces I left yes-

FIRST JOURNAL OF SIMON FRASER
FROM APRIL 12TH TO JULY 18TH 1806

terday near [at] hand were found by Mr. Stuart almost in the water, though they were upward of a foot and a half above the level when I left them on my return here, and the interval was not above 3 hours. We continued with both canoes until the place where the pieces were left yesterday, and from there Mr. Stuart continued with one canoe six men and twelve pieces for about a mile and a half, where they were obliged to unload and carry over a point of 200 yards. There they left their load and returned here. On their way down they had many trees and ambaras [obstructions] to cut and in performing that, one of the men dropped a large axe and was near drowning himself besides.

As soon as they returned we set off with both canoes, but mine broke against an embaras about 1/3 of a mile above the Portage, which obliged us to unload and take down the canoe light. This cause us a considerable delay, as all the Pieces were carried from this place to the Portage, where we formed our encampment for the night. The Indians are ahead. We did not see them since yesterday. Mr. Stuart and I went down the River for about a mile and a half to examine what difficulties we would have to encounter tomorrow. We had such bad walking that it was past eleven oclock when we came back to the tents.

Monday, July 7. Rained all day, notwithstanding which we started early with one canoe and a half load and went down for about two miles, where we unloaded, where [there was] an embaras in the middle of the River, and from thence returned to our encampment, and there went off with both canoes, but were obliged [to carry] the canoes and load over the embaras, which was a difficulty [difficult] job on account of its height, tho' not much more than 30 paces. From this we got down about a mile and a half in the usual way (of sending a canoe a head to examine, lightly loaded with six men and one of ourselves, and afterwards bringing down both together with the remainder of the loads), to a succession of falls and Rapids, where we were obliged to open a road wide enough to admit of the canoes and baggage being carried over a point of 800 yards, which was completed by the conclusion of the day, and the pieces carried better than half way. I went down a mile on foot and as far as I could see it was a succession of falls and rapids.

Gave all hands a dram to cheer up their spirits after their violent exertion during the whole day. All hands worked hard and Mr. Stuart and my share of the labor is the most difficult, as we not only work in the canoes [the] same as the others, but are obliged either one or the other to examine the River on foot before we risk the canoes, so that as soon as we arrive with the canoe at the place we return from on foot, we embark again to examine farther on.

Kenchuse arrived from the large River, where we left the other Indians making small canoes, to kill Beaver, of which he says there are many. He likewise says the distance from there to the large River is not great but bad walking.

Tuesday, July 8. Still raining all day, same as yesterday. At 11 o'clock Mr. Stuart went off with *Kenchuse* to determine the distance and the best road from here to the large River, and returned at sun set after having been at the said River [the McGregor River is meant] cold, wet and hungry, having walked [the] most part of the time in water up to the knees. He says the distance is not great, but that there is a steep hill to ascend, and that it would be difficult to carry over it, and more so to the remainder of the distance, sometimes in water up to the middle.

They did not see any vistages [vestiges] of the Knights [Sir Alexander Mackenzie's] road,[41] or see the hunters that are ahead. They seem to have gone down the River; and in tracing their Road Mr. Stuart and *Kenchuse* lost themselves, but in coming back they traced the River a long piece and [Mr. Stuart] is of opinion that the lower part will be less difficult than the past.

FIRST JOURNAL OF SIMON FRASER
FROM APRIL 12TH TO JULY 18TH 1806

Mr. Stuart has his hands much swollen, the effects of his violent exertions, and being generally wet since in this River, or else [of] his having passed amongst poisonous weeds.

At noon I began with two men to open the road about a mile farther down, and the other six men carried both canoes over the road that was opened last night, and ran them down one after another a long and dangerous Rapid with five pieces in each. This laborious task of carrying and running down the canoes, and opening the road. All hands began to carry, and took all the baggage to the end of the road by sunset excepting La Malice, who is yet at the other end of the Portage, but there are six men gone to stop there and will be here early tomorrow with him.

The people are more fatigued to day than any day yet on account of the Road being so bad, and the canoes have become so weighty that two men cannot carry them a hundred yards without being relieved. Gave all hands a dram, and I believe it is the first time that Mr. Stuart and myself could relish a glass of high wines.[42]

Wednesday, July 9. It was late before the canoes was brought over the Portage and the canoes gummed, after which we set off with one canoe six men and twelve pieces and continued for a mile and a quarter, where we were stopped by fallen trees and *embaras* [an obstruction], which rendered it necessary to unload and open a road to carry the canoes and baggage over a low point of 190 yards, after which we returned for the remainder of the baggage, and continued on in the same manner until night, alternately by land and water.

The canoes were broke and spoiled greatly this day. We met the Montagne de bouth coming before us from the large River, and [he] says that they have made pine canoes and have killed five Beaver. This place we suppose to be the low spot where Sir A.M.K. [Sir Alexander Mackenzie] carried across the neck of land to the Large River.[43] He was misinformed in saying it terminated in various branches. Mr. Stuart, who was down yesterday at the Large River [the McGregor River], traced this [i.e., the Bad] River for some time, and afterwards crossed it in many places, is of opinion that we will be able to get to its confluence with the canoes, and the Montagne de bouttes account of it agrees with his. Therefore we intend to continue by water as far as we can.

All the goods are entirely wet and the provisions are spoiling. When we arrived at this place the canoes were no more able to float, their bottoms being entirely hashed, and after getting bark and gathering some gum we patched them up for the present. The weather was cloudy all day and towards the evening it rained.

Thursday, July 10. Fine weather. After the canoes were gummed a little we continued on and had better going then we had reason to expect. The River (right branch) [the McGregor River] is narrow, but plenty of water to bear the canoes, and the current is not strong, which enabled us to continue on with both canoes with their full loads on. At 10 A.M. we arrived at the Large River [the Fraser], opposite an Island, without encountering any other difficulty than cutting several trees that laid across the channel, and we were most happy at having exempted [avoided] the long and bad carrying place and seeing ourselves once more on the banks of a fine and navigable River.

This [the Fraser] is a fine River and not unlike the Athabasca, but not so large, and the Indian we left at the height or point of land informed us that the upper end of it was the most ordinary residence of the Says — *Thau Dennehs* (Bawcanne Indians),[44] which corroberates with what the Carriers tell us of these Indians, they being enemies, when they go hunting in that quarter. I have seen one that was wounded last summer, and his brother was killed, which is likely the same that was mentioned by one of the Baucanne Indians last winter at Dunvegan as being killed there. All accounts agree that large animals, as well as those of the fur kind,

FIRST JOURNAL OF SIMON FRASER
FROM APRIL 12TH TO JULY 18TH 1806

are in great abundance, particularly towards the upper end. Could this be relied upon, and that the Baucanne Indians are really thereabouts, an establishment in my opinion would be well placed at the point of land. There is excellent fish in the three Lakes and in two of them salmon abounds in its season, and by all accounts animals are not far off. Indeed of this we had ocular demonstration ourselves, so that people would live well there, a no immaterial object [i.e., a not unimportant matter] in this quarter, and the Baucanne Indians would be much more easily got to come there than to any part of the Peace River, on account of their being afraid of the Beaver Indians; and the Big men [the McLeod Lake Indians], though they seldom meet, they live in amity.

Sir A.M.K. [Sir Alexander Mackenzie] seems to have examined the bad River [James Creek] with attention, for as far as he went down in Peace he describes it with great exactness. It is certainly well named and a most dangerous place, being much intersected with large stones, fallen trees and *embaras* [obstructions], and the current runs with such velocity, that a canoe though light cannot be stopped with poles, and it is with great difficulty it can be done by laying hold of the branches, and even that way we often drifted 100 and sometimes 300 yards from the time we began to hold the branches before we could bring to. Near its confluence it divides into three branches, all of which I suppose to be navigable, but the one to the right is the best route.[45]

We were anxiously looking for cedar and maple along the banks of the River but to no effect. I walked myself, except in very few places, from one end to the other, but saw no appearances of either, neither did any of the others. Hemlock and the Suven [?] tree we saw in great plenty, but of a lesser size than those of Trout Lake and the Lakes of the Heights of Land, which is about one third more large than he makes them. We saw Plum of small growth, and between that place and Trout [McLeod] Lake Elder of upwards of four feet in circumference.

La Montagne de boutte and Buelluraess waited for us at the entrance of the River, and we continued down to where Taba Tha was waiting for us, and there put ashore to dry the property and repair the many injuries the canoes had received coming down the bad River. Sent four men to procure gum and bark and the others were employed spreading out everything that was wet. Those who were [sent] for bark and gum soon returned with a sufficient quantity of both, and all hands set about mending and gumming the canoes. The hunters brought us five Beaver, which afforded all hands a hearty meal and La Malice, who was walking about, arrived too late to get the share he wished. We had given three to the men and the best part of another was cooking for ourselves, so their remained only one for him. He says he feels but little pain now, but that he is still weak.

Before the canoes were prepared and everything prepared it was past 5 P.M., but the current is so very swift that we ran 21 miles before night. Tabah Tha killed a Beaver and the others missed several shots on that sagacious animal, which is plentiful along this River, and it is not destitute of large animals, for we saw several Moose and Red Deer tracts [tracks] with that of the Cambaux [caribou] also.

Friday, July 11. Fine weather. We set off early and came on with great expedition, and before we entered the great Fork [where the Nechako River joins the Fraser] passed several Rapids, but the current is slack in many places. The banks of the [Fraser] River is well stocked with wood and we saw Hemlock and cedar of a large size, with some small plum.

At sunset we got to the [Nechako] River (This River is not mentioned by Sir A.M.K. [Sir Alexander Mackenzie] which surprises me not a little, it being full in sight and a fine large River and in the state we saw it equal in size to that of the Athabasca River and forms that Mr. McDougall in his journal of last spring calls the great Fork. It flows in from the right, and as far as I can

FIRST JOURNAL OF SIMON FRASER
FROM APRIL 12TH TO JULY 18TH 1806

judge about 10 or 12 miles above the first Portage. Sir A.M.K. appears to have been very inaccurate in the courses, or there must have been a vast difference in the compass he made use of and the one we had, which is old and perhaps not very good. As for the distance I say nothing; it is difficult to determine by sight, but the course of the River is different and ought to agree, at least the difference) that leads to the Carriers Lake [Stuart Lake], where Mr. McDougall was last spring, and then formed our encampment on a sandy bank and no wood, which with the rain that fell towards the night and continued until the morning rendered our situation not very pleasant. Mr. Stuart took the course of the river and minute remarks of everything.[45]

Saturday, July 12. Rained at intervals. Set off early [up the Nechako River], but the current is so strong and the canoes so leaky that we cannot advance much. In the forenoon, having seen old tracts [tracks] of Red Deer, and as the Indians by walking (for they left their canoes this morning) will be able to gain much time on the canoes, [we] put them on shore in order to hunt. They only crossed a couple of points when they came to us and said that they had seen no fresh tracts [tracks].

In the afternoon we gummed the canoes and lost nearly two hours performing that, and mending a hole that broke in the bottom of my canoe. Indeed, my foreman is so awkward that the canoe is almost continually aground or runs against stumps. Here the Indians went off with their women and children, being in hopes of finding natives along the River near [at] hand. We continued on until after sun set and encamped on the left shore opposite a high bank of clay. After unloading the canoes [I] sent four men with one of them to cross the Indians, who had embarked on the right shore. Yesterday we finished the remainder of our Pemican and today broke open the Pounded meat, which we ate without greese. Our progress is very slow, having made only 9 miles today. The River is entirely overflown, no use can be made of the poles, and the current is too strong to be steered by the paddles, and we make more use of the branches [of trees and bushes along the banks] than of both.

Sunday, July 13. Rained at intervals, and at half-past four we were upon the water, and soon passed several temperary posts erected for the summer. Yesterday we passed some likewise, and our guide *Kenchuse* is in momentary expectiations of seeing some of his countrymen. About noon we went a little out of our way in a small in hopes of seeing strangers, but there was not even any fresh vestiges [vestiges], but we saw ought not to be great.

The banks of the River is beautiful, in many places resembling that of the River Lac la Plui [Pluie; the Rainy River is meant], and the *Liard* [poplar] is the most stupendous I ever saw, as for any other wood or anything else remarkable we saw none that is not already mentioned. The narrow Gut where [there are] Rocks, [which] Sir A.M.K. [Sir Alexander Mackenzie] compares to a stupendous pile of gothic churches, we examined with attention, but according to our ideas find no resemblance.[47] They are steep rocks, and in some places almost perpendicular, of a course [coarse] and apparently hard kind of stone. We entered the River by which the Indian, whom we saw at the Height of Lands, informed us there was a more short and safer passage into the Columbia [i.e., the Fraser] at its confluence. It is about eighty or ninety yards wide, and by what we can judge, from the short distance we went up, [is] a fine navigable River with a moderate current, which I may say is the only one of that description I have seen in this quarter, for all the Rivers in the vicinity of the Mountains run with great velocity. This River likewise flows in from the right.[48]

Two old Pine canoes, which seem to have been left there in the spring. Here all the Indians (Barbuellen excepted, who was kept to paddle) debarked to go to another Lake in search of Indians, and we continued our route for about two miles, when

FIRST JOURNAL OF SIMON FRASER
FROM APRIL 12TH TO JULY 18TH 1806

we put ashore to gather gum at a place that seemed to be much frequented by the natives.

About 4 P.M., as we were advancing inside of an Island, we saw two [bear] cubs in a tree and immediately pulled ashore to fire upon them, but before we could get to them they were off, and La Garde and Barbuellen, who were the first on shore, pursued them. The latter soon met the mother and fired upon her to no effect, and she pursued him in her turn, but he being near the water he jumped in, and she after him, but soon left him, and as La Garde was advancing another Bear suddenly rushed upon him and tore him in a shocking manner. Had not the dogs passed there at that critical moment, he would have been torn to pieces. The Bear left him to defend herself against the dogs, and during the interval he ran off and jumped into the River, and from thence it was with much difficulty he could walk to the canoe. He received nine or ten bad wounds and we encamped early to dress them. We are really unfortunate in regard to the men. One of the canoes will be now obliged to continue with three, and no great help can be expected. The Indians (except the Montagne de boutte who returned to encamp with us, on account of his having his son on board the canoe) are ahead.

Monday, July 14. It was rather late before we set off, on account of our having La Garde['s] wounds to dress before our departure. At 9 A.M. we came to an Indian house that was situated on the end of an Island, and opposite on the right shore there were two tombs neatly erected. There we breakfasted, and from thence soon got to a long Rapid, where we were obliged to unload and carry one half of the loads, and put the people of both canoes upon [in one?], to take them up one after another, which nearly occupied the remainder of the day; and by the time that the canoes were gummed and ready to be off, the sun was near set. However, we set off and encamped about two miles above the Rapid.

As Tabah Tha and his wife were walking along the banks of the River, they surprissed a large grizzly bear and her two cubs. The Indian fired upon the mother and wounded her, in revenge of which she jumped upon his wife, and she instantly laid down flat upon the ground and did not stir, in consequence of [which] the bear deserted [her] and ran after her husband, who likewise fortunately escaped unhurt and killed one of the young, which he brought to the canoe. He was immediately sent back with other Indians in search of the one he wounded, which they found and killed with seven shots, and brought the meat to the canoe, which made all hands a couple of good meals.

Tuesday, July 15. Several showers of rain fell in the course of the day. At an early hour that morning we pushed off against a strong current. In the forenoon, going up a long steep bank, my foreman negligently pushed out the bow of the canoe, which made it wheel round and broke the bow against the other canoe that was inside, which caused a delay of three hours to mend, and for want of having the necessary materials it was but imperfectly done after all. *Kanchuse* and Tabah Tha, who walked on shore, saw some fresh vestiges of Indians, and the former saw a dog crossing the River. We encamped a little before sun set upon the right shore. The canoes are becoming so leaky that a man is almost constantly employed to keep [them] clear of water. Distance about 12 miles.

Wednesday, July 16. We set off early, but the canoes took as much water as ever, though they were gummed last night, which obliged us to put ashore at 11 A.M., to perform the same operation and mend the bow of the one that was broke yesterday. In the meantime everything that was wet was spread out to dry, and before everything was dry and the canoes ready to be off it was 5 P.M., at which time we pushed off and continued on for 3 miles without much current, when we got to the foot of a strong Rapid of two miles long, and which we ascended by pulling the branches, and were obliged to cut several trees that laid across the

FIRST JOURNAL OF SIMON FRASER
FROM APRIL 12TH TO JULY 18TH 1806

way. It was past 9 A.M. [P.M.] when we got to the upper end, where the Indians had arrived, and had kindled a fire both for themselves and us. As the people were taken [taking] one of the canoes of the water, the stern got into the current and filled instantly with water, and it was very near breaking before it could be emptied and taken up the hill, which was high and steep.

Thursday, July 17. Having arrived last night too late to gum the canoes we were under the necessity of performing that operation this morning before we set off, and it was 7 A.M. before we took our departure; and we did not advance above two miles when we got to the foot of a cascade and a long Rapid where our guide *Kenchuse*, a dammed blockhead that never passed [through this country] before I believe, informed us that it was fine going on the left shore. Accordingly we traversed, and went up but a very short distance when we were obliged to stop and mend the bow of my canoe, which got such a thump upon a tree that shattered it so much that it could continue no longer upon the water in the state it was in.

Here we dried [the baggage] again, and though all hands were bussy we lost seven hours on shore, after which we continued on, and by the assistance of the line and pulling by the branches went up several strong and dangerous points for the distance of better than a mile to a strong Point under a perpendicular rock where we were at a stand [still], and no possibility of ascending it, there being no bottom for the poles and no possibility of employing the line, and there were no branches to pull by, neither could a Portage be made on account of the perpendicular rocks, and to attempt crossing to the other side would be little short of madness, for the canoes would have been smashed to pieces against the large cascades and stones that were in the way. In this critical situation we had no other resource than to return down by the way we came, which was soon effected by drifting down along shore and laying hold of the branches to prevent it going too fast, and we crossed

245

over to the right shore at the same place we left in the morning, where we unloaded and carried the canoes and baggage up a very steep bank, which was with difficulty effected, and then we worked a while making a road.

Friday, July 18. Early in the morning the men cut a road of 300 yards in length, wide enough to carry the canoes, which they brought with all the baggage to the upper end. From thence they set off with only one canoe, on account of the current being strong and several Rapids to pass, which they could not ascend with less than six men, and continued for a mile and a half. In the above distance they carried the canoe and loading over a point about twice the length of the canoe, and from the upper end of the Rapid returned for the other canoe, which was effected at 1 P.M., from thence we continued up a strong and constant current, where we made a small Portage, and soon got to a high point of perpendicular rock, where we had much trouble to pass and fix [a] line. Here all hands, excepting one man that was taken [taking] care of the other [canoe], was put to one canoe, but as they were hauling it up the last cascade it wheeled round, and the foreman was obliged to cut the line, and they went down to the foot of the Rapid before they could bring to. As this happened through the awkwardness of the people, [I] made them unload everything and bring it up a very steep hill, rather than risk everything in the canoe.

We encamped upon a beautiful hill. The canoes were left on the water all tied, it being too late to take them up the Rapid, and impossible to take them up the hill on account of the steepness. The Indians are ahead, but about sun set the Montagne de boutte came before us to get provisions for himself and family. Instead of feeding us, we have been obliged to provide for them, and as yet they have been of no manner of use to us, and I am almost sorry for taking them.

LETTERS FROM NEW CALEDONIA[1]
AUGUST 1806–FEBRUARY 1807

1. Fraser to the Gentlemen Proprietors of the North West Company

[Stuart Lake, August 1806.]

Gentlemen,

Being this far advanced on my voyage I think it my duty to inform you about my situation and progress before I go further off. Being scarce of paper to write to you separately is the cause of my doing it conjunctly. Otherwise it would be my greatest pleasure writing to my friends, Separately from these Regions, as no other opportunity will offer until late in the winter. Therefore knowing it to be a satisfaction to you Gentlemen to hear where we are and what we are doing I take this opportunity of addressing you these few lines. But as the circumstances of the voyage, with a detail of the misery and vexation I have had, would be no wise agreeable or amusing to you, I will pass it over in silence, and observe only that all the Rivers and waters were very high wherever we passed, and the distance much greater than I expected by Mr. Stuarts computation. There are upwards of six hundred miles between this place and Rocky Mountain Portage by water, but comparatively short across land. The navigation is very bad and dangerous, extraordinary so when the water is high as it was when we passed.

When we arrived at Trout Lake [Fort McLeod] our canoes were so shattered and spoiled that it was not possible to proceed any further with them, which obliged us to make new canoes there. But this apparent misfortune at the time has since proved a fortunate circumstance for we lived upon fish without touching our dried provisions all the time we were there, and had we arrived here any time sooner we would have certainly starved, and even at this late period the water is so high in the Lake that there are no fish caught, and it is with difficulty that we procure dried small fish from the Natives which they take in small Lakes and Rivers, where we would starve on account of our nets being too large.

During our stay at Trout Lake a few Carriers arrived from this place, whose accounts agreed with Mr. McDougal's and enticed us to come here as the most proper place for forming establishments though much more time [is] required to come to it than to go down to the West Road River.[2]

Before our arrival at the height of land, we found a small band of Indians that had never seen white people before, they seemed quite peaceable and industrious. They informed us of another Road that lead[s] into the Columbia [i.e., the Fraser], which is much shorter and more safe than the one we came by. It falls in a little below the Knights [Sir Alexander Mackenzie's] first encampment on the Columbia [Fraser]. It is a fine navigable River, with no great current and report says that there is only a carrying place of about a couple of miles at most, from the other Lakes beyond [i.e., upstream from] Trout [McLeod] Lake to fall into it,[3] and Mr. McDougall has now directions to ascertain the truth of it, which if exact, will not only shorten the passage, but render it perfectly safe, as it will be the means of avoiding the Bad River.

We left the Columbia [the Fraser] on the 11th ulto. and entered this river [the Nechako] which at its confluence is half as large as the former, with a strong steady current and many Rapids and several carrying places. It seems to be well inhabited [we] having seen several houses on its Banks. But it not being the salmon time, we saw none of the Natives until the Forks [of the Nechako and the Stuart rivers], better than half way up, where we saw about 30 men, who had Beaver Cat and Badger

LETTERS FROM NEW CALEDONIA
AUGUST 1806–FEBRUARY 1807

Robes for coverings — and a couple had blankets of Cloth. We left the left Forks [the upper Nechako River] which is the passage to another considerable Lake called the Natley [Fraser Lake], and entered the one to the Right [the Stuart River], and around [arrived] at this place [Stuart Lake] the 26th. It is a fine large Lake, But since we arrived here, my ideas are far short of what Mr. McDougalls account of it would lead [me] to expect. In the Spring of the year when he was here, everything had a flourishing appearance — there were plenty of fish and fowl, and some meat and they told him that Beaver were plenty likewise. Since our arrival here we have seen upwards of 50 men — all in a starving state. Notwithstanding [this] they afirm Beaver to be plentiful at some distance from the Lake, But there are none as far as I can learn near the Borders.

They say that there are large sturgion in the Lake, But that they are not possessed of the means of catching them. We caught a small one in one of our nets which convinces me of their being large ones. The Indians also state that there are plenty white fish unconu [inconnu] some trout carp Jub, &c., in the fall of the year. Of all this we saw but very few as yet. The character that I can give of them is that they [the Indians] are a large Indolent thievish set of vagabonds, of a mild disposition. They are amazing fond of goods which circumstances might lead [one] to immagine that they would work well to get what they seem to be so fond of. But then they are independent of us, as they get their necessaries from their neighbors who trade with the Natives of the sea coast.

We are now busy building [the post later named Fort St. James], and as soon as the salmon comes up and we can collect a few, which I suppose will be between the 20th and 25th of this month, I propose to continue my route down to the Borders of the Atnah tribes Lands accompanied by Mr. Stuart in one canoe, [with] six men, and if we can find a place to winter there abouts

I will remain and Mr. Stuart [will] come back and one of us go and establish a Post at the other Lake [Fraser Lake] which [is] opposite to this to the westward.⁴

La Malice is the Bearer of this who I send down to meet the canoes which probably will be at Fort Chepewean [Chipewyan], in order to conduct them up to Trout Lake [Fort McLeod], and from thence we will be able to get the goods taken across land to this place in the course of the Fall and Winter. The distance is too great by the route we came to attempt bringing canoes in that way this Fall.

This [thus?] have I informed you Gentlemen of our occurrences since [leaving] the [Rocky Mountain] Portage with the plan and intentions for the ensuing part of the summer. Whether they meet with your approbation or not I cannot say, but this I know that no possible exertions of ours have been wanting. We have established the Post beyond the mountains and will establish another in the most convenient place we can find before the Fall, where people can live, and this I believe was all that were expected this summer.

To form establishments this summer certainly depends upon us — but to render them productive, will depend upon the attention you Gentlemen will pay them. We had but few trading goods on leaving the [Rocky Mountain] Portage, and tho few of you can immagine what it costs to feed the people in this quarter, there are none of you but know that exploring new countries and seeing strange Indians is expensive, was it only to procure a welcome reception. As we are at present we have scarcely a sufficient aportionment of goods to feed all hands during the winter. This you will naturally immagine to be poor encouragement for you to send goods. But this I must inform you that if no goods comes this fall to Trout Lake [Fort McLeod] it will be the retardment of another year for both establishing further on and making any [prof-

LETTERS FROM NEW CALEDONIA
AUGUST 1806–FEBRUARY 1807

its] at this place. The order that I sent to Mr. A.N. McL. [Archibald Norman McLeod] last spring would be required to prove any wise beneficial.

I cannot form any ideas of what returns will be made in this quarter for this year [but] I immagine that they will be no wise considerable. But notwithstanding I think they will be worth the pursuit, as the Indians are numerous and the country not destitute of beaver. A little from each would make considerable returns. Provisions are another object of consideration, for want of which the people will always be ill of [off], for sending out the returns, and I see no means of procuring any, excepting dried salmon which is but poor stuff, and it is a doubt to me if a sufficiency of that same can be procured. But many difficulties occur in forming new establishments that can be easily avoided afterwards. I need not inform you Gentlemen that if it is your intention to establish further on, or keep up what is already established, that proper people will be required for that purpose. Being appointed myself by the concern I cannot insist on leaving next summer, though I would wish to go down to Canada, But Mr. Stuart consented only to come for one year and even supposing we both of us [remain] which is not probable — to keep up two Posts and explore further on, more clerks will be required. But I am fully persuaded that you have considered all this yourselves, and will provide accordingly therefore I beg leave to remain

Gentlemen with respect
and esteem your very
Obt. Humble Servant

SIMON FRASER

2. Fraser to James McDougall

Sturgion Lake [Stuart Lake]
6th August 1806.

[Dear McDougall]

No doubt you expected to hear from us long ago. But we took more time to perform the voyage than we expected, the distance is great, and the road is difficult. Our progress was much retarded on account of having some of the people continually disabled or sick, so that we only arrived here the 26th Ultimo.

We found old Barbue the 6th day after our departure from your Post [Fort McLeod] at the same place where Mr. Finlay returned from in 1797, with four strange Indians that he went for to the Height of Land to await our arrival on purpose, that we might see them *en passant*. As he had instructions for this before he left the Fort, he was very proud of his behavior which indeed might have been better, had he made some provisions. One of the strangers an elderly man informed us of there being another passage much shorter and safer that leads into the Columbia [i.e., the Fraser], by the way of Trout [McLeod] Lake and Lac des mont [Summit Lake]. He said that there is only one Portage of about a mile or two to pass to get [to] a small river that empties into the Columbia [Fraser] a little below the Knights [Sir Alexander Mackenzie's] first encampment in that River. I hope you will be able to ascertain the truth of this and send Bazil with an Indian to visit the River and Portage, to know whether it is practicable or not.

Should the navigation be anywise good, the canoe or canoes will come in that way this fall. I will depend for your sending them [to explore] before the canoes arrives [from Fort Chipewyan]. If they cannot pass that way, you will send the people off across land immediately upon their arrival with as [much as] they can carry of the most necessary articles for the trade. To

LETTERS FROM NEW CALEDONIA
AUGUST 1806–FEBRUARY 1807

carry this in[to]execution you will require to provide provisions. The big men [the Trout Lake Indians] I should immagine are off to kill animals and when the Trout begins to be plenty you can [have] a quantity of it dried. Lamalice [will be] the bearer of this. I send him down to meet the canoes and to bring them up. Detain him as little as possible.

At the Fork of this River [the junction of the Stuart with the Nechako River] having put the little heads brother-in-law and Montaigne de Boute ashore to walk (on account of there being Rapids to go up) in order to lighten the canoes they disappeared and we [have] heard nothing of them since. This was on the 22nd of last month, and I suppose you saw them ere now, indeed they were of no service to us in the voyage, but they would have been of use here to kill Beaver &c. In [the] coarse of the voyage they got a good deal of goods from us in expectation that they would behave well — an account of which you will receive with this, and they must pay every article of it on account of their bad behaviour, and get nothing else until all their debts are paid or else to strip them of everything they have.

Please send back news immediately by the Big Carrier and if you could send a hunter with him he would be very acceptable. Mr. Stuart and I will be off about the 25th of this month to go down to the Atnah nation. We are in a starving state at present so that we cannot think of going any further until we collect a few salmon for our voyage which we expect daily. I beg leave to refer you to Lamalice for the news of this place. He has always been sick since I left you and of no manner of service to us but a great burden.

We have at present only a little better than a pack of furs and expectations we have none, which I hope is not the case with you. Having nothing more to say at present I remain D[ea]r. McD[ougall], your friend and well wisher

S. Fraser.

3. *Fraser to the Gentlemen Clerks of Peace River*

[Stuart Lake]
Early in August 1806.

Gentlemen Clerks of the Peace River.

As we are now forming a station across the mountain it is with pleasure I address you this short epistle before we go further off down the Columbia [i.e., the Fraser]. We are here upon the Borders of a spacious large Lake on the Carriers Lands Building [a trading post]. We arrived here only the 26th ulto. and we propose to continue our route as soon as we can collect a few provisions. But then we have nothing to expect but dry salmon which is bad stuff; there are no large animals except Carruban [caribou] which is too sly for us. Tho there are plenty of fish in the Lake at certain seasons of the year there are none caught at present on account of the water being too high, so it is with difficulty that we procure dry carp and Roes, which the Indians catch in small Lakes. But now berries begin to be ripe and the salmon is daily expected so we will soon be better off.

The Natives are numerous. We saw upwards of 30 men already and by all accounts we will see great numbers of them before long as they all flock upon the Banks of the River in the salmon time, of which they lay up great store for the winter, it being their principle food.

Lamalice is the bearer of this who is sent down to return with any canoes that will be for this quarter. I expect he will get to Athabasca about the same time with the canoes from Lac la Pluie. If not and should he meet canoes coming up for the Trout [McLeod] Lake or this place, he will return from where he will meet them, in order to conduct them to this country. In that case please Gentlemen to give the canoes a sufficiency of provisions, and any other needed assistance they may require. I hope

LETTERS FROM NEW CALEDONIA
AUGUST 1806–FEBRUARY 1807

you will not detain this man any where along the road which will much oblige your friend and very humble servant

Simon Fraser

4. Fraser to James McDougall

Naugh-al-chun [Stuart Lake]
31st August 1806.

Dear McDougall

I received your letter of the 11th of August on the 14th inst. by Kunsusse[5]— and return you the following answer, which no doubt will surprise you that I write to you at this late period from this place. But I have the mortification to inform you that we are yet in the same situation in regard to provisions as we were when you heard from me last. We have subsisted chiefly upon berries since that time. Tho we have always had seven nets in the water and properly attended, they produced nothing excepting a few carp and unconnu [inconnu], and of that same but seldom. Cowa ['Kwah, a noted Indian warrior and chief] gave us about a dozen Beaver and a few Rabids [rabbits] and having been in daily expectation of the salmons arriving, naturally led us to expect to be able to procure a sufficiency of that fish for our voyage. But now the season is so advanced and no salmon arrived that I dont expect any this year, and the Indians say it does not come up every year.

At all events I have come to the determination to be off from this place, the day after tomorrow, in order to establish another Post. God knows where. Mr. Stuart left his place the 28th with a man and Wacca [Waccan; nickname of Jean Baptiste Boucher, a half-breed] to go to Nat-leh [Fraser Lake] (the Lake on the other side of the mountains in a western [actually in a southern] direction from this), and he goes down that way and

[is] to meet me at the Fork of the River [the junction of the Stuart and Nechako rivers] from thence he will come up to this place and I am to continue further on. Until Mr. Stuarts arrival which will be in about 5 days after my departure, Blais and another man remains in charge of this post.

I am glad to hear of your being in good health, and being so well off in provisions and your being in hopes to lay up a good stock for the winter. As you are in such a fair way of making plenty of provisions, I have not the least doubt but what you will be able to furnish the people that will come to this place with a sufficiency for the voyage.

I am happy you are pleased with Maria des dent de Biche,[6] as hunter. It seems I am [i.e., I made] a good choice when I employed him to serve you as such, indeed had not his wife been sick I would have asked him to accompany me to this place and left the little heads brother-in-law who seems so fond of you. But as charity ought to begin at home, it is very just that I should be without a hunter. You say that our hunters made their appearance on the 3rd inst. and as they told you that they gave us the slip, that you turned them out of your house and sent them a hunting, without give [giving] them anything. Indeed they could not be much in want of anything, otherwise I should immagine that you would have given them something, on account of their being particular favorites.

The reason they gave for deserting seems to be all very plausible to you, but it is far from appearing in that light to me; you say you cannot think what enticed me to load them with such debts and throw away goods to no purpose in such a short time. To satify your curiosity in this you have only to look back at the enormous debt you gave out to the meadow and Indians and Big men without any prospect of their paying the fourth part of them. Pray why should you find it hard not to give those two Indians anything? And punish them as they deserve, in order to prevent them from misbehaving another time. Whatever goods that I squandered with them, would have been well bestowed had they not deserted and only hunted Beaver for us. But had their presence been of essential service to us in getting a footing in this country we certainly would have been more upon our guard.

What a childish excuse to say that you could not get Canoe Bark Risen on account of it being passed the time when Bazil was able to go. I am sure you know that Bark can be risen at all times, especially in the months of May, June, July and August.

As La malice say[s] that there are no communications by water and that the road is bad even by land the way he passed to go to your Fort, by which account I should immagine that the goods could not be got across until the 1st Ice. But at all events it must be tried, and if possible I expect La malice will come in with one Canoe (if he has provisions for 14 days) by the middle road [the Summit Lake route] which I hope you will ascertain the truth of the Indian report above.

Inclosed is a list of the goods I expect from L.L.P. [Lac la Pluie]. The contents of the second column is what you are to keep at Trout Lake [Fort McLeod], if the order is complete. If not you will keep only in proportion to that you will send here. Please make my compliments to Lamalice, Bazil, &c. Should not Lamalice be able to come in by the middle road you cannot be at a loss for getting a guide to come by land. I will expect to hear from you about the latter end of next month, therefore I conclude

My D[ea]r James
Yours as usual
S. Fraser.

SIMON FRASER

5. Fraser to John Stuart

Naukazeleh [Stuart Lake]
29th September 1806.

My Dear Stuart

I received you[r] kind favour the 21st late at night. As Attouyey was anxious to be off, I did not wish to force his inclination. I wrote to you by him but the letter was brought back to me with yours, his reason for returning was to wait a few days until the snow should melt in the mountains. But in spite of me he went off the 25th unknown to me. Soon after your departure from here I gave [him] a corduroy Jacket and some other trifles which he immediately lost at play.

The 26th L'homme de la Fourche who was kept prisoner at the village since the middle of the summer was allowed to depart by leaving his wife here, so I am now entirely deprived of the means of understanding the Indians. As yet they are all very quiet and noways troublesome. I am sorry to hear of the Indians of your place having been so troublesome and rogish [roguish] in our absence. They imposed greatly on the men to be sure. I certainly approve of the method you took to punish them and to restore the articles they had stolen. They are a thievish forward inconsiderate set of bagabonds [vagabonds], of course they require to be kept at a proper distance.

It seems to me that Blais is becoming useless and is not deserving of the least indulgence. What plausible reason can he give for not arranging the hangard [probably *hangar* is meant; i.e., the shed] before you got there, and not having attended the nets properly. The nets had maitres enough and no stones nor floats were tied with maitres when I came away. Any articles that were wanting of the goods when you got there, you have only to send me an account of it and probably I may account for it. I left a pint of shot good measure. I

LETTERS FROM NEW CALEDONIA
AUGUST 1806–FEBRUARY 1807

have been informed that the Indians have your axe, and that they intend to return it.

I have not been more fortunate than yourself in the nets, the long one is rotten and the small one not much better. They produced about the same number of fish with yours until the 20th. Since then they took from 15 to 40 pieces. Soon after your departure there was a sturgeon caught in them which was pretty big the head weighed 50 odd pounds and the body was amazing large, but now we are obliged to give up setting the nets as the salmon breaks them into pieces. It was the constant employ of one man to keep them in order.

It is only since the 20th that the Indians began to gather fish. Until then they only took for daily consumption, but now they have thousands of them drying. I have not as yet traded many but I must soon begin and the few goods I have will all go. I am at a loss how to pay them. The Indians dont seem to value goods much, they are not half so fond of goods as those of Naucauseleh — and what is worse I am afraid that they will not make any furs.

Mr. McDougall's letter surprised me not a little, after he having been in such high spirits and having such expectations for making provisions, now asking for 5 or 6 measure of powder to receive the canoes. He says he lives well and that his hunter behaves well. Of course alls well; as he thinks only for the moment. I allow that his situation is highly disagreeable, on account of Bazil being sick.

We may say that we have been unfortunate all along, Since the Spring, our people being sick. Ever since the 13th St. Pierre has been sick and now he only just begins to walk about. Saucer [Saucier] was a long time unwell, La lands [La Londe] is sick since the 24th, therefore you see that the work could not advance much. The hangard [shed] is not yet finished, the wood is scarce and far off, and almost all tremble [aspen or poplar]. It will be late before I can get a house made as the most of the men must be employed about curing fish. I am loth at present to part with any of the men but if you have sent him [McDougall] a man you have only to send back the new [news] immediately with the Indian that speaks Br [better?] indian and I will immediately send you another to replace him. Should you be in want of powder I will send you some. There are no Indians here that knows how to fire off a gun, and but very few Gibin[?].

I assure you I am tired of living on fish and I feel quite dull and lonesome since you left me. Nothing goes on to my likeing. I hate the place and the Indians. I will expect to hear from you again before you go to Trout [McLeod] Lake. The greatest curiosity I saw on my voyage to the other end of the Lake [Stuart Lake] was spoons and a metal pots, there are difference[s] between them and those of this place. I beg of you to get the little heads brother-in-law sent to me. Should it be possible to undertake coming in by the new road, send some body with the news that fish may be sent before them. All the muskets that the Indians of your place have, they got by way of the Trembler, which I imagine to be by Cooks River. I am Dear friend

Yours sincerely
S. Fraser

The Indians have given us several confused accounts of your being in a starving state. Should you not be able to procure nets for Mr. McDougall I will send him over a couple.

6. Fraser to James McDougall

Natleh [Fraser Lake]
30th September 1806.

Dear McDougall

I received your favour on the 22nd and was sorry to hear of Bazil's being so sick and your situation so disagreeable. Nothing

LETTERS FROM NEW CALEDONIA
AUGUST 1806–FEBRUARY 1807

very particular occurred to me since I wrote you last. After my departure from Naukazeleh [Stuart Lake] I met Mr. Stuart according to appointment at the Fork [of the Stuart and Nechako rivers] and as we were still in a starving condition at that time and the Indians [had] only just begun to spear a few salmon, it was not in my power to continue downwards therefore there was no alternate but to come up to this place, where we were well received as they gave us plenty of dried salmon and encouragement that they would make plenty furs when the salmon time would be over, so [I] took up my station here, and Mr. Stuart returned to Nakazleh [Stuart lake], with one man, and I have five here. St. Pierre has been sick ever since the 13th, and La londe has been [ill] since the 24th, indeed every one of them has been more or less so. I have not been able to get a house made as yet the people are employed arranging fish and making a hangard [hangar; a shed] so my Dear Sir it is not possible for me to spare a man at present. Indeed the people from Lac la Pluie will be nearly as soon there now as [a] man could be sent from here, and you will see Mr. Stuart over about the 15th of next month. He wrote me that he sent you over some powder, and no doubt he can procure you a few nets.

I have nothing particular to tell you. Mr. Stuart will give you all the news. I hope you will stretch all your invention to furnish the people with provisions when they arrive and forward the goods to this place &c. Settle the Indians in the manner you think they will work best, and try and send me the little heads brother-in-law. He will serve in the double capacity of hunter and interpreter. Will you be able to send me over some green skins for windows and Babich [babiches; i.e., leather straps or thongs] and plenty pack cords, dressed skins and c. [&c.]. The Indians of this place are naturally lazy. I am at my wits end to fall upon a proper method to make them work. I think yours are of a different desposition and that they will work well.

S. Fraser.

7. Fraser to the Gentlemen Proprietors of the North West Company

Nakazeleh [Stuart Lake]
21st December 1806

Gentlemen

As we are obliged to send two men to Mr. McDougall's at Trout Lake [Fort McLeod], with a little powder to enable him to live, it gives me an opportunity of addressing you these few lines merely to inform you of our situation.

Tho I have nothing pleasing to communicate, it cannot displease you to hear of our being still safe, notwithstanding our not receiving any news or assistance from your quarter. I wrote you pretty fully last August about our plans and intentions. I was then in expectation of going further down the River Columbia [i.e., the Fraser], and nothing but the entire want of provisions prevented my attempting it. I remained here until the beginning of September awaiting the arrival of the salmon, but as none arrived I sent Mr. Stuart with two men across land to the Lake called Natleh [Fraser Lake] to see what kind of a place it was and I started myself on the 3rd September to meet him at the Fork of this River [the Stuart] where we joined and as the accounts Mr. Stuart gave me were as favourable as could be expected I determined to go there and build. Indeed there was no alternative left, as it would have been little short of madness to attempt going down the Columbia [the Fraser] in a starving state without an ounce of any kind of provisions.

S. Fraser.

LETTERS FROM NEW CALEDONIA
AUGUST 1806–FEBRUARY 1807

8. Fraser to James McDougall

[Stuart Lake
December, 1806]

[My Dear McDougall]

I received yours of 30 of October on the 12th Inst. at Natleh [Fraser Lake] and I arrived here on the 18th. Had it not been for the disappointment of the conveyance of letters on account of the quantity of snow in the mountains you would have received the news from us long before now.

I certainly was highly disappointed and vexed that no canoes arrived to this quarter which is a considerable loss to the Company, and a severe blow to our discoveries. This is the first opportunity I [have] had of sending you a man and Powder but with this you will receive St. Pierre and 3 quarts of good Powder.

I think that it would be a very good Plan to go inland to make the Indians work but then you cannot leave the house without some person to take care of it on account of the Property. In regard to the Indians settle with them according to your own best Judgment. I have not the least doubt but what you will exert yourself to make them work beaver until the beging [beginning] of February and after that to employ the best hunters to make provisions. I am thoroughly convinced that your returns will fall far short of your expectations but that is a misfortune that cannot be helped, but then I entreat you to be particular in making the Indians dress the furs properly.

The little heads br[other]. in Law arrived at Natleh [Fraser Lake] on the 12th Conducted by two men. I dont know as yet whether he will be of any service or not. The Montaigne de Butte behaves well with Mr. Stuart. Two men that Mr. S[tuart]. sent to Forests[?] for fish brought the news that three of the Big men [Trout Lake Indians] were arrived there. Send back Gervais immediately with the news as we intend to send the news after his return to the Peace River. Should an opportunity offer forward the General letter to the P[eace]. River. Kunchusse promises to be back in 6 nights. Should you see any Possibility of getting any goods brought up in [the] Coarse of the Summer, please write accordingly.

Having nothing more to say upon this subject I must here wish you Joy as I understand that you have entered upon the Matrimonial State. I am Glad to hear that the Children are well taken care of. I assure you that I am nowise concerned about them as they are under your Protection. The only thing I fear is that you are starving, but I hope it is the Contrary with you, so I conclude my D[ea]r. James, yours sincerely

Simon Fraser.

9. Fraser to James McDougall

Natleh [Fraser Lake]
31st January 1807.

My Dear McDougall

Yours I received this afternoon p[e]r the two men from your quarter, whom to be sure took much time, this being their fith [fifth] day from Nakazleh [Stuart Lake] indeed they were not in a hurry as they had plenty provisions. One half of 22 Salmon ought to have been enough for them as the voyage can easily be performed in 2 days 3 at the most allowing the road to be bad.

Regarding what you say about the woman that Bugni has, I am noways apprehensive that the Company can put their resolve[7] in execution. But then it was wrong of you to have given him leave to take her, you Knew full well that she was taken from St. Pierre last spring, merely to give up the Custom of taking any more women from the Indians, and that he was promised that no other Frenchman would get her. Your Commerce between Blais

LETTERS FROM NEW CALEDONIA
AUGUST 1806–FEBRUARY 1807

& Lamalice last spring ought to have been a sufficient warning, not to meddle yourself any more about women.

Your conduct at T[rout] Lake [Fort McLeod] is highly blamable and your character as a Trader much blasted which you can only recover, but by your future assiduity and attention to your business, which I would be most happy at & will befriend you as much as lays in my Power. I am pleased you own your fault and seem sorry for it, & promise to do better for the future. The Company probably will blame us both as they will be highly Disappointed in their expectations regarding this Country. We are highly unfortunate every thing has been against us since Last Spring, & nothing was of so much detrement as the Canoes arriving so very late in the fall.

We had such a severe speal [spell] of bad weather it is to say [i.e., that is to say] it was so very cold for several days after my arrival here that I could not make the Indians of your place set off to return until the 25th when the first band went away & Q'ua ['Kwah] & Le Gourmand, having been upon a visit to Steela [or *Stillá*; an Indian village about 15 miles from the post on Stuart Lake] the Latter did not come back untill of late, but both of them sate [set] off yesterday straight across by the winter Road. They said they would have gone round by the way of *Scycuss* [or *Sycus*; an Indian village on the Stuart River] but that they were too ill Cloathed & would Starve before they could get to where there are beaver, but they promised me that they will work well untill the Spring, but I put no faith in what they say.

Those big men [Trout Lake Indians] must be severely treated to break them of the Custom of coming to the Carriers. The Poudres band has behaved & worked pretty well. I heard that there were two Indians who never saw the Fort in that band. Mr. Stuart apprehends that Barbue and many others will not go to the Fort untill [they can go] *en canoe*. Maitres will answer as well as a codline for a cordeau & Mr. S[tuart]. can send you plenty

265

Hooks.[8] I received the Play Book you sent, which will answer very well with the Play thing I brought before. The Tea Kettle I could have done without.

Your Journal of Last winter at the [Rocky Mountain] Portage & Trout Lake [Fort McLeod], as well as the one of last summer & this winter you must get them brought over to [make a] copy, which must be sent to the Peace River by next opportunity, which I expect will be in the Later end of march, as the Company require it.

Saucier & Gagnon are to be the bearers of this who starts tomorrow morning to take each a Load of fish to Mr. Stuarts [the post on Stuart Lake] and in the meantime to get their Equipments & they will bring back a load when they return. Those that came from there say that they lost their way in several places. If true those that go there must have a Guide, & I have no doubt but what you can secure one of those beggars that go over from here for that purpose. Expedition is required the season is pretty far advanced and much to be done yet.

I send my Journal over to Mr. S[tuart]. to Copy and it must be done in order to send it down by the next opportunity that it may go out to headquarters in the light Canoe.[9] Besides I have another Plan in view, that is if it could be done with ease [namely] to get all the goods that will be required for going down the Columbia [i.e., the Fraser] in the Spring, as well as whatever will be necessary for your Post for the Summer Trade, brought over from T[rout]. Lake [Fort McLeod] upon the snow, as I fear much time would be Lost by going there by the New Road in the Spring. I don't know which would be most advantageous, to get the pieces brought over in the winter or go for them in the Spring en canoe. At all events bark must be had, to make a Canoe at Nakazleh [Stuart Lake], as I expect Mr. McLeod will send us a canoe maker, & I have been informed that there are plenty good Bark [trees] very near your place, which is absolutely necessary you should ascertain as soon as possible. Here we Know where there is where with to make a Canoe.

I cannot think of any thing else so I conclude My Dear McDougall all as usual

Your well wisher
Simon Fraser.

N.B. Anything that the Children are in want of and that can be had please give it to them & Charge the same to my acct. Saucier will deliver you the hand saw.

10. Fraser to John Stuart

Natleh [Fraser Lake]
1st February 1807.

My D[ea]r friend

Yours of the 12th Jany. I received only yesterday so you see they took much more time than they ought to. I am sure you will be getting out of Patience before you receive this. It is with the greatest pleasure that I always receive letters from you, they contain much useful information and instruction. Tho' the subject of your last cannot be agreeable it is satisfactory knowing how matters stood at T[rout]. Lake [Fort McLeod] upon your arrival there — which you have written in a copious & lively manner. Notwithstanding your mind being obscured in thought you wrote with ease.

I sympathize with you my friend under your Present affliction for the loss of Mr. R. Stuart your Late Dearest of Brothers, and hope he has only left this world of Trouble and vexation to go to ever lasting bliss. We cannot shun that Power which Rules our fate therefore it should be our only Consolation to be Prepared for our last and awful end.

It is a true observation of yours that when the head fails the Body soon goes to wreck, which has been the decay of Trout Lake [Fort McLeod] since last November. That business is so intricate that a person cannot easily see into it. However it seems that Lamalice had an ascendancy over Mr. McD[ougall]. but then I am sure that he can change both his palate & his manners to the will of his master & his interests. It seems then that the debt he was said to have made a the [Rocky Mountain] Portage was only put in effect at Trout Lake, while Mr. McD[ougall] was at the Indians. I immagine when you take account of the Dry goods that you will find they suffered less or more like the stores.

Had Lamalice behaved honestly he would have come to Nakazleh [Stuart Lake]. It is not a good excuse that he was not ordered. It was our last directions to him when he Started from Nakazleh in the summer that he was to come and winter there and if any person a long the Road wished to detain him not to mind them unless absolutely Kept.

McD[ougall] owns that he gave Bugni leave to take the woman that St. Pierre had last winter. This was like the rest of his Conduct. He knew full well that she was taken from St. Pierre merely to give up the Custom of taking any more women from the Indians and that St. Pierre was Promised that no other Frenchman would get her.

I received my order (the Coat and Trowsers are amazing large) my Equip[men]t. also which is extremely bad & the Trousers so small that I cannot put them on much less make use of them, and tho' you were pleased to send me your Capot instead of mine it is also too small for me. I own the Eq[uipmen]t to be Useless, But then I should rather think that it is the fault of those who put it up at L L Pluie [Lac la Pluie] than the Companys. Upon the note you mention a pair of Corduroy Trousers which I did not receive & [I] received a handk[erchie]f there is no mention of. I also

LETTERS FROM NEW CALEDONIA
AUGUST 1806–FEBRUARY 1807

received the small axes & 10 pounds of sugar & some Tea, with which I will content myself.

At present, a good [fishing] net cannot be had [from the Indians] for a small ax. I traded one of small meshes which appears very good for an half ax. I only got 50 Salmon for a small axe today. I sent off Saucier & Gagnon with 200 Salmon for you & 60 as provisions for themselves, but I am afraid they will take much time to go there on account of the Road being stoped [stopped] or filled up with snow between Nakazleh [Stuart Lake] and your place [Fort McLeod]. All the Salmon that is here has been Picked [over] & the best sent over before therefore, I beg of you not to Complain of what I send now and indeed to be free with you [I] dont expect you will have Occation [occasion] to eat Sal[mo]n yourself as you are a good Economist you will Provide something better c. [&c.] and [I] hope your returns will prove better than you expect. The Powder & Treisées bands will give you better than five Packs, as I am informed they have made a Pretty good hunt.

Yes my friend I have once more entered upon the matrimonial state and you would have a hearty laugh if you heard of our Courtship, this I will inform you of if you have not heard of it already but I defer it at present having something else to say and I expect to have the p[l]easure of seeing you before the embarkation as you expressed a wish of coming to take the longitude of this Place & if you can settle your Post in such a manner that it will not suffer by your absence I will expect you by the return of the express from the Peace River.

I now inform you of a Plan I have in view for the summer expedition which is this, to get all the goods required what had to be brought over[10] to Nakazleh [Stuart lake] as soon as possible upon the Ice. By going round by the New Road [the Giscome Portage route], when the navigation is open would cause the loss of much time & I expect that the Ice will break up in this River [the Nechako] nearly a month before the Lakes of the mountains.

269

Probably a canoe would take more time than we think by that Route & Guides would be wanted as well as a canoe at Trout Lake [Fort McLeod], but by starting from Nak[azleh]. the canoes that will be made in the western Division will both answer for going down, but then perhaps the one Canoe that would go up would bring everything from Trout lake to the confluence of this River, where the other canoe & any Provisions that may be Procured in this quarter will be left en cache.[11] I leave it to your judgement to determine which Plan would be the best. I think to get the goods over immediately would be the most expeditious. 10 pieces [of] goods exclusive of Provisions will answer for going below viz. 3 Bales, 1/2 Bale Kettles 1/2 Case Guns 1 Cassette 1 Case Iron 1/2 Rolls Tobacco, 1 Keg Powder, 1 Bag Ball, 1 Bag Shot, and 1/2 Keg high wines & I doubt if this same can be spared. Trout Lake [Fort McLeod] must not be left destitute for the summer & something will be required for Nakazleh [Stuart Lake]. I have not the list of what came there in the fall nor do I know what is there now, but then if you think this is a good Plan you [will know what] would be necessary & that can be spared for the 3 Bales & the Cassette. The sooner it would be sent over the better before any other work is begun. Besides the above articles a supply will be wanted for Nakazleh.

This can be done and to that end every man that can be mustered ought to be sent over with a load. All could be brought over in one Trip each man. Can Provisions be had & what quantity, perhaps it would be more easy and sure getting Provisions by going there in a Canoe. Supposing a few furs would be had at the Lower houses they cannot go out this year. I will send over the few furs that are here immediately with fish to Nak[azleh]. to be in readiness to send over all the furs that are there and to bring across any goods that we may want.

With this I send you over my Journal since the 5th April [1806] except from the time we arrived at Nakazleh [Stuart

LETTERS FROM NEW CALEDONIA
AUGUST 1806–FEBRUARY 1807

Lake] until the 20th August which I expect you will be able to bring up. It is exceeding ill wrote worse worded & not well spelt. But there I know you can make a good Journal of it, if you expunge some Parts & add to others and make it out in the manner you think most Proper. It will make away with a good deal of your time and Paper but I think it necessary to send it to headquarters in the light canoe as it will give our Gentlemen a good deal of information about the Country. You will also receive the two letters you sent me by Blais. I would keep them to copy but I heard you say that you could make up a good Journal from your letters, but then you will send them back in the spring. Your last letter I will copy & send it over another time. With this I enclose what I have of the mens accts.

Please send over Mr. McD[ougall's] Journals of last winter at the [Rocky Mountain] Portage and Trout Lake [Fort McLeod] &c. of last summer [and] this winter to be copied by himself. There are some of them I did not see as yet & it would be necessary for you to look over them and point out anything that is not necessary to be in them. All this will be giving you much trouble and work, but then it will be of service to the Company & some credit to ourselves to have the Journals in better order. Was I possessed of your abilities I would willingly undertake doing all myself. I will send over more of my Journals by next conveyance.

I have succeeded in sending back Qwa ['Kwah] le Gourmand & Several others of the Indians of Nakazleh [Stuart Lake], & many of the Stragglers that were here dispersed as they have ate up all the salmon these of this place had. They now go to trade at Steela [Stillâ], so I apprehend not being able to Procure any for the summer. Had I men here I would go & trade there also. As I cannot think of any thing more at Present I conclude my Dear Stuart your friend & servant,

whilst
Simon Fraser.

P.S. I will be in want of a few small Kettles at this Place therefore you can send one half Bale which will serve for both these places & some common Cloth & Motton [?] if any will remain after the men have all their Equipments. We have found Birch here but tho' the Bark is not very good we can get enough to make a canoe.

I will send you herbs by next opportunity I have none now Dried but then you ought to have sent me a Token of Tobacco first. As for a Calumet [long-stemmed pipe] you have Pierre to make one. Do you know one thing I have a secret to tell you. Guess what it is. I believe you cannot therefore I must give you a hint of it, that is I would thank you for some of that Medicine you made use of Last winter with Directions how to take it, as I have a small Touch of come riddle come Raddle. Your sincerely S.F.

I will Depend upon you for cords to tye our Salmon, Leather, Babiche &c.

If you send people with pieces they will return from Nakazleh [Stuart Lake]. Mr. McD[ougall's] hunter does nothing. He had no person to send to the Powders band this Trip. I send over 100 Beaver. It is bad weather continually snowing which will cause the people to take much time to perform any voyage. I am Positively informed that the Nascudenees have horses that they get from the east. Many of the Natlians [Natliotens] are in mourning for the Deaths of some of their Eminant men. We have some broils with them. Nothing spoils Indians so much as the men having intercourse with them.

Yours &c. S.F.

LETTERS FROM NEW CALEDONIA
AUGUST 1806–FEBRUARY 1807

11. Fraser to James McDougall

Natleh [Fraser Lake]
10th February 1807.

D[ea]r McDougall

I received your favour yesterday forenoon, and indeed it was high time for the bearers to return. [It was] their 9th day; the voyage might easily be performed in 5 days.

Waka and Minard started in the morning at about a couple of hours [after] sun [rise] with a few furs and the other two men will be off in the afternoon with each a load of salmon for the purpose of conducting the furs to Trout Lake [Fort McLeod] as soon as possible but the people that I send over at present must all return that I may go & trade salmon at Steela [Stillâ] after which they will be employed to convey the furs to Trout Lake. Should any person arrive from Mr. Stu[ar]ts before that time you can send them back with a Pack each. Particular care must be taken that the Furs be well envelloped & that the rats and mice does not cut them in the Store. It is very Proper that the men should be prevented from Trading with the Indians, and dont allow any of them to trade without permission.

The Gourmand that says that I give the goods for so very little in return, ask him what he got from me. The day before he went away he asked me for something of every article I was possessed of, but I refused him everything. They are sweet mouths, thieves lyers and in short have every bad quality, therefore you have no occasion to beleave them. It matters very little whether a person is hated or beloved by them, as they are a lazy set of vagabonds. Qua ['Kwah] owes 8 skins from this place, Le Traiteur 3 do. & his big Brother 6 do. & LaVielle Naschoes mother 5 1/2.

Almost all the Natlians [Natliotens] are gone over to Steela [Stillâ] to a Grand feast to Burn & enhume [inhume] a couple of Chiefs that died of late. When they return from there they will go to the mountains to Kill Carribou.

Please tell Bannonu [?] that it was his mothers fault that I bet [beat?] L——. As she wished to prevent her from accompanying me, [she said] that if she came with me, that she had medicine which she got from her sister and she would make her die.

I will expect the men back on the 16th early.

I am D[ea]r. McDougall Yours

Sincerely
Simon Fraser.

MISCELLANEOUS PAPERS

1. Fraser's Notes on His Family[1]

The 3rd William Fraser of Culbokie was married to Margaret McDonell, daughter of John McDonell of Ardnabee, had issue nine sons viz. William, Simon, John, Archibald, Peter, Alexander, Donald, James & Roderick.

William Fraser 4th. William Fraser of Culbokie was married to Margaret Stuart daughter to Alexander Stuart of Achchoillie had sons and daughters.

Simon Fraser the 2nd Son with his family immigrated to America in 1773, And purchased lands in Vermont near Bennington, about 12 months after landing in Albany. Soon afterward the Revolutionary War broke out and in 1777 he joined the Royal cause under General Bourgoin [Burgoyne], and by the recommendation of General [Simon] Fraser he got the appointments of Superintendency of Indian affairs and a Lieutenancy in the Army, and soon after promoted to a Captaincy, was taken prisoner at the Battle of Bennington & Confined 13 months & 10 days in Albany Jail when he died owing to bad usage. He was married to Isobel [Isabella] Grant, daughter to Daldregan, had issue 4 sons & 5 daughters, viz. William, Angus, Peter & Simon, Margaret, Isabella, Hanah, Nelly & Nancy. The family came to Canada after the peace in 1783. William, was married to Jane Fraser, daughter to Malcolm Fraser of Three Rivers, had issue two sons & two daughters, viz. Simon, William Malcolm, Maria Grace, & Jane. Angus was not married. Peter was married but had no issue. Simon is married to

SIMON FRASER

Catherine McDonell, Daughter of Allan McDonell of Matilda of the leek family, have issue five sons & three daughters viz. Simon William, Allan, Roderick, James Ambrose & John Alexander, Isabella, Margery & C[atherine]. Harriet. *John Fraser* was Captain in General Wolf's army, shared in the honours of the battle of Quebec, was paymaster to the troops in the District of Montreal, and afterwards many years Chief Justice there. He was married to a French lady, daughter of Dechambeau of Montreal, had issue 1 son & 4 daughters viz. William, Margaret, Jossette, Fleurie & Ellen. William married a Lady in England, had issue one son & two daughters. He was Lt. Colonel in the 2nd Battalion of the 60th Regiment.

Margaret was married to Captain Banner.

Jossette was married to Delerey of Quebec.

Fleurie was married to James Cuthbert of Bartier.

Ellen was married to Captain Ployart.

Archibald Fraser was Lieutenant in Fraser's Regiment under General Wolf, he was at the taking of Quebec, afterwards went home & was Major of the Glengarry fencibles. Served in Ireland during the Rebellion of 1798.

Peter Fraser was Doctor of Medicine, he died in Spain.

Alexander Fraser was Captain in General Caretts [?] Army in the East Indies & died there.

Donald Fraser was Lieutenant. Killed in battle in Germany.

James Fraser was also Lieutenant, died in the East Indies, was taken prisoner by the Nabob and suffocated in the black hole at Calcutta in 1756.

Roderick Fraser the youngest of the family went to sea & died.

[signed]

Simon Fraser, Grand Son
to the above 3rd William Fraser
of Culbokie.

Saint Andrews near Cornwall
19th January 1846.

Memo. Miss Bell [Isabella] Fraser [the explorer's sister] first took sick on the 9th September 1840 with a violent pain in her breast. Thursday 10th the pain continued without abating much. Sunday 13th she was no better, on the 14th the Priest & the Doctor were brought in the afternoon, they have no hopes of her recovery. Tuesday the Priest came again. Wednesday 16th at 2 o'clock the Priest anointed her. The 17th she was getting weaker & weaker in the agonies of death. Friday 18th at about 12 O'clock at night she died. Miss M. G. [Maria Grace] Fraser arrived from Coteau du Lac a quarter before ten o'clock. The 21st at 9 o'clock in the Morning the funeral took place.

Nancy Fraser [Simon's youngest sister] Died on Sunday the 2nd day of June 1844 about 5 o'clock in the evening. She had been unwell since Monday the 8th of April having gone to church on Saturday the 6th and walked home on Monday. She took to bed some time in the beginning of May.

She was born in Albany, in the year 1774, which made her 70 years of age, her Father and Mother came out from Scotland in the year 1773 in the vessel called the Pearl, in which vessel so many of the Highland Families came to America, the same year, viz. McDonell of Leek, Culochi, Apacallador, & Crowling &c. My Father purchased land in Vermont State in the year 1775 — about this period the Revolutionary War broke out. In 1777 my father joined the British cause, under General Bourgoine, and received a Commission by the recommendation of General Fraser, and soon afterwards he was [taken] prisoner, at the Battle of Bennington under Colonel Baum at Moutoomscock [Waloomscoick is meant; the name is now spelled Walloomsac] & was Committed to Albany Jail, where he was very Cruelly used along with many other British officers, and from there he was sent on board the Sophas a small vessel to Rhode Island,[2] [where he died of ill treatment after an imprisonment of 13 months and 10 days].[3]

2. Isabella Fraser's Claim for Compensation, 1787[4]

Evidence on the claim of Isobel [Isabella] Fraser Widow of Simon Fraser deceased late of Albany County [heard on December 19, 1787].

William Fraser, eldest son of Simon Fraser deceased appears and Sworn.

Says this is a claim put in for his Fathers Estate by a friend of the Family, and was put in, in the Name of his Mother. Says his Father died without a Will leaving Isobel his Widow, and eight Children. Witness is the eldest, the rest of the Children are with him. 5 were Infants in the Summer of 1784 all agree he should act for them.

The late Simon Fraser was a Native of Scotland came to America in 1773.

Was settled at Mapletown Albany County when Rebellion broke out. From the first he sided with British Government collected many persons who came to an Agreement to join the British Troops as soon as they could. He joined at Skenesborough in July 1777, served till he was taken Prisoner at Bennington — he died in Albany Gaol.

Witness joined the British Army in 1777 served in Sir John Johnson's Regiment as Lieutenant — has now half pay.

His Mother came into this province in 1784.

Witness was himself at Cataraqui in the Fall of 1783, and the ensuing Winter.

Resides at Coteau de Lac.

Produces Letter from Judge Fraser of the active and zealous Loyalty of Simon Fraser deceased, and of the Sufferings of himself and family on that account and gives his opinion of the Truth of the account of Losses set forth in the Schedule. Produces Certificates from Colonel Campbell to Simon Fraser's

Services, and of his Sufferings by which his Death was, as Colonel Campbell thinks, occasiond. His Father had 160 Acres at Mapletown Lease Land — taken of Alexander Colden.

Lease for ever at 1 shilling an Acre Rent taken in 1774. Most of it clear when he took it, he bought Improvements, paid £240 York for them.

He cleared about 12 Acres afterwards in the whole 124 Acres clear.

The Title was under New York Government.

His Mother has sold 100 Acres of it.

60 Acres of the best part she could not dispose of this had been taken on the Division of the 2d. Townships Mapletown and Bennington in the year 1775 — there was a Dispute about Boundaries.

His Father had — 2 Yoke of Oxen — 1 Yoke smaller Oxen — 6 Cows — Calves Heifers altogether about 20 head.

Horse Mare and Colt — 24 sheep. Utensils — some Furniture — Corn and Hay in Stack.

All taken from the premises after Battle of Bennington, his Father was then a prisoner in Bennington they were taken on account of this having joined the British Army.

[In an accompanying schedule the property lost is listed in detail. The total estimated value was £573/14/-; this included £192 for the 60 acres of land lost as a result of the local boundary dispute. The Commissioners evidently reduced the claim to £322/14/2, but William Fraser later submitted a supplementary claim for a further sum of £145. *See* Audit Office 12, vols. 63–8, p. 83.]

3. *Jules Quesnel's Description of New Caledonia and of the Journey Down the Fraser River in 1808*[5]

[A note on this letter reads:"Par faveur de Mr. Simon Fraser", which indicates that it was carried across the continent by Fraser himself.]

[To J.M. Lamothe, Montreal]

Nouvelle Caledonia
1er Mai 1809

Cher Ami

J'ai reçu ta Lettre de L'Année Derniere le 1er Octobre et ai été flatté d'apprendre que ta santé avoit été toujour bonne; puisse t'elle toujour durer est le souhait que je te fais de tous mon Coeur! je te felicite Cher Ami de l'agrement que tu a a Montréal et tu fais bien d'en profiter autant qu'il est dans ton pouvoir. Pour moi je serez peutetre Longtemp sans pouvoir avoire le même agrement, mes Intérets me forcant de rester dans le Nord Longtemp, puisque j'ai tanc fais que d'y etre venus, et malgre le peu d'espérance qu'il y a pour les jeunes gens apresant dans ce Pays ici, je suis Resolu de Continuer jusqu'au bout la Cariere que j'ai eu le Malheur d'Entreprendre a moin que s'a soit au préjudice de ma santé alors je sacrifirais volontier mes Intérets pour préservé ma santé sans quoi il est Impossible d'Etre Heureux.

Il y a des Endroits dans le Nord qui, malgré les Desagrément atacher au Pays en Général, il est sependant possible de passer le temps quelquefois agréablement; mais dans selui-ci il n'y a rien a avoire que de la Misère et de l'Ennui. Eloigné de tous le monde, nous n'avons seulement pas le Plaisir de savoir les nouvelles des autres Endroits, nous ne vivons Entierement que qu'au saumon séchéz au Soleille par les Sauvages qui est aussi leurs Seule Depandence pour la Vie, car pour D'Animaux il n'y en a pas, et nous yrions souvent sans soulier, si nous ne procurions du Cuire de la Rivière de la Paix, et pour Combler le tous, nous ne fesons aucun bon Retoure car il y a tres peu de Castore, et les Sauvages accoutumez a vivre au saumon sont trop paresseux pour travailler comme font seux de toute autres Endroit. Ainsi tu peu juger sans t'en dire davantage si ma situation est Agréable, mais je ne regarderais pas encore la Misère de la Fatigue, ni même de la mauvaise nouriture, si le Saumon avec la mauvaise Qualité d'avoire un tres Mauvais Gou, n'avait pas aussi cela de faire tors a la Santé, car les Hommes les Plus Robuste qui ont été 3 Ans dans se Pays ici sont déjas apeine capable de faire leurs Devoir, et malgré que je suis d'un bouillant tempérament je m'apperçois dejas que ma santé Décline.

C'est assez sur se sujet — il faut que je t'apprenne aprésant que j'ai été en Découverte cette Eté avec Mser. Simon Fraser, et John Stuart que tu a Connus je Crois, nous étions accompagner par 12 Hommes et en trios Canot Dessendimes cette Riviere qui jusqu'a présant passois pour la Columbia, Mais trouvant la riviere bien vite Innavigable, nous laissames nos Canots et Continuames notre route apied, dans Les Montagnes les Plus affreuse, et que nous n'aurions jamais pus passer si Les Natifs de qui nous fumes bien Reçu ne nous eurent aider. Apprés avoire passé tous ces Mauvais Endroits non sans beaucoup de Misère comme tu peu panser, nous retrouvames la Riviere encore navigable est embarquames tous dans des Canots se bois et Continuames notre Route avec plus d'aises, jusqu'a la Décharge de cette Riviere dans la Mer Pacifique. En arrivant, comme nous nous disposions a aller plus avant Les Sauvages de ces Endroit qui sont tres Nombreux mirent opposition a notre passage, et se fut le plus Grand Aubaine du monde qui nous retiras de se mauvais pas, sans être obligé de Tuér et d'Etre tous Tuéz nous même. Nous fumes bien Reçu de tous les autres Sauvages en Retournant et arrivames tous en parfaite santé dans notre Nouvelle Caledonia. La Decharge de Cette Riviere est en Latitude 49° pres de trois Dégrés au Nord de la Véritable Columbia.

SeVoyage n'a pas tourné au soins de la Societe, et ne leur seras jamais d'aucune avantage, cette Riviere n'etant pas navigable, maid les But pour lequel nous avon Entrepris le voyage nous l'avons Effectuer, ainsi nous n'avons aucun Reproche a nous faire.

Je suis au bout de mon Papier, ainsi je Conclus, et suis ton sincere ami

J. Quesnel

4. Fraser's Declaration to the Earl of Selkirk, 1816[6]

My Lord

In Spring 1815, I came up from Montreal in company with Mr. Alexander McKenzie, and went with him as far as Red River, with a view to convey information to the Gentlemen of the North-West Company, that a Treaty of Peace had been made with the United Sates of America.

When we arrived at Red River, we learned that a number of Settlers there wanted to go to Canada, being disgusted with their situation in that Country. — Captain Miles McDonell delivered himself up to Mr. A. McKenzie, a number of the Colonists came out on the North West Canoes without any solicitation on the part of any of the Gentlemen that I know of. I never saw any violence committed on the Settlers or Hudson's Bay people. Alexander McDonell was appointed to assume his old situation [in charge of the Red River Department of the North West Company], there being no cause for his removal. I know of no violence that he committed. I heard that he was at a great distance when the disturbances took place between Governor Semple & the Half-Breeds [in June 1816]. — Once the partners leave this place the concern has no authority over their actions. I have no knowledge, nor did I ever hear that our people committed any violence on the H[udson's]. B[ay]. people; but I often heard the H. B. Company's people burnt and pillaged our property. The Agents have not the power of directing nor did I know of their giving any orders to commit any violent acts, but on the contrary, often heard them cautioning our people, not to be agressers. — I am not acquainted with the circumstances of the Colonists having gone away, nor the particulars of Governor Semple & several of his people having been destroyed by the Half Breeds; upon my way out from Athabasca in the Spring to the Red River in the latter end of June last, Indians informed me of the fact.

[Signed] Simon Fraser

Fort William
16th August 1816.
To the Earl of Selkirk.

5. Petitions for Land Submitted by Fraser in 1818[7]

(a) *To Sir Peregrine Maitland*, Knight, Commander of the Honorable Military Order of the Bath, Lieutenant Governor of the Provance of upper Canada, Major General Commanding His Majesty's Forces therein &c. &c. &c.

In Council

The Petition of Simon Fraser of the Township of Cornwall in the Eastern District Gentleman —

Respectfully Sheweth,

That your Petitioner is one of the first Settlers in the said Township of Cornwall, where he now resides and where he has Erected Mills and made other improvements.

That your Petitioner has received two hundred acres of Land from the Crown as a Son of an U. E. Royalist, is desirous of obtaining an additional Grant of His Majesty's waste Lands in this

SIMON FRASER

Province, under the present Regulations, wherefore your Petitioner Prays that your Excellency may be pleased to Grant him such quantity of Land in addition as your Excellency may deem meet,

And your Petitioner shall ever Pray

Simon Fraser.

York 2d November 1818

[Notes on the petition show that it was received from Fraser himself on November 3, 1818, and that he had already received lot 35 in the 1st concession in Osgoode, containing 200 acres. Endorsations include the following: "Read in Council 4th November 1818. Ordered 200 Acres in addition."]

(b) *To Sir Peregrine Maitland*, Knight Commander of the Honorable Military Order of the Bath, Lieutenant Governor of the Provance of upper Canada, Major General Commanding His Majesty's Forces therein &c. &c. &c.

In Council

The Petition of Simon Fraser of the Township of Cornwall in the Eastern District Gentleman.

Respectfully Sheweth

That improvements have been made by your Petitioner upon Lot No. 11 North Side 2d Street Cornwall with intention to present the same to Isabella Fraser Petitioner's Sister and the better to confirm the same to her he was advised to Petition in her own name, but being informed that no Land is now Granted to Women the Petition is withheld and your Petitioner humbly Prays that your Excellency may be pleased to Grant the said Lot to his Brother Angus Fraser who now resides in the Township of Cornwall

And your Petitioner Shall ever Pray

Simon Fraser

York 3d Novr. 1818

[Endorsations on the petition include the following: "Read in Council 4th November 1818." — "Petitioner's Brother must apply himself and accompany his Petition with a Certificate from two Magistrates that the Lot is vacant and clear of difficulty and in the meantime it is Ordered that the Lot prayed for be kept open." — "In a Petition by Angus Fraser Read 16 June 1819 — to whom the Lot is Granted."]

6. *Letter from Fraser to Donald Æ. MacDonell, 1840*[8]

St. Andrews
27th January 1840.

My Dear Friend,

Since my last on the 23rd Instant, I received a Letter from Doctor William J. Scott, who informed me that Dr. Holmes of the [Military Medical] Staff upon his way home, informed him that the Medical Board at Cornwall made a favourable Report of my case, which probably will obtain favourable consideration at Home. This information makes me think that it will be necessary for me to support my claim by Petitioning Lord Hill, the Commander in chief of Her Majesty's Forces.

However I expect your information on that head will be better than mine. Only yesterday I received the Debates on the Union [of Upper and Lower Canada] which I thank you kindly for.

Every one here says that they never had so little information from the Parliament as this session.

It is reported here that the Clergy Reserves have been disposed of, one half the proceeds for the National Churches and the other amongst all other Denominations. So I do not see what the Catholic's have gained by their support of the Dominant Church. I admit that the Presbyterians have as good a right to them as the Church of England. But it is very mortifying for the Roman

Catholic's to be Huddled in an empty space with all other Hundred Creeds.

I understand that Fothergill's Toronto Almanac sells at a reduced price if convenient I would be obliged to you to bring me one.

I cannot find out from Mrs. Bickie exactly what she would be at, but she keeps a correspondence with some person in Toronto. I believe she begins to repent of her undertaking to obtain the Control of her affairs. She keeps all secret.

In expectation of seeing you soon Home, I remain

Dear Sir,

Yours very sincerely

Simon Fraser.

P.S. I wrote the above yesterday and upon my way to Cornwall this morning. I called at the St. Andrew Post Office where I received your Letter, inclosing Mrs. Bickie's Letter, so that I cannot deliver her letter till this evening and I am afraid that I could not get her reply [in] time enough to overtake you at Toronto, but I shall endeavor to forward you a reply as soon as possible, and at worst it will only be occuring [incurring] the expense of double postage, if it comes back after you to St. Andrews.

After your departure in November from St. Andrews for Toronto, I received your Letter inclosing fifty Dollars, and a Letter for Mrs. Bickie, both which I delivered to her. For some time afterwards she seemed rather more contented. but she broke out again with invectives against you. She was three or four different times in Cornwall since the beginning of sleighing and each time she was rather more violent, portending that she was getting the management of her affairs into her own hand, but I could never exactly find out what proceeding she was taking against you.

The other day she expressed her regret that she was obliged to put you upon your oath, but that you compelled her to do so by your injustice. I thought by that expression that she was regretting having undertaken any steps against you. Mrs. Bickie shewed me a copy of the will which does not state anything about the disposal of the moveable effects of the deceased Mr. Bickie, so that perhaps it may be a question who the effects should go to. It does not appear that Miss Finlay has any claim on them – however you know best how that is.

Simon Fraser.

Tuesday 28th January.

Excuse the badness of the writing being in a cold room.

7. Fraser's Application for a Military Pension, 1841

(a) *His Petition to the Governor General.*[9]

To His Excellency the Right Honorable Baron Sydenham of Sydenham in the County of Kent and Toronto in Canada Governor General of the British North American Provinces &c. &c. &c.

The Memorial of *Simon Fraser* Captain in the 1st Regiment of Stormont Militia of upper Canada.

Most Humbly Sheweth,

That your Memorialist volunteered under the authority of Colonel Turner, Particular Sevice, Commanding the Militia Forces in the Eastern District of upper Canada, as Captain in the above Regiment Commanded by Lieutenant Colonel Donald Æ. McDonell, upon the Expedition to Lower Canada in the Month of November 1838, to join the Force under Colonel Campbell in that Province to aid in subduing the Rebels at Beauharnois.

That on the evening of the 7th of November, after the landing of the volunteers at the mouth of Salmon River in Lower Canada, and marching from thence to Dundee, when the

SIMON FRASER

Detachment was halted for the night, your Memorialist after seeing his Company in quarters was returning to the Commanding officers quarters to ascertain the orders for the next mornings march, when your Memorialist sustained a fall by which his right knee is so much injured that your Memorialist has certainty to believe he will never recover the usefulness of it, in confirmation of which he begs leave to refer to the certificates of the Commanding officer and the Surgeon who were present at the time he met with the accident. And subsequently a Court of enquiry, and a Board of Military Medical officers, ordered by the then Commander of the Forces, Sir John Colborne, assembled at Cornwall and examined your Memorialist.

Your Memorialist trusts that altho, His Excellency the Lieutenant Governor of upper Canada, and His Excellency the present Commander of the Forces in Canada to whom your Memorialist has applied, made answer that your Memorialists case does not appear to come under any of the clauses of the Royal Warrants for granting Pensions and allowances to officers for wounds received in action.

That your Memorialist met with the injury which has disabled him while on active service, and on the march to meet the enemy, consequently prays that your Excellency will be pleased to take such steps for his relief as will enable him to obtain a pension from Her Royal Majesty by placing him on the pension list the same as if he had been wounded in action.

  And your Memorialist,
    As in duty bound will ever pray
      Simon Fraser Capt.
        1st Stormont Militia

Saint Andrews
County of Stormont
Province of Canada
March 25th, 1841.

MISCELLANEOUS PAPERS

(b) *Supporting Statement by Lt.-Col. MacDonell.*[10]

I hereby certify that during the Expedition of the 1st Regiment of Stormont Militia into Lower Canada in the month of November 1838. That Captain Simon Fraser of said First Regiment of Stormont Militia while acting under my Orders and in the actual discharge of his duty on the night of the Seventh of November was severely injured in the right Knee by a fall. By which injury he has been rendered incapable of doing his duty as Captain in the said Regiment, and also of transacting his usual business.

    Donald Æ. MacDonell
     Lieut. Colonel Commanding
      1st Regiment Stormont Militia
St. Andrews, Cornwall,
7th July 1841

(c) *Notification that the Pension had been Granted.*[11]

      [Civil Secretary's Office]
      19 July 1841

Sir,

I am commanded by the Governor General to acquaint you that the certificates transmitted with your letter of the 9th Inst. having been submitted to the Attorney General for his report that officer has declared them in conjunction with those previously sent, sufficient to establish your claim to a Militia Pension under the act for the Upper Part of the Province, & that directions have accordingly been issued to the Receiver General to place your name on the Pension List from & after this date.

      I have &c.
      John Hopkirk

Capt. S. Fraser

8. *Memorandum by Simon Fraser and John McDonald of Garth, 1859*[12]

We are the last of the old N[orth]. W[est]. Partners. We have known one another for many years. Which of the two survives the other we know not. We are both aged, we have lived in mutual esteem and fellowship, we have done our duty in the stations allotted us without fear, or reproach. We have braved many dangers, we have run many risks. We cannot accuse one another of any thing mean & dirty through life, nor [have we] done any disagreeable actions, nor wrong to others. We have been feared, loved & respected by natives. We have kept our men under subordination. We have thus lived long lives. We have both crossed this continent, we have explored many new points, we have met many new Tribes, we have run our Race, & as this is probably the last time we meet on earth, we part as we have lived in sincere friendship & mutual good will.

J[ohn]. McD[onald].
Simon Fraser

1st Augt. 1859.

9. *Letter of John A. Fraser, Son of Simon Fraser, to the Editor of the "Hastings Chronicle", 1862*[13]

To the Editor of the Hastings Chronicle.

Dear Chronicle, — I see by to-day's *Globe* that the "gold fever" is making head in Toronto, and that a committee has been formed out of the "smitten" to obtain information respecting the overland route to British Columbia.

Through your journal, permit me to say a few words respecting the Fraser River, and the overland route to it; and if those Toronto gentlemen to whom I have referred find anything in my remarks worthy of notice, my object in writing these lines will be accomplished.

In the year 1792, at the age of 16, my father became an articled clerk to the Northwest Fur Trading Company, which had its head quarters at Montreal. In the year following he was sent to Lake Arthabasca, which was then the principal trading post of the Company west of Grand Portage. In 1802 he became a partner, and in 1805 he came down from Fort Arthabasca [Chipewyan] to Fort William, and was then nominated to cross the Rocky Mountains — to extend outposts and form trading connections with the Indians. In Aug. 1805 he left Fort William, and reached the foot of the Mountains; his route lay through the Lake of the Woods, Lake Winnipeg, up the Sascatchewan for a short distance, past Cumberland House on the Sascatchewan, then up English River as far as Isle a la Croix, — then up Buffalo Lake, then over Portage La Cache [La Loche] into the Arthabasca River and Lake to Fort Arthabasca [Chipewyan], which was the rendezvous of that department,—then up the Fraser river [the Peace River is meant] to the foot of the mountains to a place which he named the Rocky Mountain portage, where he left two clerks (named James McDougall and Arch'd McGillivray), and 12 men. He thence continued his route with 6 men to the summit of the mountains, and reached a small Lake of about 12 superficial miles in extent, which discharges down both sides of the mountain, and is either the source of [or] a tributary to the Peace River, and is situate in about latitude 55°. At this Lake, which he afterwards called McLeod's Lake (out of compliment to one of the Northwest partners) he left three men to form acquaintance with the Indians, and in November returned with his remaining three men to the portage at the foot of the mountains, where he had left the 14. At this portage he passed the winter of 1805-6. In the month of May 1806 he sent two canoes loaded with furs to Arthabasca, with a report of his proceedings, and went again up the mountains with six men and a clerk named John Stewart [Stuart], and reached McLeod's Lake [Stuart Lake is meant] by a devious course to the South. In this course he touched Fraser River — which takes its name from him—but which he then supposed to be the Columbia. He went up a tributary of the Fraser River, and called it Stewart's River. Doubts now arose in his mind as to the "Fraser" — which he called the "great" River—being the Columbia. About 120 miles up the Stewarts river [the Nechako and Stuart rivers are meant] he built a house, and called the place "New Caledonia." Here he left Mr. Stewart and two men, and crossed westerly into the open country, and built another house near a Lake which he called Fraser's Lake. He was now, with four men, in the midst of Indians who had never before either seen or heard of the "pale face." On the border of this Lake he witnessed an Indian ceremony which, after a lapse of more than half a century, is as fresh in his mind as if it occurred yesterday. He was brought by the Indians along the Lake border to where they had a very large burying ground, when one of the Chiefs of their tribe was being buried. An immense number of warriors were assembled, and after a most solemn and impressive ceremony, my father was invited by signs to approach the grave; he did so, and gave immense satisfaction by engraving his name on a post which had been planted over the remains of the departed warrior. What a commentary is this upon human ambition, when we reflect that even the fame of Napoleon, time will as effectually obliterate as it has the name of the warrior whose remains a whole nation met that day to honor!

From this Lake my father returned and passed the winter with Mr. Stewart [Stuart]. In the early part of 1807 he sent despatches, with what furs had been collected, to Arthabasca, and asked for an increased force of clerks, and goods. In the Fall of 1807 he received two canoes loaded with goods, and two clerks, named Julius [Jules] Quesnel and Hugh Jones [Faries] (the former was afterwards an M.P. for Montreal). These gentlemen brought despatches from the Company, recommending my father to trace with all possible speed the "great" River to the sea, — they being apprehensive that the Americans would get ahead of the British in that quarter — particularly as in the previous year (1806) Captains Lewis and Clark had gone down the Columbia, and were extending American authority along the western coast of America; and Astor, on the part of the Americans also, was looking anxiously towards that section. The Company therefore urged my father to spare no expense in achieving the object of their desires.

In the summer of 1807 my father built another Trading house on the Fraser River, in about latitude 54°. In May 1808 he started from Stewart's [Stuart] Lake with four canoes and 16 men, exclusive of Messrs. Stewart and Quesnel, leaving Ferres [Faries] and two men in charge of a post at the mouth of the Stewart River [Fort George, at the mouth of the Nechako River is meant], — reached the ocean early in July and remained but a short time there, on account of the hostility of the Indians. From the time he left Ferres [Faries] until he arrived at the sea, he met numerous and very large bodies of Indians, speaking several different languages. They assembled to see the wonderful "pale faces" that were come amongst them. An idea may be formed of how they regarded white men from the fact, that when hundreds of them were congregated together, at the discharge of a single rifle they would all fall upon their faces on the ground, so great was their astonishment.

This hasty sketch will apprise you of three facts: — 1st, that Fraser River takes its name from my father, now an aged man of 86 years. 2nd, that he gave the name of "New Caledonia" to the country through which it flows. 3rd, that his exertions and enterprise in all probability secured to the British Crown what promises to be a Province surpassing in every element of natural greatness even our own Canada, the "brightest jewel" in the British Crown.

Yours truly,
John A. Fraser.

Belleville,
Feb'y 10th, 1862.

10. Memorial of Fraser's Last Will and Testament, 1862[14]

A Memorial, to be registered, of the Last Will and Testament of Simon Fraser of the Township of Cornwall in the County of Stormont and Province of Canada, Esquire, in the words and figures following that is to say

In the Name of God, Amen.

This is the last will and testament of me Simon Fraser of the Township of Cornwall in the County of Stormont and Province of Canada, Esquire, made this seventh day of August in the year of our Lord one thousand eight hundred and sixty two, as follows that is to say

I give devise and bequeath all my messuages land tenements and hereditaments and all my household furniture. ready money, securities for money, goods and chattels, and all other my real and personal estate and effects whatsoever and wheresoever unto the following persons their heirs executors administrators and assigns to and for them respectively and their own repective absolute use and benefit according to the nature and quality thereof respectively Subject only to the payment of my just debts, personal and testamentory expenses, the charges of proving and registering this my last will and Testament and the maintenance of my lawful wife during her natural life. And I hereby appoint Roderick MacDonald of the Town of Cornwall in the said County of Stormont, Esquire, executor of this my last will and Testament, and hereby also revoke all other wills.

I hereby give devise and bequeath unto my elder son Simon William Fraser his heirs executors administrators and assigns the West half of Lot number twenty one fronting on the River aux Raisin and on the North Bank of said River, in the seventh Concession of the said Township of Cornwall — reserving thereof and therefrom nine acres of firewood on the northern extremity of the Rear or North part of the same. Reserving also the right of entry upon the said Lot for the purpose of cutting and carrying away the said firewood.

I also give devise and bequeath unto my daughters Margery Fraser and Catharine Harriet Fraser, for their joint use and benefit the nine acres of firewood above reserved, together with the right of entry on the said Lot for the purpose of cutting and carrying or drawing the said firewood away, or having same cut or drawn away by any person they may appoint for that purpose — the said right to hold good during the natural life of my said daughters or either of them. Further I give devise and bequeath unto my said daughters their heirs executors administrators and assigns that certain point or tract of land known as the mill point being the Southern part of the north parts of Lots numbers nineteen and twenty in the fifth [sixth?] concession of Cornwall aforesaid and being on the south side of the middle branch of River aux Raisin — which said point may be otherwise known and described as follows that is to say Commencing at the water's edge at the Western extremity of the mill pond thence westward to the nearest point of the public Road (now travelled from St. Andrew's church Westwards) on the north Bank of said River or north side of said River, thence along the Eastern side of said Road Eastwards and Southwards to the southern limit of the said North parts of Lots numbers nineteen and twenty, thence Easterly along the said limits to the water's edge of said River aux Raisin, thence along the waters edge of said River northerly following the Windings of the same to the place of beginning, together with all buildings thereon standing and the mill privilege and all rights and reservations thereto appertaining and belonging.

Further I give devise and bequeath unto my said daughters Margery and Catharine Harriet their heirs executors administrators and assigns the North part of Lot number nineteen and the East half of the North part of Lot number Twenty in the fifth Concession of the Township of Cornwall aforesaid and on the south side of the Middle Branch of the River aux Raisin.

Further I give devise and bequeath unto my son Allan Fraser his heirs execturos administrators and assigns the south half of the East half of Lot number twenty one on the south side of the Middle Branch of River aux Raisin in the sixth Concession of the Township of Cornwall aforesaid.

Further I give devise and bequeath unto my son Roderick Fraser his heirs executors administrators and assigns the North half of the said East half of Lot number twenty one reserving however thereout and there from a strip of land thirty feet wide along the Eastern side line of said East half of said Lot number twenty one from the southern limit of said north half northwards to where the said strip shall intersect the Public highway which said strip shall be for the use and benefit of said Allan Fraser his heirs administrators executors and assigns forever.

Further I give devise and bequeath unto my son James Ambrose Fraser his heirs executors administrators and assigns all that portion of the West half of the North part of Lot number twenty in the fifth Concession of the said Township of Cornwall and on the south side of the Middle Branch of the River aux Raisin not heretofore given devised and bequeathed under and by virtue of this last will and testament.

Respecting the reservations made on the West half of Lot number twenty one, devised to my son Simon William Fraser, in favour of my daughters Margery and Catharine Harriet, it is my wish and intention that said reservations shall end and terminate with the natural lives of my said daughters or the survivor of them.

Further I give devise and bequeath unto my lawful wife Catharine Fraser her heirs executors administrators and assigns all my goods and chattels personal estate and effects not heretofore mentioned in this my last will and testament.

Further I give devise and bequeath unto my son John Alexander Fraser his heirs executors administrators and assigns all my right title and interest claim and demand whether in possession or expectancy to any property real or personal, or both, which I may now have or which may hereafter come to me in consequence of my having been the discoverer and explorer of the River Fraser West of the Rocky Mountains in British territory in North America.

Which said Last Will and Testament is dated the seventh day of August in the year of our lord one thousand eight hundred and sixty two and is Witnessed by John Macdonald of the Township of Cornwall in the County of Stormont, Esquire, and John R. McDonald of the same place, Esquire.

And this memorial thereof is hereby required to be registered by me John Alexander Fraser, one of the devisees therein named, of the said Township of Cornwall, Gentleman.

Witness my hand and seal this fifteenth day of October in the year of our Lord one thousand eight hundred and sixty two.

Signed and sealed in
the presence of
John R. McDonald
Mary Margaret McDonald

[Signed]
John A. Fraser

SIMON FRASER

11. Petition Submitted by Harriet Fraser, Daughter of Simon Fraser, in 1887 and again in 1890[15]

To His Excellency the Governor General of Canada, in Council assembled:

The Petition of Harriet Fraser, of St. Andrews, in the County of Stormont, Spinster, Humbly Sheweth:

That Your Petitioner is the only surviving daughter of the late Simon Fraser, who died at St. Andrews in the year 1862.

That in the year 1792 the late Simon Fraser entered the service of The North-West Fur Trading Company and was soon after sent to Lake Athabasca. He remained in that vicinity for some years. In the year 1802 he became a partner in the Company.

In 1805 Mr. Fraser took part in the Conference of the leading members of the Company who met at Fort William to consider the project of extending their operations beyond the Rocky Mountains and of occupying the country Westward to the ocean in advance of the American Traders who had then penetrated as far North as the Columbia River and were eagerly pushing their way further up the coast.

The members of the Company having decided to extend their out-posts across the Rocky Mountains and to establish trading connections with the tribes of Indians west of the Mountain Ranges, his partners deputed your Petitioner's father to undertake the task of exploring that region, of establishing trading-posts in that then unknown Territory and of occupying the country as British Traders.

Mr. Fraser's diary shows that he left Fort William on his long and perilous adventure in August 1805, passing through the Lake of the Woods, Lake Winnipeg up the Sakatchewan past Cumberland House then up English River as far as Isle [à] la

Croix. Up Buffalo Lake then over Portage La Cache [La Loche] into the Athabasca River and Lake to Fort Athabasca [Chipewyan] up the Peace River to the foot of the Mountains to a place which he named the Rocky Mountain Portage, where he left two clerks Mr. James McDougall and Mr. Archibald McGillivray, and twelve men in charge. He then continued his route with six men to Lake McLeod, so named by him, where he left three of his men to form acquaintance with the Indians.

In the year 1806 having returned to the Portage for additional men, Mr. Fraser penetrated westward to the Fraser River, which receives its name from him, as its discoverer. He explored the Stewart [Stuart] River calling it after John Stewart [Stuart], a clerk who was with him, and at the distance of 120 miles from its mouth he established a trading post, leaving Stewart and two men in charge, calling the place "New Caledonia." Continuing his exploration westward he established another Post at Fraser's Lake. The despatches he sent to Fort Athabasca [Chipewyan] gave increased interest to his undertaking and he was pressed to push on to the ocean and trace out the Fraser River, which at first he supposed was a branch of the Columbia. In the Fall of 1807 two canoes with goods, in charge of Messrs Quesnel and Ferres [Faries], were sent to his assistance. (The former was afterwards Member for Montreal.) They brought letters urging Mr. Fraser to continue his explorations and to occupy the country in advance of the Americans, as Lewis and Clark had in the previous year gone down the Colubmia River, and were extending the authority of the Republic through that region. And John Jacob Astor was also enlarging his operations northward.

In the Summer of 1807 Mr. Fraser built another trading house on the Fraser River in about Latitude 54. In May 1808 he started from Stewart [Stuart] Lake with four canoes and sixteen men traversing the Fraser River to the ocean. The Indians of the Interior had never before seen the "Pale faces," and it required great prudence and skill to avoid a conflict and eventually to win their friendship.

The North-West Fur Company having thus added what is now British Columbia to their sovereignty it remained under their control till the fusion of that Company with the Hudson Bay Company in 1821, and thirty-seven years after it became a Crown Colony.

After the retirement of your Petitioner's father from the Company he was offered the honor of Knighthood in recognition of his services. His circumstances did not, however, warrant the acceptance of a title, and he died extremely poor leaving his family unprovided for. Your Petitioner and two brothers are now the sole survivors.

Remembering the advantages gained by the neighboring Republic in all our diplomatic controversies, touching the boundary line between the two countries from the State of Maine line in the East to the San Juan boundary in the west, can it be claimed that had British Traders not occupied the country West of the Rocky Mountains in advance of the Americans, we should to-day have the Pacific Ocean for our Western boundary, and should possess within our Confederation the fine Province of British Columbia? Canada has never been ungrateful to those sons who have secured advantages for their country, and your Petitioner therefore hopes that some recognition of her father's services may even now be shown by making provision for the support of his only surviving daughter.

And your Petitioner will as in duty bound ever pray.

Harriet Fraser.

Ottawa,
June 1887.

PORTRAITS OF FRASER

The portrait of Fraser reproduced in the frontispiece was first published in 1904 by Father Morice in his *History of the Northern Interior of British Columbia*. His caption states that it was "From a photo by James Hawes, Cornwall, C.W., kindly furnished by Hon. R.W. Scott." It would seem to be almost certain that the original painting was at one time in the possession of the Fraser family at St. Andrews. Cornwall, which is only a few miles from St. Andrews, would be the logical place to take a picture to have it photographed; Scott was closely related to the Frasers, and would naturally turn to the family when he was asked for a picture of the explorer.

The Fraser centenary exhibit displayed in New Westminster in 1908 included a watercolour portrait of the explorer. The Vancouver *Province* stated that this had been presented by Catherine Fraser, Simon's granddaughter; but as the original is not in the collections of the Archives of British Columbia, it must have been merely lent for the occasion. It seems highly probable that the picture displayed was that reproduced in the frontispiece. Every detail in it matches the description of Fraser published in October 1908 in the *Westward Ho! Magazine* by E.O.S. Scholefield; and we know that Scholefield had much to do with the centenary arrangements. Scholefield, incidentally, mentions the colour of Fraser's eyes and hair, which shows that he based his description on a coloured original.

A different likeness of Fraser was reproduced in 1914 in the first volume of Sholefield and Howay's *British Columbia*; but the pose is identical, and in all probability the original was derived from the portrait printed by Morice. This is the portrait of a gentleman, rather than that of an explorer and fur trader. The rather snub nose has become straight; the rough sideburns have disappeared; the tousled hair is much neater in appearance. Details, however, are somewhat shadowy, and perhaps this prompted the Provincial Archives to have some artist carry the transformation one step further. The much larger and sharper portrait that resulted hangs in the historical museum in Victoria.

Copies of a fourth likeness are in the possession of Mr. Donald C. Fraser, of Fargo, N.D., and the Provincial Archives in Victoria. This is a relatively crude sketch which has every appearance of being an amateurish attempt to copy (and perhaps improve upon) our frontispiece. Neither copy of this version appears to be old, and it is extremely unlikely that either can have been in existence in Fraser's lifetime.

SELECT BIBLIOGRAPHY

Bancroft, H.H., *History of the Northwest Coast*, vol. II, San Francisco, 1884. Pages 87-119 comprise the first detailed account of Fraser and his explorations to appear in print. This was based on transcripts of Fraser's first and second journals and of his letters from New Caledonia that Bancroft had secured in Victoria in 1878.

Masson, L.R., *Les Bourgeois de la Compagnie du Nord-Ouest*, first series, Quebec, 1889. Includes Fraser's "Journal of a Voyage from the Rocky Mountains to the Pacific Coast, 1808". This was the first printing of Fraser's narrative.

Morice, A.G., *History of the Northern Interior of British Columbia*, Toronto, 1904 (3rd edition, Toronto, 1905). Still the most detailed account of Fraser's activities in New Caledonia, where Father Morice served as a missionary for many years.

Scholefield, E.O.S., "Simon Fraser": a series of four articles in the *Westward Ho! Magazine*, Vancouver, vols. III and IV (issues dated October and December 1908, and January and March 1909). A notable attempt to write a biographical sketch of Fraser and to give an impression of his character and personality. This interesting account is virtually unknown today, as it is buried in the file of a long defunct periodical.

Scholefield, E.O.S., and Howay, F. W., *British Columbia from the Earliest Times to the Present*, 4 vols., Vancouver, 1914. Scholefield wrote the first volume, which includes the account of Fraser. In this general history the emphasis is naturally on details of exploration rather than biography or character. Four of the letters from New Caledonia were first printed in this history.

Denton, V. L., *Simon Fraser* (Ryerson Canadian History Readers), Toronto, 1928. A brief routine account (28 pages), intended primarily for school use.

Sage, Walter N., "Simon Fraser, Explorer and Fur Trader", in *Proceedings*, Pacific Coast Branch, American Historical Association, 1929, pp. 172-86. This paper presented important new information about Fraser. Still a useful and interesting account, although many details can now be added or corrected.

Public Archives of Canada, *Report for the Year 1929*, Ottawa, 1930. Bancroft's transcripts of Fraser's 1806 journal and of the letters from New Caledonia were here printed for the first time.

Morton, A. S., *A History of the Canadian West to 1870-71*, London, 1939. Places Fraser's work in perspective and reviews it in some detail. Unfortunately, there are very serious errors in chronology; botht the 1806 and the 1808 expeditions are wrongly dated.

Spargo, John, *Two Bennington-Born Explorers*, n.p., 1950. The two explorers are Fraser and Daniel Williams Harmon, who were born within a few miles of one another. The account of Fraser gave many new details about his family's tribulations in Bennington and of his life after he retired to St. Andrews.

Mackenzie, Alexander, *History of the Frasers of Lovat*, Inverness, 1896. A comprehensive genealogical work (761 pages) that includes an account of Simon Fraser's branch of the family, the Frasers of Culbokie and Guisachan.

Fraser, Alexander, *The Clan Fraser in Canada*, Toronto, 1895. A useful local supplement to Mackenzie's *History*.

NOTES

Introduction

1. For the ancestry in detail *see* Alexander Mackenzie, *History of the Frasers of Lovat*, Inverness, 1896.
2. H.J. Somers, *The Life and Times of the Hon. and Rt. Rev. Alexander Macdonell* ... Washington, D.C., 1931, pp. 98–9.
3. He seems also to have been appointed Superintendent of Indian Affairs; *see* Simon Fraser's notes on his family, printed in this volume.
4. John Spargo, *Two Bennington-Born Explorers*, n.p., 1950, pp. 91-2.
5. *Minutes of the Albany Committee of Correspondence, 1775-1778*, Albany, 1923, vol. I, p. 889.
6. *See* "Genealogy of the [Grant] Family of Glenmoriston"; manuscript in the possession of Donald C. Fraser; photocopy in Public Archives of Canada.
7. John Fraser to Haldimand, May 31, 1784; *Haldimand Papers*; transcript in Public Archives of Canada.
8. Mackenzie, *History*, p. 619.
9. Fraser to Haldimand, May 31, 1784.
10. The original petition and order are in the Public Archives of Canada.
10a. It should be noted that Judge Fraser and Simon McTavish were related, but whether or not this had anything to do with young Simon's entry into the service of the North West Company is not known. Simon McTavish came to America in 1764, as a boy of 13, with his sister Elizabeth and her husband, Lieut. Hugh Fraser. As already noted, Hugh and Elizabeth Fraser took up land at Bennington, and Simon Fraser (father of the explorer) settled nearby in

1774. Hugh and Simon Fraser were kinsmen of some sort; it has been said that Hugh was a cousin of the explorer's grandfather, but no proof of this is yet available.

11. W.S. Wallace, *Documents Relating to the North West Company*, Toronto, 1934, p. 171. Fraser's few surviving papers include an incomplete inventory of "Equipment &c. of Fort Liard September 1803" (now in the possession of Mr. Donald C. Fraser); this suggests that he was serving at this post at the time the list was compiled.
12. Thompson to Sir James Alexander, May 9, 1845. Quoted in A.S. Morton, "Duncan M'Gillivray and David Thompson", *Canadian Historical Review*, XVIII (1937), p. 157.
13. Mackenzie to John Sullivan, October 25, 1802. Quoted in A.S. Morton, "The Columbian Enterprise and David Thompson", *Canadian Historical Review*, XVII (1936), p. 273.
14. Original manuscript in the Archives of British Columbia; photostat copy in the Public Archives of Canada.
15. 3rd edition, Toronto, 1905, pp. 60-2.
16. Fraser to the Gentlemen Proprietors, December 21, 1806 (printed in this volume).
17. Fraser to McDougall, December 1906 (printed in this volume).
18. *The Report of the British Columbia Centennial Committee*, Victoria, 1959, p. 187.
19. Narrative, June 15, 1808.
20. *Ibid.*, June 26, 1808.
21. The name is used in notes by Stuart appended to A.C. Anderson's *History of the Northwest Coast*; manuscript in Archives of British Columbia.
22. David Thompson, "Remarks on the Countries westward of the Rocky Mountains with reference to the rough Chart of David Thompson". Manuscript in the Library of the Royal Commonwealth Institute, London; Photostat copy in Public Archives of Canada.
23. E.E. Rich (ed.), *Part of Dispatch from George Simpson, Esqr ... 1829*, Toronto and London, 1947, pp. 38-9.
24. H.H. Bancroft, *History of the Northwest Coast*, vol. II, San Francisco, 1884, p. 89.

NOTES

25. *Westward Ho! Magazine*, III (1908), p. 222.
26. *Ibid.*, p. 444.
27. Fraser to Stuart, February 1, 1807; printed in this volume.
28. Bancroft, *History of the Northwest Coast*, vol. II, p. 93.
29. L.R. Masson, *Les Bourgeois de la Compagnie du Nord-Ouest*, 2nd series, Quebec, 1890, pp. 128-9.
30. Translation; for the original French text, see pp. 280–82.
31. *Sixteen Years in the Indian Country; The Journal of Daniel Williams Harmon*, Toronto, 1957, p. 116.
32. *Ibid.*, p. 121.
33. Masson, *Les Bourgeois*, second series, p. 96.
34. Fraser to Lord Selkirk, August 16, 1816; printed in full elsewhere in this volume.
35. *Ibid.*
36. See *Report of the proceedings connected with the disputes between the Earl of Selkirk and the North-West Company at the assizes, held at York in Upper Canada, October 1818*. Montreal, 1819.
37. J.G. Harkness, *Stormont, Dundas and Glengarry: A History, 1784-1945*, n.p., 1946, p. 396.
38. *See* her petition to the Governor General in Council, printed elsewhere in this volume.
39. *Westward Ho! Magazine*, IV (1909), p. 143.
40. The date of the issue of the *Freeholder* in which the obituary appeared is not known; only an undated clipping survives. Fraser's death was noted in the Toronto *Globe* and the Montreal *Gazette* on August 25, 1862. The notice in the latter reads as follows: "At his residence, St. Andrews, in the township of Cornwall, on Monday, the 18th instant, Simon Fraser, Esq., after a short illness, aged 86 years."
41. The description by Harry Jones is quoted in a letter from R.W. Haggen to W.N. Draper dated November 27, 1930; copy in the Archives of British Columbia.
42. *British Columbian*, June 1, 1865.
43. *Cariboo Sentinel*, Barkerville, June 6, 1865.
44. W.W. Walkem, *Stories of Early British Columbia*, Vancouver, 1914, pp. 278-9. Stevenson's story is probably substantially true. The land registry records at Cornwall Township show that the properties Fraser left to his family were all mort-

gaged in 1862-3, and all the mortgages were later foreclosed. In 1871 Roderick, Harriet, James and Margery Fraser bought back the hundred acres in the sixth concession lying within the loop of the Rivière aux Raisins, and this was subsequently divided for them into four 25-acre plots.

45. *Colonist*, April 21, 1888.
46. *Ibid.*, August 12, 1902.
47. The original petition is in the records of the Privy Council (P.C. 715, dormants, 1896)
48. *Hamilton Times*, August 15, 1907.

THE GREAT JOURNEY: EXPLORING THE FRASER RIVER

Journal of a Voyage from the Rocky Mountains to the Pacific Ocean performed in the year 1808

1. The point of departure was Fort George, which had been built at the mouth of the Nechako (here referred to as "Fraser's River") in 1807. Fraser thought that the main river, which he was about to descend, was the Columbia.
2. In recording solar observations a capital "O" is often used to indicate the sun. Spelled out in full, this entry would read: "Sun Lower Left", meaning a reading based upon an observation directed at the lower left edge of the sun. If a very exact observation were required, a second reading would be taken on the sun's upper right edge (O.U.R.); the correct bearing would be the mean of the two.
3. "The place where the goods alone are carried, is called a *Decharge*, and that where goods and canoes are both transported overland is denominated a *Portage*." (Alexander Mackenzie)
4. Mackenzie mentions that each canoe usually carried two oil cloths with which to cover goods and furs, and protect them from spray and rain.
5. The correction is based on the entry for the same date in the *Second Journal*.

NOTES

6. Simple shelters are meant, usually consisting of a framework covered with rush mats. The winter dwellings were the famous "keekwillie" houses; for a diagram, photograph and description of these *see* Diamond Jenness, *The Indians of Canada*, 4th ed., Ottawa, 1958, pp. 91-3; 354-5.
7. The valley of the North Saskatchewan River is meant; the name Fort des Prairies was applied at different times to different posts on the river. The "friends" to which Fraser refers were David Thompson and his men, who in 1807 had set out from Rocky Mountain House, on the North Saskatchewan, had crossed the Rocky Mountains by way of Howse Pass, and had established Kootenae House on the upper waters of the Columbia River. Fraser evidently thought it possible that the Thompson River might be the lower portion of the river upon which Thompson had built his post.
8. Details given in the *Second Journal* indicate that Fraser camped for the night four or five miles upstream from Riske Creek.
9. The distances given for this date in the *Second Journal* total 41 1/2 miles. Although Fraser over-estimated his progress, the actual distance covered—probably about 35 miles—was nevertheless notable. His camp for the night cannot have been far from Churn Creek.
10. This camp, at which Fraser spent two nights, was in the vicinity of China Gulch.
11. The camp-site was probably not far from Deadman Creek.
12. French Bar Canyon.
13. It is almost certain that Leon Creek was the point where he landed, and near which he left his canoes.
14. Probably in honour of Angus Shaw (d. 1832), one of the partners of the North West Company.
15. Except for the words "attention" and "applause", Masson scored out the whole of the last half of this sentence so heavily that the text cannot be deciphered with any certainty. In his printed version Masson altered the wording to read: "They seemed to speak with a fluency which attracted a kind of attention indicative of applause."

16. Fraser's camp must have been near the site of the present town of Lillooet. The Askettih village was across the Fraser River, on the east bank.
17. Masson ends the sentence with the word "journey" and the remaining words are scored out heavily.
18. Although he does not mention the fact until later, Fraser had now reached the point where the Thompson River joins the Fraser. Lytton is the modern town in this vicinity.
19. It is fitting that Thompson, in his turn, should have been the person who named the Fraser River in honour of Simon Fraser. As already noted, Thompson had built Kootenae House on the upper waters of the Columbia River in 1807. At that time, however, he did not know that the river was the Columbia, and in the existing state of geographical knowledge, Fraser's speculation that Kootenae House might stand on the upper reaches of the Thompson River was entirely reasonable.
20. As this "little fellow" is referred to frequently, and as Fraser used the phrase as if it were his name, it is spelled with capital hereafter.
21. This mishap probably occurred in the vicinity of Jackass Mountain, a dozen miles downstream from Lytton. From Lytton to Yale the river is an almost continuous series of rapids and canyons.
22. Undoubtedly a branch of the Lower Thompson Indians, who inhabited the valley of the Fraser River as far south as the vicinity of Spuzzum. The *Handbook of the Indians of Canada* (Ottawa, 1913), refers to the Thompson Indians as the *Ntlakyapamuk*; there may be some relationship between this name and *Nailgemugh*.
23. Fraser was now in the most difficult and dangerous part of the Fraser Canyon, which centres upon Hell's Gate and the Black Canyon. His description of the return journey through this same region is equally vivid (see the entry dated July 10). Fifty-one years later, travel at this point was still hazardous in the extreme. Commander R.C. Mayne, who ascended the river from Yale to Lytton in 1859, printed a description that rival's Fraser's own in his well-known

volume, *Four Years in British Columbia and Vancouver Island* (London, 1862, p. 106): "The mode of rounding these cliffs, which literally overhang the river, is peculiar, and makes one's nerves twitch little at first. There are two or three of them, the trail coming up to them on one side, and continuing again on the other. The difficulty, of course, was to pass the intervening space. This was managed by the Indians thus: they suspended three poles by native ropes, made of deer-hide and fibre, from the top of the cliff, the inner end of the first and third resting on the trail, and the middle one crossing them on the front of the bluff. Of course there was nothing to lay hold of, and the only way was for the traveller to stretch out his arms and clasp the rock as much as possible, keeping his face close against it; if he got dizzy, or made a false step, the pole would, of course, swing away, and he would topple over into the torrent, which rolled hundreds of feet beneath."

24. That is to say, the boundary between the areas occupied by the Interior Salish and the Coast Salish Indians. *Hacamaugh* is Fraser's name for the Thompson Indians, an Interior Salish tribe; *Ackinroe* is his name for the first Coast Salish Indians that he met.

25. These rugs or blankets were characteristic of the Coast Salish Indians living on or near the Fraser River. A special breed of dog, now believed to be extinct, was raised to furnish a supply of hair for weaving.

26. Fraser had now reached the site of Yale, which is about a mile downstream from Lady Franklin Rock. No record of any visit by white men to this vicinity before Fraser's arrival is known to exist.

27. This island was probably near the present village of Hope. Fraser's description of his journey down the river from Lady Franklin Rock to the site of New Westminster is described in such general terms that it is impossible to identify the various mentioned with much confidence.

28. Masson spells this word "Stremotch" and identifies the mountain as Mount Baker (10,750 feet). Sholefield believed that the stretch of the river that widened into a lake was

near Chilliwack, and that the mountain was Sumas Peak. David Thompson's famous *Map of the North-West Territory of the Province of Canada*, drawn in 1813-14, seems to support Scholefield's opinion. The Fraser was in freshet at the time Fraser explored its lower reaches, and until dikes were built, many years later, huge areas of low-lying land between Hope and the river's mouth were flooded whenever the water was high. It is surprising to note that Fraser makes no mention of the three important rivers that flow into the Fraser from the north between Hope and New Westminster—the Harrison, Stave and Pitt rivers. What appears to be the Harrison River is marked on Thompson's map, and this detail was doubtless taken from the notes by John Stuart that Thompson is known to have used when compiling this portion of his chart.

29. Musqueam Indian village still exists. A small stream flows through the present Indian reserve, but there is no lake. No doubt the lake seen by Fraser was formed by the freshet and flooding.
30. We have no clue as to the precise location of this second village, but it was evidently further along the shore of the Strait of Georgia, towards Point Grey.
31. The main ocean was, of course, much more distant than Fraser imagined. Cape Flattery and the open Pacific are about 140 miles from Musqueam.
32. Possibly the little island in the Fraser near the mouth of the American Creek. It is clear that Fraser spent most (if not all) of this very trying day between Hope and Yale.
33. For Fraser's description of his difficulties at this point on the way down the river, *see* entry dated June 26.
34. Not identified.
35. Illustrated in Diamond Jenness, *The Indians of Canada*, 4th ed., Ottawa, 1958, p. 107.

NOTES

Second Journal of Simon Fraser from May 30th to June 10th 1808

1. Not identified.
2. Fraser's name for the Sekani Indians that lived in the vicinity of McLeod Lake.
3. The bearings recorded would be compass readings, not corrected for magnetic deviation. The entries, which vary in form in the transcript, have been made uniform for the sake of clarity.
4. There is no such word; the original manuscript probably read *tourniquettes*, the French word for whirlpools or eddies.
5. The distances recorded for this day total 29 1/2 miles. Fraser almost always over-estimated the distance he had gone, but this total is probably not far wide of the mark. The "dangerous rapid ... called Rapid du Trou" was the canyon near Chimney Creek.
6. A word was evidently omitted in the transcript. Fraser probably wrote that there were "few Rapids" or "no Rapids".
7. The name of one of the canoes is meant—perhaps the *Determination*. We know that Fraser was in the habit of naming his canoes; the *Perseverance* is referred to by name several times later in this journal.
8. *See* the note appended to the entry dated June 3 in the preceding narrative. The "people" Fraser had in mind were David Thompson and his men. "Capt. Lewis" was Captain Meriwether Lewis, of the Lewis and Clark expedition, which in 1805 had travelled from the Missouri River to the Pacific Coast. After spending the winter near the mouth of the Columbia River, he returned to the East in 1806.
9. The game was thus a variation of thimblerig, or the shell game.
10. Thin spruce roots, which were used by the fur-traders to sew the bark in their canoes. As the journal shows, the canoes were constantly in need of repairs, and the three essential materials were watap, gum (a suitable resin), and bark.
11. By the Askieteghs (Askettihs) Fraser meant the Lillooet Indians. *Suchanchs* may refer to the Shuswap Indians. Both were Interior Salish tribes.

SIMON FRASER

12. The text breaks off abruptly in the transcript. The distances recorded in this entry for June 4, total almost 13 miles. The party encamped for the night four or five miles upstream from Riske Creek.
13. Shrub: "A prepared drink made with the juice of orange and lemon (or other acid fruit), sugar and rum (or other spirit)."—*Oxford English Dictionary*.
14. Fraser is here describing what is known locally as the Iron Canyon (more correctly, the Iron Rapids), between Riske Creek and the Chilcotin River.
15. Presumably this should read: "I suppose to be the River".
16. Fraser was wrong in this assumption; Mackenzie saw neither the Chilcotin River nor any of its tributaries.
17. *Chevreau*, literally, kid; goats are probably meant, as deer have already been mentioned.
18. Fraser thought that he had travelled over 41 1/2 miles on June 5, but the actual distance was probably about 35 miles. He camped for the night a short distance above Churn Creek.
19. The distances given for this day's travel total nearly 15 miles. The next two nights were spent in the vicinity of China Gulch.
20. The distances notes for the day total about 13 1/2 miles. The encampment was probably near Deadman Creek.
21. Fraser estimated that he travelled nearly 30 1/2 miles on June 9. When his courses are plotted, it seems quite clear that Leon Creek was the stream passed shortly before he landed for the night.

BACKGROUND OF THE GREAT JOURNEY

First Journal of Simon Fraser from April 12th to July 18th 1806

1. Walking was much easier at night, when the frost had formed a hard crust on the snow. See the next entry.
2. Moberly Lake, which lies about 14 miles south of the site of Rocky Mountain Portage House, would seem to be the only possible identification of Beaver Lake.

NOTES

3. Fraser was sending these bales upstream, to the point above the canyon from which he intended to leave on his journey across the mountains as soon as the river was clear of ice.
4. A "piece" was a package or bale of provisions or trade goods, usually weighing about 90 pounds. Fur shipments were made up in "packs" of about the same weight.
5. A group of Sekani Indians that frequented the upper waters of the Beaver River (the Moberly River of today) and of the Sinew River (now the Pine River), and the adjacent valley of the Parsnip River.
6. A Sekani group, occupying the country around the Parsnip and Nation rivers. Although the murder of a Carrier Indian is mentioned here, the Big Men were usually on friendly terms with the Carriers, who were their neighbours to the west.
7. In Fraser's day this group controlled the Peace River from the mouth of the Smoky River as far up as Rocky Mountain Portage House. Although they were Sekanis, they had been much influenced by the Crees, and were slowly driving their kinsmen, called by Fraser the Meadow Indians, farther and farther up the river.
8. This should perhaps read: Mari de Dents de Biche; i.e., Deer Tooth's Husband.
9. It seems clear that the Indians were referring to the Skeena River. The lake may have been Bear Lake (a much smaller body of water than it was thought to be in Fraser's day), but was probably Babine Lake. The "Iron works and ornaments" that Fraser saw in the possession of the Indians would come from trading-vessels on the Coast, which frequented the waters near the mouth of the Skeena.
10. No record of any such expedition is known to exist.
11. The exact meaning of this word is not clear. Possibly *peignes* is intended; this can mean the ends of sticks or poles composing a trellis or lattice. The ribs and framework of the canoe formed a lattice of sorts, and the ends of the ribs had to be secured (tied or sewed) to the gunwales. The word is used again in the entry dated June 16, where the spelling appears to be *paigneis*.

12. This would be the Halfway River, which joins the Peace about half-way between the site of Rocky Mountain Portage House (near the modern Hudson Hope) and the mouth of the Beaver (Moberly) River.
13. Meaning that there was no one at Rocky Mountain Fort. This post was 6 miles up the Peace River from the present town of Fort St. John, and about 4 miles from the mouth of the Beaver (Moberly) River. Rocky Mountain Fort was abandoned for a time in 1805, when Fraser built a post at Rocky Mountain Portage, about 45 miles further up the river.
14. The spelling should probably be either *Chatillon* or *Chatelain*.
15. "Above" here means up the Peace River, which was the route Fraser and his party would take when they left to explore the country across the Rocky Mountains; "below" means down the Peace, to Dunvegan and Fort Chipewyan.
16. McLeod, the senior partner of the North West Company in the region, would be leaving Dunvegan soon to attend the annual rendezvous at the "New Fort" (which in 1807 was named Fort William), on Lake Superior.
17. By "public" letters, Fraser meant those relating to the business affairs of the North West Company; the "private" letters would be personal letters to friends and relatives.
18. An exaggeration; the distance is about 12 miles.
19. Fraser was following the same route he had taken in the autumn of 1805, when he led a party to McLeod Lake and there built the post later named Fort McLeod.
20. By an odd coincidence, Alexander Mackenzie also lost his note-book, exactly 13 years before, on May 27, 1793, when he was ascending this same stretch of the Peace River. The following note is appended to the entry for May 27: "From this day, to the 4th of June the courses of my voyage are omitted, as I lost the book that contained them. I was in the habit of sometimes indulging myself with a short doze in the canoe, and I imagine that the branches of the trees brushed my book from me, when I was in such a situation,

NOTES

which renders the account of these few days less distinct than usual."

21. This name, now borne by a village in the Peace River district, is supposed to have been derived from the name of a Beaver Indian guide, Pooscapee, who was called Pouce Coupé by the French-Canadian voyageurs.

22. Presumably this should read "main branch"; otherwise what follows does not make sense. In the printed version of Mackenzie's journal for May 31, 1793, he states clearly that he followed the smaller but swifter of the two branches of the Peace, because his guide told him that a portage from it would take him to a large river that Mackenzie believe would lead him to the Pacific Ocean. Fraser undoubtedly had a copy of Mackenzie's journal with him, but this and other discrepancies between his references to it and the printed text suggest that he may have had a manuscript version that differed in some respects from the printed text.

23. The actual distance is 65 miles as the crow flies, and about 85 miles by the twisting course of the river.

24. Meaning Stuart, La Malice and Fraser himself, who normally travelled separately, one in each of the three canoes. Each canoe had a crew of three men.

25. The voyageurs were given a short rest every hour or so, during which they would light up their pipes. As a result of this custom, "pipes" became a measure of distance, or, more correctly, of the time required to perform a certain journey. Thus, instead of giving the length of a lake as 20 miles, it might be described as a "lake of three pipes".

26. Mackenzie himself makes no attempt to conceal the fact that he dozed at times; see above, footnote 20.

27. Fraser may have been thinking merely of the northern part of McLeod Lake, which is separated from the lake proper by a narrows. The whole lake is about 12 miles in length.

28. In the entry in his journal dated May 23, 1793, Mackenzie describes the *bois picant*: "It rises to about nine feet in height, grows in joints without branches, and is tufted at the extremity. The stem is of an equal size from the bottom to the top, and does not exceed an inch in diameter; it is covered with

small prickles, which caught our trowsers, and working through them, sometimes found their way to the flesh." Devil's club would appear to fit this description.

29. The word "in" should be "brother-in-law".
30. Probably *peignes* is meant. See above, footnote 11.
31. Another reference to Mari de Dents de Biche, "Deer Tooth's Husband". See above, footnote 8.
32. It is impossible to identify with any certainty the various lakes, rivers and mountains referred to by Fraser in his account of his journey from the mouth of the Pack River up the Parsnip to the small stream that leads to Arctic Lake. The total distance is about 75 miles by air, but considerably more by the winding course of the river.
33. On June 8, 1793.
34. This is clearly a garbled reference to the Sinew River (now the Pine River). As a glance at the map will show, Fraser was right in believing the Indians when they stated that the rivers entering the Parsnip from the left (east) had their sources near those of tributaries of the Pine.
35. The transcript actually reads: "at least fifty yards under" in place of "at least fifty yards wide" — a good example of the careless copying that characterizes it.
36. The three small lakes at the height of land are now appropriately named Arctic Lake, Portage Lake, and Pacific Lake.
37. This much easier travel route was by way of the Crooked River to Summit Lake, and thence by the Giscombe Portage to the Fraser River. See below, footnote 48.
38. Mackenzie's "Bad River", so named because of the great difficulties he experienced in descending it. James Creek flows into Herrick Creek, which soon joins the McGregor River, which is a northern branch of the Fraser River. All three streams, together with nearby Captain Creek, were named in memory of Captain James Herrick McGregor, of Victoria, B.C., a land surveyor who lost his life in the Great War. The name Bad River is still used locally. Fraser either saw it when the water was unusually high or exaggerated its size; a surveyor who explored the region in 1910 described it as "a very swift-running stream ... average width about 25 feet".

NOTES

39. The stem and framework at the bow of the canoe.
40. A puzzling remark, as there is no wide spot on James Creek that could be described as a lake. An area flooded temporarily by the freshet must be meant.
41. A rough roadway that Mackenzie's men cut through the wood, in order that they might carry their canoes and bypass a part of James Creek that they could not follow because of rapids and obstructions.
42. Undiluted spirits.
43. Some of the confusion in detail between the accounts given by Fraser and Mackenzie would seem to be due to the fact that Fraser considered that Herrick Creek was a tributary of James Creek, rather than the other way about, whereas Mackenzie considered that Herrick Creek was part of the McGregor River (the "great river"). Mackenzie states in his journal (June 17, 1793) that his last portage to the "great river" was in an "east-north-east" direction; this would seem to be impossible unless he were portaging from James Creek, some distance above its mouth, to Herrick Creek. Moreover, his first courses and distances on the "great river" fir the contortions of Herrick Creek.
44. Jenness believes these Indians were a group of Sekanis who lived at the headwaters of the Smoky River.
45. The reference is to the various channels into which Herrick Creek (which, as already noted, Fraser makes a part of James Creek, or the Bad River) divides about half a mile below the mouth of James Creek.
46. So far as is known, none of Stuart's journals or notes has survived.
47. At this point, without warning, Fraser interpolates several remarks that relate to earlier stages in his journey. The rocks and cliffs that seemed to Mackenzie to resemble huge gothic churches were on the Fraser River, below its confluence with the McGregor (see Mackenzie's journal, August 13, 1793).
48. The reference must be to the Salmon River, which joins the Fraser a dozen miles (as the crow flies) above the mouth of the Nechako. The Indian evidently had in mind

319

a portage from Summit Lake to the Salmon, instead of a direct portage (the Giscombe Portage) from Summit Lake to the Fraser.

Letters from New Caledonia August 1806–February 1807

1. Seven of the eleven letters have been copied from transcripts secured in Victoria in 1878 by H.H. Bancroft, the historian; these are now in the Bancroft Library at the University of California, Berkeley. The text of the other four (those dated December 21, 1806, and January 31, February 1 and February 10, 1807) is from letter-book copies, in Fraser's own handwriting, in the Archives of British Columbia.
2. Fraser means that from the mouth of the Nechako it would take much longer to travel up the Nechako and Stuart rivers to the post on Stuart Lake, than to go on down the Fraser River to the West Road River.
3. Fraser had in mind a route that followed the Crooked River to Summit Lake, crossed a portage to the Salmon River, and followed the latter to its junction with the Fraser. See the further reference in the next letter.
4. The lake to the westward would be Babine Lake, but Fraser meant Fraser Lake, which is south of Stuart Lake.
5. The Carrier Indian who had come to Stuart Lake with Fraser, and who presumably had accompanied La Malice to Fort McLeod when Fraser sent his first letter to McDougall. The name is spelled in several different ways in the transcript, including *Ran Chuse* and *Kenchuse*.
6. Mari de Dents de Biche; i.e., Deer Tooth's Husband.
7. The cost of maintaining Indian women and half-breed children at the North West Company's trading-posts was causing much concern, and on July 14, 1806, the proprietors had resolved "that every practicable means should be used throughout the Country to reduce by degrees the number of women maintained by the Company". No "Partner, Clerk, or Engage" was thereafter to "take or suf-

NOTES

fer to be taken ... any woman or maid from any of the tribes of Indians ... to live with him within the Company's Houses or Forts & be maintained at the expence of the Concern".

8. Fraser is referring to fishing tackle.
9. The express canoe, carrying letters and other documents to Kaministiquia (Fort William).
10. The manuscript actually reads: "be had brought over".
11. In this confused passage, Fraser is referring to the mouth of the Nechako River, which he proposes to use as a transfer point. Goods and supplies from both Stuart Lake and Fort McLeod that were needed for the expedition down the Fraser River could be brought there, and the exploring party could then get away without further travel or delay. This plan was carried into effect. Fort George was built at the mouth of the Nechako later in 1807, and Fraser set out from the post on his great journey down the Fraser River in 1808.

MISCELLANEOUS PAPERS

1. From the original documents, in the handwriting of Simon Fraser, now in the possession of Mr. Donald C. Fraser, of Fargo, North Dakota.
2. It seems very unlikely that this transfer to Rhode Island ever took place; all other accounts agree that the explorer's father died in prison in Albany. The Rev. Duncan Fraser, of Canton, N.Y., has suggested that *Sophas* may be a mistake for *Esopus* (probably contracted to *Sopus*), a town on the Hudson River south of Albany. The Americans established a maximum-security prison at Esopus, and seem also to have used prison ships there.
3. These notes are now incomplete; the text breaks off in the middle of a sentence at the bottom of the page. The last sentence has been completed from a garbled version of part of the notes that appears in a letter from General George Fraser to Dr. W.N. Sage, dated November 12, 1929.

4. From a microfilm copy in the Public Archives of Canada. The original document is in the Public Record Office, London (Audit Office 12, vol. 28, pp. 421-4).
5. The original letter is in the Public Archives of Canada.
6. Selkirk Papers, 8919-20. From the transcript in the Public Archives of Canada. The original papers were destroyed by fire in 1940.
7. The original petitions are in the Public Archives of Canada.
8. The original letter is in the Public Archives of Canada. McDonell was a Member of the Legislative Assembly of Upper Canada.
9. The original petition, in Fraser's handwriting, is in the Public Archives of Canada.
10. The original statement, in McDonell's handwriting, is in the Public Archives of Canada.
11. Civil Secretary's Letter Book, 1841, p. 397.
12. Quoted from the original memorandum, which is preserved in the McCord Museum, Montreal. John McDonald died in 1860.
13. This letter was printed in the *Chronicle*, which was published in Belleville, on February 12, 1862. It evidently attracted some attention, as long extracts from it were printed in several other journals. It will be noted that "Athabasca" is spelled "Arthabasca" throughout.
14. The original memorial is preserved in the Stormont County Land Registry Office, in Cornwall, Ontario.
15. The petition was submitted in printed form. When submitted a second time, in 1890, the date "June 1887" was struck out and "29th Jany. 1890" substituted in ink. The text has been taken from the copy in the records of the Privy Council Office; this was signed by Harriet Fraser, below the printed signature.

INDEX

Ackinroe Indians, 117–19, 127, 311
Albany, 23, 25, 72, 275, 277, 321
Albany Committee of Correspondence, 25
Albany Council of Safety, 25
Albany Jail, 275, 277
Alexandria, 34, 49
American Creek, 312
Arctic Lake, 229, 318
Argenton (voyageur), 185, 188, 190
Askettih Indians, *see* Lillooet Indians
Aspen, 167, 259
Athabasca, 12, 28, 31–32, 61–64, 291–92, 322
Atnah Indians; 85–87, 92–93, 98, 104, 140–44, 146, 151–53, 158, 165, 173, 177, 179, 210, 249, 253; vocabulary, 162

Bad River, *see* James Creek
Bagot, Sir Charles, 70
Balsam trees, 216
Bancroft, Hubert Howe, 51, 54–57, 303
Baptiste (voyageur), 43, 174
Barbin (or Barbein) (Indian), 218–19, 226–27
Barkerville, 73
Baucanne Indians, 238–39
Bazile (voyageur), hired, 183–84; illness, 223–24, 259–60; mentioned, 38, 188, 192, 195–99, 201, 218–21, 252, 257
Bear Lake, 61, 189–90, 210, 315
Bears, 189, 195, 230; men attacked by, 243–44
Beaver and beaver skins, 88, 94, 96, 100, 114, 139, 144, 152, 155, 168, 184–85, 189, 194–97, 199–200, 210, 219, 222–23, 225–27, 236–37, 240, 248–49, 251, 253, 255, 257, 263, 265, 272
Beaver Indians, 185, 195–97, 199, 211, 239
Beaver Lake, *see* Moberly Lake
Beaver Lodge, 228
Bennington, 23–25, 275, 277–79
Bennington, Battle of, 26, 275–79

Beyson (voyageur), 184, 186–88, 192–93, 195, 198–200, 205
Big Bar Creek, 177
Big Men (Sekani Indians near McLeod Lake), 36, 152, 185, 210, 213, 218, 239, 256, 263, 265, 315
Birch trees, 84, 171, 175, 220, 272
Black Canyon, 310
Blais (voyageur), 38, 202, 217–18, 220–22, 228, 256, 258, 264, 271
Blondin (Indian chief), 131–32
Boucher, Jean Baptiste, *see* Waccan
Bourboné (Bourbonnais?) (voyageur), 44, 180
Bourbonneur River, *see* West Road River
Bridge River (Shaw's River), 100
Brissère (voyageur), 184
British Columbia, first mainland settlement, 21, 34–36; claim that Fraser secured it for the British, 71, 73–75, 293–94, 300; Fraser honoured by, 77–79
Buffalo, 92, 161, 184

Cameron, Duncan, 11, 70
Camerontown, 73
Campbell, Colonel, 69, 278, 287
Canoes, building and repairs, 37–38, 79, 213, 218, 221–22; bark for, 185–86, 197, 218–21, 266; sturgeon-nosed, 143; names for, 161, 166, 176, 178, 313
Carcajous, 189
Cariboo gold fields, 54, 71, 73–74
Caribou, 94, 152, 208, 210, 234, 240, 254
Carp, 217–22, 249, 254–55
Carp Lake, 48, 217–21
Carrier Indians, 37, 39–42, 85, 91, 94, 145, 151–52, 158, 165, 168, 185–86, 190, 210, 217–22, 229, 238, 315
Carrier Lake, 37, 241
Cedar trees, 84, 122, 152, 166, 239–40
Chatillon (or Chatelain), 196, 316
Chilcotin Indians, 91, 105, 144–45, 168
Chilcotin River, 48, 94, 144–45, 168, 314

Chimney Creek, 88, 313
China Gulch, 309, 314
Churn Creek, 144, 170, 309, 314
Columbia River, 34, 37, 48–49, 298, 309–10, 313
Corless, Richard F., Jr., 79
Cornwall, 27, 66–67, 69, 322
Cornwall Township, 27, 65–67, 78, 283–84, 294–97
Cottonwood Canyon, 84, 148
Cottonwood River, 84
Cowichan Indians, 46
Crooked River, 318, 320
Cypress trees, 84, 155, 166

Dallaire (voyageur), 43, 111, 200–03
Deadman Creek, 309, 314
Deer, 83, 87–88, 94, 105, 118, 139, 144, 147, 152, 168, 187–90, 197, 208, 240–41, 311
Devil's club, 318
Dogs, as food, 105–06, 136, 140–41; for hunting, 147, 189, 208; wool from, 119, 121, 123, 136, 311
Douglas, (Sir) James, 73
Ducks, 177
Dunvegan, 11, 36, 60, 183, 188, 192, 200, 316

Eagles, 175
Elder trees, 175, 216

Farcier (voyageur), 186–88, 190, 193–94, 196, 198
Faries, Hugh (clerk), 43, 148, 293, 299
Finlay, James, 34, 227, 252
Finlay Forks, 34, 36, 38
Finlay River, 34, 189, 196, 208–10, 215–16
Firearms, 84, 86–87, 89, 116, 137, 191, 270; fired to impress the Indians, 41, 100, 115, 131, 134, 143, 152–53; accidents, 86, 101, 153
Fisher, 189
Flax, wild, 175
Fort Chipewyan, 48, 57, 60, 252, 291, 299, 316
Fort des Prairies, 92, 309
Fort Fraser, founded, 43, 250, 262; naming, 48; letters from, 260, 264–73
Fort George, founded, 43, 308, 321; mentioned, 44, 46, 48, 60, 79, 148, 293
Fort George Canyon, 83
Fort Liard, 306
Fort McLeod (Trout Lake Post), founded, 36; returns from, 195, 200–01, 203;

Fraser at, 218–23, 247; mentioned, 48, 185, 227, 231–73, 316, 321, *passim*
Fort St. James, founded, 42, 48, 249, 254, 292, 299; letters from, 247–64
Fort Vermillion, 195–96
Fort William, 31, 35, 60–65, 283, 291, 298, 316
Fraser, Alexander (uncle of Simon), 276
Fraser, Allan (son of Simon), 73, 276, 296
Fraser, Angus (brother of Simon), 26–27, 66–67, 73, 275, 284–85
Fraser, Angus (great-grandson of Simon), 76
Fraser, Archibald (uncle of Simon), 22, 275–76
Fraser, Catherine (Macdonell) (wife of Simon), 67, 71, 276, 297
Fraser, Catherine (granddaughter of Simon), 55–56, 301
Fraser, Catherine Harriet (daughter of Simon), birth, 72; pensions, 75–77, 298–300; death, 76; mentioned, 35, 75–76, 295–97
Fraser, Donald (uncle of Simon), 276
Fraser, Donald C. (great-great-great-grandson of Simon), 55, 76, 302, 305–06
Fraser, Elizabeth (McTavish), 305
Fraser, Hannah (sister of Simon), 275
Fraser, Harriet (daughter of Simon), *see* Fraser, Catherine Harriet
Fraser, Helen (daughter of Simon), 72
Fraser, Hugh, 23–24, 305–06
Fraser, Isabella (Grant) (mother of Simon), 23, 26–27, 275, 277; petition as Loyalist, 27, 278
Fraser, Isabella (sister of Simon), 27, 66, 275, 284; death, 277
Fraser, Isabella (daughter of Simon), 73, 276
Fraser, James (uncle of Simon), 276
Fraser, James Ambrose (son of Simon), 72, 75, 276, 296, 308; death, 75
Fraser, Jenny (sister of Simon), 27
Fraser, John (uncle of Simon), 22, 276, 305; wife and family, 276
Fraser, John Alexander (son of Simon), letter, 71, 290–97; goes to Cariboo, 73; death there, 74; mentioned, 54, 72–73, 77, 297
Fraser, Margaret (Macdonell) (grandmother of Simon), 22, 275–76
Fraser, Margaret (Peggy) (sister of Simon), 27, 66, 275
Fraser, Margaret (granddaughter of Simon), 76

INDEX

Fraser, Margery (daughter of Simon), 72, 75, 276, 295–97, 308; death, 75
Fraser, Nancy (sister of Simon), 27, 275; death, 277
Fraser, Nelly (sister of Simon), 275
Fraser, Peter (uncle of Simon), 276
Fraser, Peter (brother of Simon), 27, 275
Fraser, Roderick (uncle of Simon), 275–76
Fraser, Roderick (son of Simon), 72, 75, 296; pension, 75–76; death, 76
Fraser, Simon, *passim*; birth and ancestry, 22–27, 276; career in North West Company, 29–30, 35–47, 60–65; letters and journals, 37, 44, 48, 52–58; settles at St. Andrews, 66–67; properties there, 27, 66–67, 74–75, 294–97; wife and children, 67, 72–77, 276, 294–97; militia service and pension, 68–71, 287–89; offer of knighthood, 68, 300; death, 71, 75, 307; character, 51–52; portraits, 301–02; monuments to, 13, 78
Fraser, Simon (father of the explorer), 23–26, 275, 277–79, 305
Fraser, Simon, 14th Lord Lovat, 22, 68
Fraser, Simon William (son of Simon), 72, 76, 276, 295–96; death, 76
Fraser, William (grandfather of Simon), 22, 275
Fraser, William (brother of Simon), 26–27, 66, 275–76, 278–79
Fraser, William (uncle of Simon), 275
Fraser Lake, 42–43, 249–50, 255, 262, 299, 320; named, 292
Fraser River, *passim*; named, 48; cascades and rapids described, 85–87, 95–97, 104, 107, 112, 145, 155, 158–59, 169, 180, 245; Fraser first sees, 238; found not to be the Columbia, 34, 129, 281; gold rush to, 54, 71, 73–74
Fraser's Highlanders (78th Regiment), 22
French Bar Canyon (Rapide Couvert), 96, 98, 143–44, 173, 176, 178–79
French Bar Creek, 176

Gagnier (voyageur), 44, 153
Gagnon (voyageur), 38, 44, 56, 185–88, 192, 194–95, 198, 218, 228, 266, 269
Geese (outardes; Canada geese), 226–27
Georgia, Strait of, 46, 125, 312
Gervais, *see* La Garde, Gervais, and Rivard, Gervais
Giscombe Portage, 318, 320
Gosselin (voyageur), 192–99
Grandbois (voyageur), 225

Grant, Donald, 27
Grant, Peter, 27

Hacamaugh Indians, *see* Thompson Indians
Haldimand, Sir Frederick, 26
Halfway River, 316 .
Harkness, John Graham, 67
Harmon, Daniel Williams, 15–17, 44, 60, 304
Harrison River, 312
Hawks Creek, 155
Hazelnuts, 115
Hébert, Louis, sculptor, 77
Hell's Gate, 47, 310
Hemlock trees, 84, 149, 216, 239–40
Herrick Creek, 39, 318–19
Hope, 311–12
Horses, 23, 84–85, 91–94, 100, 105, 139, 142, 144, 153, 159–65, 168, 272
Hudson's Bay Company, rivalry with North West Company, 29–30, 33, 61–63; union with North West Company, 44; erects monument to Fraser, 78

Indians (*see also* names of individual tribes); their accounts of the country, 46, 87–88, 97, 102–03, 106, 152, 177, 189, 194, 210, 219; bows and arrows, 40, 87, 99, 104, 119–20, 125, 152, 166; coats of mail (leather), 101, 122, 124, 126, 140, 148; cremation of dead, 273–74; fishing nets and fishing methods,116, 121, 134, 175, 219, 230, 232, 234, 269; nets to catch animals, 118; gambling, 92, 162; honesty, 92, 93, 110, 165; houses, 92, 119, 123–24, 126, 165, 309; shades or shelters, 92, 95, 103–04, 119, 309; shield, 105; slaves, 86–8, 120, 152, 166, 185; smoking, 41, 88, 154; sword of sheet metal, 106; thieving, 124–25, 135, 249, 258, 273; tombs, 93, 106, 114, 118, 120, 123, 166; villages described, 103, 119, 122–23, 126
Iron Rapids or Canyon, 94, 314

Jackanet River (Fraser River), 48
Jackass Mountain, 138, 310
James Creek (Bad River), 38, 232, 239, 318–19
Jones, Harry, 74, 307
Juniper, 84, 152, 166

SIMON FRASER

Kascka Indians (Nakanés), 195
Keith, George, 58, 61
Kenchuse (Carrier Indian guide), *see* Ranchuse
'Kwah (Indian chief), 40, 255, 265, 271, 273

La Certe (voyageur), 44, 162, 170–71, 173–74, 180
La Chapelle (voyageur), 43, 111
La Fleur, J.B., 192
La Garde, Gervais (voyageur), 38, 44, 172, 187–88, 190–91, 214, 218, 223, 243
La Londe (voyageur), 38, 184, 186–88, 192–95, 218, 228, 259, 261
La Malice (voyageur), 35–36, 38, 51, 197, 201–03, 205, 213–14, 216, 218, 221–32, 234, 237, 240, 250, 253–54, 257, 265, 268, 317, 320
La Pistole (voyageur), 187–88, 190, 201–02
La Rammée (voyageur), 184, 186, 190–91, 193–95, 200
Lady Franklin Rock, 120, 134, 311
Lamothe, Joseph Maurice, letter to, 58–59, 280–82
Le Gourmand (Indian), 265, 271, 273
Leon Creek, 46, 54, 142, 179, 309, 314
Lewis and Clark expedition, 21, 293, 299, 313
Lillooet, 46, 54, 310
Lillooet Indians (Askettihs), 98, 107–08, 140, 179, 313
Little Fellow (Indian guide), 109, 113, 115, 120, 122, 125, 127, 133–35, 137, 141–43, 310
Little Head (Indian chief), 184–202, *passim*
Lone Cabin Creek, 175
Lower Thompson Indians (Nailgemughs), 114, 310
Lytton, 310

McBride, (Sir) Richard, 77
Macdonald, John (witness of Fraser's will), 297
McDonald, John (Nor'Wester), 65
McDonald, John of Garth, 70, 290
Macdonald, Sir John A., 15, 73, 75
McDonald, John R. (witness of Fraser's will), 297
Macdonald, John Sandfield, 13, 73
MacDonald, Roderick, 294
Macdonell, Alexander (Bishop of Upper Canada), 22

McDonell (i.e., Macdonnell), Alexander (Nor'Wester), 282
Macdonell, Captain Allan, 67, 276
MacDonell, Donald Æ., 68–69; letter to, 285–87; statement by, 289
McDonell, John (great-grandfather of Simon Fraser), 275
Macdonell, Miles, 61, 64, 282
McDougall, James (clerk), at Fort McLeod, 185, 217–18, 248; expedition to Stuart Lake, 35–37, 200, 241; journals, 266, 271; letters to, 252, 255, 260, 263–64, 273; mentioned, 39, 60, 200, 202, 205, 222–23, 259, 268, 291, 299, 320
McGillis, Hugh, 11, 65, 70
McGillivray, Archibald (clerk), 192, 198–99, 205, 291, 299
McGillivray, Duncan, 34
McGillivray, John, 11, 61, 70, 192
McGillivray, Simon, 62, 64
McGillivray, William, 61, 64–65
McGregor, Captain James Herrick, 318
McGregor River, 39, 236, 238, 318–19
McKenvin, John, 184–200, *passim*
Mackenzie, Sir Alexander, 17, 21, 23, 31–34, 36–39, 42, 48, 151–52, 168, 215, 226, 239, 252, 308, 314, 316–19; Fraser's critical remarks on, 51, 57, 207, 210, 228, 237, 240–42
Mackenzie, Alexander (nephew of Sir Alexander), 61, 65, 282
McKenzie, Kenneth, 62, 65
McKenzie, Roderick, 52–53, 58
McLellan, Archibald, 63
McLeod, Archibald Norman, 36, 63, 183, 192, 251
McLeod Lake (Trout Lake), discovered, 36; named, 48, 291, 299; mentioned, 37–38, 184, 200, 206, 216, 229, 317
McLoughlin, Dr. John, 65
McNiff, Patrick, 27
McTavish, Simon, 28, 31–32, 61, 305
McTavish, Frobisher & Co., 28, 33
Mallatisse (voyageur), 192
Maple trees, 239
Mapletown, 23–24, 27, 278–79
Mari de Dents de Biche (Indian), 186, 222, 256, 315, 318, 320
Marmot (siffleur), 107, 171
Masson, Honourable L.F.R., 15, 27, 53, 309
Mayne, R.C., 310
Meadow Indians, 162, 184, 187, 189–90, 195, 208, 315

326

INDEX

Ménard (voyageur), 38, 189–90, 196, 198–99, 203, 218
Moberly Lake (Beaver Lake), 184–99, *passim*
Monck, 4th Viscount, 73
Montagne de Boutte (Indian), 217–22, 225, 237–38, 240, 243, 246
Moose (orignals), 94, 96, 162, 168, 189–90, 194, 196, 201, 230, 240
Morice, Reverend A.G., 39, 301–03
Mosquitoes, 122
Mount Baker, 311
Musqueam, 47, 78–79, 125–26, 312

Nailgemugh, *see* Lower Thompson Indians
Nakazleh, *see* Fort St. James
Nation River, 213, 315
Natleh, *see* Fort Fraser
Nazkoten Indians, 84, 147
Nechako River, 37, 39, 43, 48, 149, 200, 240–41, 248–49, 253, 256, 269, 292–93, 319–21; called the Fraser, 48, 83; Fraser ascends, 240–46
New Caledonia, 44, 49, 54, 59–60; named, 48, 292–93, 299; letters from, 247–74, 280–82, 320
New North West Company, 33
New Westminster, 73, 77, 125, 301, 311–12
Newcastle, Duke of (Colonial Secretary), 73
North West Company, history and organization, 28–30; plans for westward expansion, 31–33, 35, 49; annual rendezvous, 31, 33, 35, 61, 316; policy re women at posts, 264, 320

Onions, 84, 100, 118, 144
Ossian, manuscripts relating to, 22
Otter, 139
Oysters, 122

Pacific Lake, 38, 230, 318
Pack River, 36, 38, 215–18, 224, 318
Parsnip River, 34, 36, 79, 208, 210–11, 215–17, 219, 224, 315, 318
Peace River, 32, 34–36, 38, 57, 195; Fraser ascends, 204–11
Pearl (ship), 23, 277
Pemmican, 61, 184, 188, 212, 224, 228, 231, 241
Pine River (Sinew River), 229, 318
Pine trees, 84, 96, 147, 171, 175, 179
Pitt River, 312
Plum trees, 239–40

Point Grey, 47, 312
Poplar trees, 96, 167, 171, 242, 259
Portage du Baril, 94, 144, 167
Portage du Trou, 145
Portage Lake, 230–31, 318
Powell, Dr. I.W., 54–55, 78
Pulagli (Indian village), 131

Quesnel, Joseph, 44
Quesnel, Jules Maurice, 83–183, *passim*; career, 43–44; letter by, 59, 280–82
Quesnel River, 84, 148; named, 48

Ranchuse (or Kenchuse; Indian guide), 229, 236, 242, 245, 320
Rapide Couvert, *see* French Bar Canyon
Rapide du Trou, 145, 156, 313
Raquette Relevée (Indian), 187, 199
Rattlesnakes, 152, 166
Rebellion of 1837–38, Fraser's service in militia, 69, 287–89
Red River Settlement, 61–64
Riske Creek, 94, 167
Rivard, Gervais (voyageur), 38, 183, 186–91, 212, 218, 221–22, 228, 263
Rocky Mountain Fort (Peace River), 219, 316
Rocky Mountain House (North Saskatchewan River), 34, 309
Rocky Mountain Portage and Rocky Mountain Portage House, 35–38, 43, 183–204, *passim*, 291

St. Andrews, 11–14, 67, 70–78, 285–89, 298, 301
St. Pierre (voyageur), 38, 201, 203, 213, 218, 220–21, 231, 259, 261, 263–64, 268
Sage, Walter N., 304, 321
Salmon, 42, 84, 87–88, 96, 100, 103, 105, 108, 115–16, 118–21, 130–31, 133, 138–39, 144–48, 154, 162, 164–65, 172, 189, 239, 248–49, 251–55, 259, 261–62, 269, 271–73
Salmon River, 69, 189, 287, 319–20
Saucier (voyageur), 185–98, 218–25, *passim*, 228, 259, 266–67, 269
Sauteux (Saulteaux) Indians, 105
Scholefield, E.O.S., 51, 54–55, 68, 301, 303
Scott, Sir Richard W., 27, 76, 301
Seals, in Fraser River, 122
Selkirk, Earl of, 57, 61–65; Fraser's declaration to, 282–83
Semple, Robert, 63–65, 282–83
Seton River, 101

327

Seven Oaks Massacre, 63–64, 68, 282–83
Shaw, Angus, 309
Shaw's River, *see* Bridge River
Sheep and/or goats, 23, 163, 174–75, 179, 208
Shoshoni Indians, 105
Shuswap Indians, 145, 313; *see also* Atnah Indians
Simpson, Sir George, 50
Sinew River, *see* Pine River
Siveright, John, 65
Siwash Creek, 119
Skeena River, 315
Smallpox, 115
Smith, Sir Donald (later Lord Strathcona), 75
Snails, 107
Soda Creek, 54, 146, 151
Soda Creek Canyon, 87, 154
Spruce trees (épinette), 155, 179; *see also* watap
Spuzzum, 118, 310
Stave River, 312
Stein River, 107
Stevenson, Robert, 74–75, 307
Stuart, John, *passim*; career, 44, 49; notes and journals, 35–36, 48–49, 57, 205, 241, 306, 312; skill as a canoe builder, 37, 193–94, 206, 220; letters to, 258, 267; report by, 173
Stuart, Robert, 267
Stuart Lake, McDougall's visit to, 37, 200, 241, 248; Fraser there, 39–42, 71, 247–74, *passim*; 291–92, 299; mentioned, 48, 219
Stuart River, 37, 39, 42, 148–49; named, 292, 299
Sturgeon, 121, 259
Sumas Peak, 312
Summit Lake (Lac des Monts), 252, 257, 318, 320
Swans, 212
Swhanemugh Indians, 138
Sydenham, Baron, 287–88

Tabot Tho' (Indian; brother-in-law of Little Head), 217–25, *passim*; 240, 244–45, 256, 260, 263
Tacoutche Tesse (Fraser River), 48
Tauten Indians, 85–88, 98, 146, 151; vocabulary, 162
Thompson, David, 11, 34, 48–49, 70, 309, 312; names Fraser River, 48–49, 310
Thompson Indians, 104, 107–09, 139, 311
Thompson River, named, 48, 310; mentioned, 109, 138, 140, 159, 161, 309, 310
Tobacco, 41, 154, 184, 187, 193, 270
Toeyen, 39–41
Trade goods, awls, 107, 109; blankets, 96, 107, 175; brayettes, 96, 175; brooches, 105; calico bed gowns, 115, 122; files, 103; kettles, 103, 107, 121, 270, 272; knives, 105, 109; list of, 270; from the Coast ("iron work"), 189–90, 200, 210, 223, 315
Trout, 217, 220, 225, 232, 249, 253
Trout Lake, *see* McLeod Lake
Trout Lake Post, *see* Fort McLeod
Tudyah Lake, 217

Vancouver, Captain George, 34

Waccan (or Wacca, or Waka; nickname of Jean-Baptiste Boucher), 44, 157, 172, 255, 273
Walkem, W.W., 74
Wananshish (voyageur), 38, 201–02, 218, 221–22
Watap (spruce roots), 104, 120, 147, 164, 192, 195; described, 313
Watson Bar Creek, 178
West Road River, 48, 83, 248, 320
Williams Lake Creek, 156
Willow trees, 175

X Y Company, 33

Yale, 46, 134, 310–12

www.ingramcontent.com/pod-product-compliance
Lightning Source LLC
Chambersburg PA
CBHW021143160426
43194CB00007B/669